BECKETT AND THE MODERN NOVEL

Samuel Beckett's narrative innovations are among his most important contributions to twentieth-century literature. Yet contemporary Beckett scholarship rarely considers the effect of his literary influences on the evolution of his narrative techniques, focusing instead on Beckett's philosophical implications. In this study, John Bolin challenges the utility of reading Beckett through a narrow philosophical lens, tracing new avenues for understanding Beckett's work – and, by extension, the form of the modern novel – by engaging with English, French, German, and Russian literature. Presenting new empirical evidence drawn from archives in the United Kingdom, Ireland, and the United States, Bolin demonstrates Beckett's preoccupation with what he termed the 'European novel': a lineage running from Sade to Stendhal, Dostoevsky, Gide, Sartre, and Céline. Through close readings of Beckett's manuscripts and novels up to and including *The Unnamable*, Bolin provides a new account of how Beckett's fiction grew out of his changing compositional practice, even as he moved beyond early exemplars.

JOHN BOLIN completed his M.Phil. and D.Phil. at Exeter College, Oxford. From 2008 to 2011 he lectured at Oxford, where he was the Bamborough Junior Research Fellow at Linacre College. He currently lectures at the University of Wollongong in New South Wales.

BECKETT AND THE MODERN NOVEL

JOHN BOLIN

CAMBRIDGE
UNIVERSITY PRESS

CAMBRIDGE UNIVERSITY PRESS
Cambridge, New York, Melbourne, Madrid, Cape Town,
Singapore, São Paulo, Delhi, Mexico City

Cambridge University Press
32 Avenue of the Americas, New York, NY 10013-2473, USA

www.cambridge.org
Information on this title: www.cambridge.org/9781107029842

First published 2013

Printed in the United States of America

A catalog record for this publication is available from the British Library.

Library of Congress Cataloging in Publication data
Bolin, John, 1979–
Beckett and the modern novel / John Bolin.
p.   cm.
Includes bibliographical references and index.
ISBN 978-1-107-02984-2 (hardback)
1. Beckett, Samuel, 1906–1989–Criticism and interpretation.   I. Title.
PR6003.E282Z5763   2013
848'.91409–dc23   2012016514

ISBN 978-1-107-02984-2 Hardback

For my mother and father

Beckett always saw himself – his post-war, as well as his pre-war self – as part of a continuum with the European literary and artistic past. We cannot, therefore, understand the remarkable leaps of the imagination that he made to produce some of the most radical work in prose ... of the twentieth-century without knowing where he is leaping from.

(James Knowlson, *Images of Beckett*)

No theory is good except on condition that one use it to go on beyond.

(André Gide, *Journals*)

Contents

Acknowledgments

Above all, I wish to thank Ronald Bush, who supervised my doctoral thesis on Beckett: for his careful reading of this project in its various stages, for his guidance and advice, and for the example of his own work, I am deeply grateful. I am also indebted to those experts and friends who helped me think through and revise my writing on Beckett in detail. My special thanks to John Pilling, James Knowlson, Shane Weller, David Walker, Erik Tonning, Matthew Feldman, Mark Nixon, Jeri Johnson, and the anonymous readers for Cambridge University Press.

The writing of this book was made possible by institutional and individual support during my years as a student and a research Fellow. My thanks to the University of Oxford, which granted me a Clarendon Fund bursary and an Overseas Research Studentship; to Exeter College, Oxford, for offering me the Amelia Jackson Senior Studentship and several assorted bursaries; to Linacre College, Oxford, which awarded me the Bamborough Junior Research Fellowship so that I could revise my manuscript; and to Lady Wheare, for her patronage during my student days. For their criticism, friendship, and guidance, I am grateful to Bernard and Heather O'Donoghue, John and Christine Kelly, Peter McDonald, David Bradshaw, Paul Giles, Vaughan Roberts, and Patrick and Sarah Hayes.

During the years I was preoccupied with this project, I had the pleasure of working as a Lecturer at St Catherine's College, Oxford and Lincoln College, Oxford. I am thankful for the stimulating conversations I enjoyed with the students and faculty during my time there.

For their assistance, I am grateful to Richard Workman and his colleagues at the Harry Ransom Center at the University of Texas, Austin; to the staff members at the Beckett Archive at the University of Reading; to the archivists at Trinity College, Dublin; and to the librarians at the John J. Burns Library at Boston College. I am also thankful for the hospitality of Dr and Mrs LaFrance during my time in Boston, and the kindness of the friends who facilitated my stay in Texas. My grateful thanks to the Estate of Samuel Beckett, and to Edward Beckett for providing me with the cover image of this book. I also wish to acknowledge the Board of Trinity College, Dublin. Every effort has been made to ensure that all quotations from copyrighted material fall within the definition of fair dealing for the purposes of literary criticism.

I am grateful to my commissioning editor, Ray Ryan, and to Louis Gulino, Marielle Poss, and the other staff members at Cambridge University Press for their commitment to this project.

I have many other debts, too many to list here. I am extremely grateful to Katherine for her patience and her concern for my work. This book is dedicated to my mother and father.

Abbreviations

In the citations from Beckett's letters, SB indicates Samuel Beckett, TM Thomas McGreevy, MM Mary Manning, and GD Georges Duthuit.

WORKS BY SAMUEL BECKETT

Dis	*Disjecta* (London: John Calder, 2001).
DFMW	*Dream of Fair to Middling Women* (London: John Calder, 1993).
DN	*Beckett's* Dream *Notebook*, ed. John Pilling (Reading: Beckett International Foundation, 1999).
LSB 1	*The Letters of Samuel Beckett: 1929–1940*, vol. 1, Martha Dow Fehsenfeld and Lois More Overbeck, eds. (Cambridge: Cambridge University Press, 2009).
LSB 2	*The Letters of Samuel Beckett: 1941–1956*, vol. 2, George Craig, Martha Dow Fehsenfeld, Dan Gunn, and Lois More Overbeck, eds. (Cambridge: Cambridge University Press, 2011).
M	*Murphy* (London: John Calder, 2003).
MC	*Mercier and Camier* (London: John Calder, 1999).
N	*First Love and Other Novellas* (London: Penguin Books, 2000).
NB	*Watt* Notebooks, Harry Ransom Center, University of Texas at Austin, box 6 (folders 5–7); box 7 (folders 1–4).
PTD	*Proust and Three Dialogues with Georges Duthuit* (London: John Calder, 1999).
T	Trilogy: *Molloy, Malone Dies, The Unnamable* (London, Montreal, New York: John Calder, 1994).
W	*Watt* (London: John Calder, 1998).
WTS	*Watt* Typescript. Harry Ransom Center, University of Texas at Austin, box 7 (folders 5–6).

WORKS BY OTHER AUTHORS

AP   Joyce, James, *A Portrait of the Artist as a Young Man* (London: Penguin Books, 1992).

BBG   Pilling, John, *Beckett before Godot* (Cambridge: Cambridge University Press, 1997).

BC   Pilling, John, *A Samuel Beckett Chronology* (New York: Palgrave Macmillan, 2006).

C   Gide, André, *The Counterfeiters*, trans. Dorothy Bussy (London: Penguin Books, 1966).

D   Gide, André, *Dostoïevsky*, trans. Dorothy Bussy (London: Secker and Warburg, 1949).

DF   Knowlson, James, *Damned to Fame: The Life of Samuel Beckett* (London: Bloomsbury, 1996).

DP   Ackerley, C. J., *Demented Particulars: The Annotated* Murphy (Tallahassee, FL: Journal of Beckett Studies Books, 1998).

GC   Ackerley, C. J. and S. E. Gontarski, *The Grove Companion to Samuel Beckett* (New York: Grove Press, 2004).

J   Gide, André, *Journals.* 1889–1949, trans. Justin O'Brien (Harmondsworth: Penguin Books, 1967).

L   Gide, André, *Lafcadio's Adventures*, trans. Dorothy Bussy (New York: Vintage International, 2003).

LC   Gide, André, *Logbook of the Coiners,* trans. Justin O'Brien (London: Cassell, 1952).

N   Sartre, Jean-Paul, *Nausea*, trans. Robert Baldick (London: Penguin Books, 2000).

OLSK   Ackerley, C. J., *Obscure Locks, Simple Keys: The Annotated* Watt (Tallahassee, FL: Journal of Beckett Studies Books, 2005).

PS   Gide, André, *La Symphonie pastorale* in *La Symphonie pastorale* and *Isabelle*, trans. Dorothy Bussy (London: Penguin, 1963).

U   Kenner, Hugh, *Ulysses* (London: George Allen and Unwin, 1980).

Introduction

I wouldn't have had any reason to write my novels if I could have
expressed their subject in philosophical terms.
(Beckett in an interview with Gabriel d'Aubarède, 1961)[1]

The suggestion that Fielding was deficient in comprehension of the
novel as a form, because we have no notes (no?) from his hand on
the subject, is very nice.
(Beckett, 'Ex Cathezra', 1934)[2]

As Frederik Smith has recently pointed out, Beckett's readers have paid
significantly less attention to his literary influences than to his philosophical ones.[3] New book-length studies on Beckett and Dante (Daniela
Caselli), Beckett and Proust (James Reid), and a long-established recognition of Joyce's influence (Barbara Reich Gluck) are still notable excep-
tions to the dominant tendency to position Beckett in relation to thinkers
like Berkeley, Descartes, Leibniz, Geulincx, Schopenhauer, Heidegger,
Sartre, and Derrida to glean a philosophical meaning from his work.[4]
One result of this approach is that Beckett's readers have often considered him from a thematic perspective; for example, by asking what the
value or non-value of 'nothing' is in the text – an argument which has
been consistently deployed by critics and philosophers from the postwar
period to the present day to co-opt Beckett and argue that 'a certain kind
of literary practice constitutes a genuine resistance to nihilism.[5] For all
the differing conclusions among Beckett's prosecutors and defenders in
this debate – from Lukács to Badiou – this fundamentally philosophical
approach unites a significant portion of Beckett's readers in a common
agon, even as they argue across the so-called modern/postmodern theoretical divide that began troubling literary studies in the seventies and
eighties. As David Pattie contends, despite their differences both 'mod-
ernist' and 'postmodernist' camps use Beckett in a similar manner: 'as
a lens through which to focus the critic's attention on perhaps the most
basic theoretical inquiry: "How do we make meaning in the world?"'[6]

Moreover, such questions have often led Beckett's readers to similar conclusions as they claim 'a positive estimation of the impact of Beckett's
writing, either as a document of eternal struggle or as a heroic attempt to
escape the authority of fixed meanings' (Pattie, 244).[7]

This common theoretical project has neglected Beckett's literary
influences but it has also marginalised his importance in a generic continuum which he himself emphasised (even as he denied that he had a
message expressible in philosophical terms)[8] – that is, it ignores Beckett's
place as an innovator in the *novel*. Starting with Kenner's account in the
early sixties, studies engaging with Beckett's fiction have neglected the
attempt to discuss Beckett's engagement with a theory of the novel and
with the lineaments of the genre itself.[9] This trend has continued into
the twenty-first century, even as the philosophical frameworks deployed
for this purpose have shifted from, say, Cartesian to poststructural-
ist. It is telling that *Palgrave Advances in Samuel Beckett Studies*, which
neatly addresses the state of Beckett criticism circa 2004, has no section on Beckett as a novelist, though there are essays on 'Beckett and
Performance' (S. E. Gontarski) and 'Sources of Attraction to Beckett's
Theatre' (Katharine Worth), as well as 'Feminist Readings of Beckett'
(Elin Diamond) and 'Beckett and Homoeroticism' (Peter Boxall). The
closest thing to an account of Beckett's engagement with the novel is
H. Porter Abbott's essay on 'Narrative'. Several recent studies on Beckett's
fiction have taken a similar tack. Jonathan Boulter's *Interpreting Narrative
in the Novels of Samuel Beckett* (2001), for example, reads Beckett's novels
'in the light of phenomenological-hermeneutical theory, primarily that of
Hans-Georg Gadamer'.[10] James H. Reid's *Proust, Beckett and Narration*
(2003) ends up relying less on Beckett's relation to what Christie
McDonald has rightly called the 'Proustian revolution' in the novel than
on reading Beckett's *Three Novels* and *À la recherche du temps perdu* as
works in which 'first-person narration takes the form of an interplay
between the tropes of allegory and irony as defined by Paul de Man'.[11]

By pointing out the nature of recent approaches to Beckett I do not
wish to deny the insights that reading him through philosophy, or
reading his fiction through narrative theory have provided. It is inevitable, and desirable, with a writer like Beckett to read him alongside
such theories. Nor do I seek to overemphasise another kind of theoretical approach which the reader may already suspect lies waiting in the
wings after my repeated use of the term 'novel': that of genre theory.
But what if the kinds of questions Beckett *himself* was asking, especially
at the beginning of his career, were more involved with literature than

philosophical meaning – or to put it more specifically, What if Beckett's novels began as a question of how a particular literary *form* can address reality? What of Beckett himself as a theorist – of a rather different kind than the philosopher or reader of philosophy his critics have often described?

These are the questions with which I began this study, but before I proceed, a few words are necessary on the limits and aims of this book as it now stands. In what follows I consider Beckett's development chronologically, focusing on his experimentation with the novel in the formative period from the early thirties to 1950 – the period leading up to and including the *Three Novels*. Beckett did of course go on to write another novel, *Comment c'est* (begun 1958). But this work belongs to a later phase of his thought and career, when he had already worked through the process of 'getting [him]self in perfection ... after so many years of expression in blindness', and was addressing different concerns from the ones that led him to *The Unnamable* – a book that positions the novels from *Murphy* up to *Malone Dies* within a kind of self-enclosed, collective form.[12] Much that is in this study has a bearing on *Comment c'est*. But in order to provide space for the detailed formal and stylistic analysis and the use of manuscript evidence this book relies on for its argument, I was forced to confine myself to the novels I have included.

Since the late sixties, Beckett's readers have viewed these fictions mainly with relation to an Anglo-Irish literary tradition, an approach that has been given new life by two recent studies, Patrick Bixby's *Samuel Beckett and the Postcolonial Novel* (2009) and Frederik Smith's *Beckett's Eighteenth Century* (2002). But despite the importance of this tradition for Beckett, his consideration of the novel was focalized through a distinctly European lens from the beginning. Starting with *Dream*, Beckett drew key novelistic targets as well as several of his chief exemplars from the Continent in order to challenge what he termed the 'tradition' of the 'European novel'.[13] This study brings attention to new influences in this regard, and attempts to reposition Beckett's early novelistic theory and practice within an important, even a defining context: a countertradition running from Sade to Stendhal up to Dostoevsky, Gide, and Sartre – writers who are pitted against antagonists like Goethe, Zola, and Balzac.

Beckett's challenge to and emulation of such Continental novelists fed into one of his key concerns: cultivating tensions between the novel's components (for example, between its narrator and characters) and exploiting its competing claims (such as its pretense to a fidelity to reality, and its status as a formal construct). Beckett's attempt to exploit and intensify such tensions led him toward a preoccupation with what *Dream*'s narrator calls the 'architectonics' of the form, especially the novel's structure and the dynamics of its narration.[14] Narration and narrators are therefore a key focus of this book. As Leslie Hill has pointed out, Beckett's readers have neglected these aspects of Beckett's fiction, but they have done so at their peril.[15] As Beckett continued to write, he became increasingly preoccupied with staging the relation that underpins all novels: the fluctuating current of feeling between the voice and the story it tells.

The tensions the novel has often belied reappear writ large in Beckett's own books, but this is not only a result of his attempts at formal critique and innovation. The shape of Beckett's novels, especially during the formative years of the thirties, is also the outworking of pressures within his own psyche: chiefly, the conflict between an abiding urge to write out of what he termed 'feeling' and, against this desire, his tendency to follow the academic, highly cognitive procedures with which he began his apprenticeship in the novel. In this sense, this study assumes that the work cannot be completely separated from the life. Yet I am less interested in a 'biographical' Beckett than, to borrow from Sarah Lawall, the figure who 'assumes form as the work is created' – that is, the writer who exists in and through the work as a body of perspectives and intensities.[16] The story I will tell involves Beckett's changing approach to the practical difficulties of how one goes about writing a novel as well as the internal pressures that directed this development. But it also concerns the way that feeling itself came to play a larger role (though an often ignored or misunderstood one) in Beckett's work with the tradition of the novel.

I mentioned that I will be following a series of tensions within Beckett's thought and fiction. But in a very real sense Beckett's work in the novel, and after, proceeds from one key paradox. It is to the roots of this paradox to which we now turn.

The most obvious source for Beckett's early thought about the novel are his two essays on novelists: his 1929 piece on Joyce and his 1930 monograph on Proust. But before I rehearse Beckett's account of these writers yet again, it may be helpful to ask a secondary question regarding their importance to his own practice. Compare the theory in these essays to the way *Dream of Fair to Middling Women* works: despite *Dream*'s style (which 'stinks of Joyce' as Beckett himself admitted),[17] Beckett's first novel presents serious problems for anyone attempting to connect Beckett's treatment of the form and that outlined by 'Dante ... Bruno . Vico . . Joyce' or *Proust* – a fact that Beckett's readers have struggled to come to terms with for the understandable reason that they would like to appreciate Beckett in the light of his own theory and in the face of his reticence to talk about it. As Shane Weller has recently demonstrated, there is no disguising the fact that, despite the efforts of such eminent critics as Christopher Ricks to argue to the contrary, Beckett's novel presents a very different approach to the form from that of the Joyce it borrows. Rather than a principle of identification, *Dream* operates on, and posits through Belacqua and 'Mr Beckett', a principle of 'incoherence' – a movement toward formal and thematic 'disintegration' and 'dissonance' rather than the coherence and unitary power Beckett praised in Joyce's great symphonies.[18]

There is one point to make clear: the Beauty of *Work in Progress* is not presented in space alone, since its adequate apprehension depends as much on its visibility as on its audibility. There is a temporal as well as a spatial unity to be apprehended (*Dis*, 28).

The only unity in this story is, please God, an involuntary unity (*DFMW*, 133).

And Beckett's theory in *Proust*? In that work, Beckett defends his early French master's attempt to engage with the 'manifold component aspects' of the self in space and, most importantly, time.[19] Proust's novel is 'modern' because he engages with a reality that is inherently complex and multiple: a 'mobile' subject before a 'mobile' object – Marcel as 'the individual [composed of] a succession of individuals' confronting a 'multiple' Albertine (*PTD*, 49). But Beckett also recognises that, like *Work in Progress*, Proust's novel reveals a revelation of unitary meaning through a principle of 'apprehension', a term that Beckett originally cribbed from Stephen's aesthetic as communicated to Cranly in *Portrait* (*Dis*, 28). And it is of course this ultimate resolution by means of art – the recovery of the lost past and the fragmented self via the aesthetic – that Beckett posited as the other element in Proust's 'equation'. Christie McDonald puts it this way:

In *À la recherche du temps perdu*, Proust charts the way writing transforms the particulars of feeling and thought into form, retroactively conferring the recognition of aesthetic truth through an epiphanic vision.[20]

How did Beckett get from these theoretical origins to the wildly parodic and ironic anti-novel of disintegration that is *Dream*?

Another paradigm asserts itself when we remember that, for all the differences between Joyce and Proust (and between Beckett's essays), Beckett had a common novelistic target in both pieces: the realist novel. In taking aim at this tradition he rehearsed a critical gesture performed by theorists like Jacques Rivière in *La Nouvelle Revue Française* (which Beckett read and later published in, twice),[21] and his friend and the editor of that review, André Gide – from whom we shall see Beckett in fact derived this gesture. To mention only the obvious, Beckett's Joyce of 1929 and his Proust of 1930 are valued as 'innovators' because of their experimentation in the face of nineteenth-century novelistic realism and its inheritors: Beckett's 'parenthetical sneer' at the 'Ladies and Gentlemen' who have shunned Joyce for the 'rapid skimming and absorption of the scant cream of sense' is dutifully reiterated with greater ire in *Proust*'s rejection of the novel of 'surface' that records only 'the offal of experience' (*Dis*, 26; *PTD*, 78). And this attack on 'the grotesque fallacy of a realistic art' and 'the penny-a-line vulgarity of a literature of notations' was important enough for Beckett to redeploy it in 'Mr Beckett's' savaging of both English and French exemplars in *Dream*: *i.e.*, the 'divine Jane [Austen]' and Balzac (*PTD*, 76; *DFMW*, 119).

Beckett's concerted antipathy to the 'realist novel' as a trivial work of 'surface' and his endorsement of 'complexity' was not, of course, native to the English tradition; it was French, and specifically, it was the scepticism born of the tumultuous period of theory and experimentation that engulfed the French novel in the late nineteenth- and early twentieth-centuries, and whose fruit – the novels of writers like Céline, Camus, Sartre, or Robbe-Grillet – was later recognised to hold affinities with Beckett's own fiction. But if Beckett's 'mature' works in some ways resemble the novels of these writers, it is not only because (with the exception of Robbe-Grillet) he read them; it is because they share common roots, and specifically, a common father in the theory and practice of the novel.

I

Beckett himself acknowledged the influence of Proust, Joyce, and Dante. But he was less forthcoming about his enduring and significant debts to one of his greatest masters, whose importance to Beckett's novels and novelistic theory has, as a result, gone largely unnoticed: André Gide.[22] According to Stanley Gontarski and Chris Ackerley in their *Grove Companion to Samuel Beckett* (2004), Gide 'provided a model', but Beckett's only direct mention of the older writer is a scornful aside in his discussion of memory and habit in *Proust*.[23] To my knowledge only one critic – John Pilling – has argued for the importance of Gide to Beckett's novels, and as he has pointed out on more than one occasion (when highlighting some of the other references to Gide he has discovered in Beckett's work), such allusions as the above in fact indicate 'a *staged unconcern* … designed to mask the real interest [Beckett] had in Gide'.[24] If Pilling is right, what was Beckett's aim in feigning an 'unconcern' with the older writer? What did he have to hide?

James Knowlson's biography indicates that Beckett was probably introduced to Gide's work by Beckett's tutor and the professor of Romance languages at Trinity College, Dublin, Thomas Rudmose-Brown. Gide was part of 'Ruddy's' (at the time unusual) interest in modern authors, and Beckett's teacher at least was not immune to the magnetic force of Gide's personality; several of Rudmose-Brown's trademark utterances have a particularly Gidean ring (*DF*, 50).[25] Beckett also studied Gide for the final Moderatorship exams in which he was so successful, finishing, in his tutor's own words, 'in a blaze of glory and [with] a large gold medal in Modern Literature in Michaelmas 1927' (*DF*, 75). Two clues stand out from this period: first, after returning from his position in Paris at the École Normale Supérieure, Beckett chose to lecture on Gide and the modern novel in the autumn of 1930, which also means that he had been again bearing down on Gide's fiction as he prepared for the lectures the preceding summer (*DF*, 126). As we shall see, Beckett's choice in this regard was not an arbitrary one – a fact Beckett's former student, Rachel Burrows, suggested in her 1982 interview with Gontarski and others:

EDS.: Would Beckett have been the one who chose to have the interest in the modern novel [in his lectures]?
RB: Yes.
EDS.: In Gide?
RB: Yes. Yes he would.[26]

Second, this interest in Gide's importance as a modern novelist was not a fleeting one. One of the primary indicators of Beckett's ongoing engagement with Gide and his theory is that throughout the early to mid-thirties Beckett made numerous attempts to compose a monograph on Gide to complement his book on Proust. (The first of these attempts took place in early February of 1932, when Beckett proposed the idea to Prentice.) More telling still – and despite Ackerley and Gontarski's claim for a lack of allusion – Beckett's interest in Gide started to appear in his fiction as he parodically deployed what he termed Gide's 'modern' treatment of character and narration. He implanted allusions to Gide's writings in *Dream* and *Murphy* even as he imitated what he called Gide's '*New structure*' of the novel (MIC60, 37; Burrows's emphasis).

If Beckett's theoretical interest in Gide was as profound as I have indi-cated, this would reveal not only a new source for and an illumination of his artistic theory, but a rather different context for his early novels from those by which they have been so far understood. What if one were to perceive Beckett's early fictions, and by extension his later novels, as an attempt to develop beyond the proto-modern paradoxes of the late nineteenth- and early twentieth-century context of French aesthetic the-ory, with its post-Symbolist disdain for the novel, and its post-Naturalist disgust of linearity, closure, and 'coherence'? What might Beckett have learned from Gide's endeavour to generate narratives of 'complexity', his fascination with Dostoevsky and the convoluted structure of the *roman d'aventure*, his penchant for self-undermining narratives, or his approach to fiction as a form of *ironic critique*?

II

Beckett's book on Gide was never written, but the key components of his thinking about the older writer can be reconstructed through notes taken by his pupils on his 1930 lectures. The portrait that emerges provides a compelling model for reading Beckett's own fictional development: Gide's major works are understood as a series of ironically self-conscious responses to the problem of representation – fictions that ultimately end in contradiction and stage their own *failure*. I say *problem* of represen-tation because for Gide the novel's power lies in its capacity to engage a reality that is seen as complex and finally unknowable, a notion that put him in conflict not only with major forerunners in France but, in Gide's view, the European novelistic tradition in general.

Born in 1869, Gide came of age in a generation of French writers and intellectuals that profoundly distrusted the novel, preferring poetry to what they saw as a degenerate tradition committed to the transcription of surface reality and enslaved to reductionist philosophies. Gide's eager-ness to take up the novel was therefore shadowed at the beginning by a keen sense that his predecessors (chiefly Balzac and Zola) set an example of mastery that betrayed the novel through positioning it as a servant of or a rival to the discourses of science and history. In doing so, these writ-ers simplified the novel in the interests of achieving 'a final and conclu-sive' – and therefore, in Gide's view, false – 'solution' to the problem of the form's means and ends.[27] As Beckett pointed out to his students, the sceptical energies of Gide's mature fiction – his vicious parody of teleolo-gies and 'systems' in works like *Les Faux-Monnayeurs* and *Les Caves du*

Vatican, for example – should be understood in the light of this generational doubt; Gide's work, Beckett argued, originates in the assertion that there are forms of 'thought [which go] further than science', and that human actions 'cannot be reduced to motive[s]' (MIC60, 14). As we shall see, one measure of Beckett's abiding concern with this historical context for Gide's project is his commitment to attacking in his own novels those writers whom he described as Gide's adversaries – a critique that extends from *Dream*'s opening salvos to the final pages of *The Unnamable*.

For Beckett, a key driver of Gide's innovations in the novel thus consists in a double response to the past. First, Gide rejects a realist or Naturalist model (the two terms are not distinguished in Beckett's lectures) obsessed with reality's comprehensibility, its 'surfaces' (MIC60, 47). Second, and in tension with this rejection, Gide makes an attempt to work with his fictional inheritance, 'to renew [the] tradit[ional] structure of novel' by unleashing its potential as 'the most *lawless*' of genres (MIC60, 31; *C*, 166). But before considering how Gide approached this double task of critique and renewal the question should be asked: What lies behind Gide's view of reality, and specifically individual experience, as complex and fundamentally unknowable? In Beckett's reading a major root for this tendency was Gide's struggle with his Puritan upbringing, whose strictures sharpened contradictions in his personality even as its doctrines nurtured his congenital affinity for paradox. Beckett's lecture-hall flourish that Gide's tormented 'Protestantism explains most of his characters' or his argument that Gide should be read as a 'Protestant' first and an 'Iconoclast' second will likely find more critics than adherents (MIC60, 37; 31). Yet – in a manner that is illuminating for Beckett's own work and theory – there is much in his claim that Gide's commitment to accepting the unexplained, his refusal of logic to adequately account for human nature, and his cultivation of a poetics that admits 'failure' and contradiction are indebted to paradoxes at the heart of Protestant doctrine. For Beckett, Gide's most important trait as a novelist is a 'humility' that allows him to accept the unknowable in a manner not dissimilar to the Christian acceptance of the mystery of grace, or that enigma (which recurs continually in Gide's writing) that Beckett terms the 'Evangelistic paradox of renunciation': '[that to] save [one's] life [one must] lose it' (MIC60, 27).[28] In this view, both Gide's personal struggle with Christianity – which generated a powerful conflict in his character between the ideal and the sensual, and the sacred and the transgressive – and the antilogies within Protestant doctrine itself are relevant to his rejection of any attempt to seek a unified sense of self and world and in the novel. Just as important, in Beckett's account Gide's

vexed Christianity is inseparable from his cultivation of a poetics that rein-
scribes paradox, a comportment of 'humility' and ultimately the author's
'renouncement' [*sic*] of mastery in the form of the novel (MIC60, 23).

Gide's fascination with the ideal, with paradox, and with sacrifice
is indeed a key to his early fictions. But his Protestantism is also here
enmeshed with his first alliance with a received aesthetic paradigm: that
of Symbolism.[29] Under the spell of Schopenhauer's teachings on the rejection of the phenomenal world, Gide positioned himself as a devotee of
the new art of intuition, pure form, and essence as opposed to the 'contingent' world traditionally explored by the novel. 'In those days', Gide
wrote later,

the movement in progress was a reaction against realism.... Supported by
Schopenhauer ... I considered everything that was not *absolute* – that is to say,
the whole prismatic diversity of life – *contingent* (this was the fashionable word).
It was very much the same with every one of my companions.[30]

Beckett argued that as early as *Le Voyage d'Urien* (1893) Gide bade 'fare-
well to symbolism' and developed an original style (MIC60, 10). But he
also hints that Symbolism offered Gide a way of reconceiving the novel
that lingered in his later work. Instead of considering the form as a linear or teleological narrative, Gide co-opted a Symbolist poetics to envi-
sion the novel as an arrangement of elements in a complex of interacting
relationships. Beckett noted that this approach might be understood in
terms of a rejection of Stendhal's mirror, a claim Gide himself made
with reference to what he called the 'composition' of the work of art
(MIC60, 27):

Today the novel must prove that it can be something other than a mirror carried
down the road – that it can be superior and a priori – that is, deduced; that is,
composed, that is, a work of art.[31]

This is Gide's first serious reformulation of the idea of the novel: as a structure whose 'realism' is of a 'higher sort' than that of a mimetic representation of time or space. Gide's fascination with this view also derived
from what Beckett called his 'classical' tendencies, which Symbolism
would only have strengthened (MIC60, 39).[32] The work of art in this view
requires 'the submission ... of the word in the sentence, and the sentence
on the page, and the page in the whole work' to a greater pattern.[33]

Yet even as Gide's fascination with the novel as a work of composition
led him toward an interest in an alternative type of unity in the form,
he was compelled to reflect upon and stage this unity as another type of
artifice. In *Les Cahiers d'André Walter* (1891), Gide first experimented

with a text made up of disjointed fragments and fictional diary entries (which incorporate passages from an 'earlier' diary that the protagonist has kept even as they draw on Gide's own diary) to dramatize an authorial consciousness caught in an act of writerly composition. It was the first time he deployed an important paradigm that also became important to Beckett: that of the diary novel. But it was in a subsequent diary fiction, *Paludes* (1895) (originally subtitled *Traité de la Contingence*), that Gide deployed this strategy to distance himself from the Symbolism with which he had once allied himself. For Beckett, *Paludes* was a major work and the first of three books he identified as setting forward 'new problem[s]' for the novel (MIC60, 31).[34] In a manner that anticipates 'Mr Beckett's' difficulties in *Dream*, though, the problem that Gide's novel presents is the very difficulty of writing '*Paludes*'. Using a writer-surrogate (who is composing a work called '*Paludes*') Gide replaces plot as traditionally understood with a continual reflection on the gradual progress of the work within the work. Shifting between the narrator's fictional composition, his diary, his creature Tityre's journal, and Tityre's poetry, Gide arranges the act of composition on what Beckett termed multiple 'planes': 'action', he noted, 'instead of being treated methodically, is treated symphonically' (MIC60, 33). *Paludes* is clearly 'a novel [about] writing a novel', but the importance of this strategy is more than playful self-reflexivity; the book's multiple levels enable Gide to complicate the novel's drive toward 'conclusiveness' through a form that inevitably stages its own order and ending (MIC60, 33).

Paludes was written during a period of significant change in Gide's life. Following several trips to North Africa beginning in 1893, he began to formulate the counter-Symbolist/counter-Protestant doctrines that Beckett mocked in Gide's followers in 1930, 'opposing a pagan to a Christian ethics and an art close to life to an art far from life' and exploring such themes in *récits* like *Les Nourritures terrestres* (1893–7) and *L'Immoraliste* (1902) (Delay, 321–2).[35] As Beckett knew, however, there was a more complicated (and novelistic) dimension to Gide's development at this stage than the one suggested by his challenge to the Symbolists to engage with life. In his *récits* and diary novels, Gide had already begun to explore the reflexive current between the voice and its story in the novel – and specifically the power of narrative to mislead its narrator. Having rejected the logic of psychological or historical determinism in the novel, Gide sought to create narratives driven by a logic of ideas – moral experiments, to be sure, but ones designed for *failure*. 'At the time of my ... *Immoralist* and *Strait is the Gate*', he later claimed, 'I was almost exclusively concerned to delineate a position, a moral datum [, and] to develop my proposition to absurd lengths, to exhaust its implications.'[36] Gide accordingly created speakers who were recognizable avatars of his own complex personality and derived from his own impulses – speakers intended to portray the eventual *breakdown* and *disorientation* of their respective ideas or passions: 'All my books are ironic books; they are books of criticism. *Strait is the Gate* is the critique of a certain mystical tendency;... the *Symphonie pastorale*, of a form of self-delusion; *The Immoralist*, of a form of individualism'.[37] It is in this context that Beckett's praise of Gide as the 'most self-conscious, self-critical of [French] artists' should be understood (MIC60, 31). 'Refus[ing] to abdicate as a critic ... in [the] novel', Gide staged his speakers' undermining of their own stories in the very act of telling them (MIC60, 41). As Germaine Brée puts it of *L'Immoraliste*'s Michel, the narrator of each of these tales 'exhausts himself trying to understand how a succession of seemingly unimportant moments has assumed the inscrutable configuration of the ineluctable'.[38]

Yet Gide could not fail to recognise that, like the linear structure of the Naturalistic novel he intended to challenge, *this* form, too, was inevitably a simplification of reality – not least in its failure to acknowledge the authorial consciousness presiding over his narrator and engineering his downfall. Gide had long considered the nature of experience and of the self to be complex and ramified, involving multiple eventualities that were open to the possibility of disruption through chance, 'inconséquence', and the unforeseen. But for all their self-undermining power, his monologues ended by presenting reality as a predetermined series of relations or outcomes; there was a 'coherence in Gide', Beckett explained, 'that in spite of [his] humility he [could not] avoid' (MIC60, 25).[39] And it was through confronting this failure that Gide engaged the two poles of the paradox that, for Beckett, defined his importance as a novelist: the tension between the form-giving principle that is necessary for art, and the urge to accommodate an unaccountably complex and unknowable reality.

Gide's entire work is marked by that rivalry between the real world and the representations we make of it.... Reality presents two problems to a writer such as Gide: first, it is unknowable in itself; and second, it is impossible to communicate our perceptions of it, since the means we use impose human patterns on what extends beyond human perception (Walker, *Gide*, 178).

How, Gide asked, could the writer accommodate an unknowable reality through narrative, and especially through the novel – a feat that he considered no European writer had yet achieved?

One response to this impossible dilemma had been emerging in Gide's work for some time: to deepen the novel's ironic game with narration so as to *play at* the representation of disorder, all the while ironically exposing the novel as a work of careful composition. Gide also began to complicate the novel's hierarchical structure by setting it up as a site of shifting and uncertain authority – for example, by generating a conflict between the narrator and his characters that trespasses what J. M. Coetzee has called the novel's various narrative 'estates'.[40] Beckett spent a significant amount of time on these experiments, describing the contradictions that attempts to introduce a 'struggle [between the] artist and [his] idea' generated in Gide's fiction, especially in *Les Caves du Vatican* (1914) (MIC60, 39). In this novel, Gide stages the narrator's difficulties with controlling the events and composition of his tale even as he introduces actions at the level of the diegesis that hint at the possibility of chance and the characters' 'free will' (MIC60, 40). In doing so, Gide attempts to bring an element of '*imprévisibilité*' into the form even as he directs his fiction's critical powers against various paradigms of the novel – the quest novel, the Naturalist novel, and even anti-novels such as *Les Caves du Vatican* itself (MIC60, 9). By including figures and elements that mirror even the anti-novelist narrator who controls *Les Caves du Vatican* (Lafcadio, Protos, the Millipede), Gide's fiction achieves a self-critical form that *stages* its own anti-realism.

These innovations suggest Gide's importance in the modern novel, but for Beckett the complex form of *Les Caves du Vatican*, like that of Gide's next and greatest work, *Les Faux-Monnayeurs*, is also heavily indebted to the works of another 'modern' writer: Fyodor Dostoevsky. Dostoevsky's innovations began to seep into French literature in the 1870s and 80s. But although these books created a fervour among Gide's contemporaries, the complex depiction of character and the use of nuanced and dramatic interior monologue in works like *The Devils* (1871) and *The Brothers Karamazov* (1880) had yet to spawn much fruitful imitation by the time of Beckett's lectures.[41] And while it is true that of all the novelists then writing in France, Gide became Dostoevsky's most avid pupil, it should be noted that (as Gide pointed out in his 1922 lectures on his Russian master) he found those things in Dostoevsky that he had long been searching out in himself.[42] Gide's study of Dostoevsky, and Beckett's study of *that* relationship will be examined in detail in the following chapters, but four of the most important ideas that Beckett's Gide found in Dostoevsky should be listed here. These notions are traceable to Gide's vision of the modern novel's origins in a double refusal: a rejection of the European model of social realism *and* the Symbolist aspiration to create a 'pure' form free from contingence (*C*, 167). Instead, the Dostoevskian novel is an inherently 'lawless' and ramified form, rejecting linearity and admitting the contradiction and chaos of the real (*C*, 167). It forgoes a transcription of a social and civic world to focus on the obscure inner reality of its characters. It is thus an inherently 'psychological' form, and depicts consciousness as *dis*-unified and divided (MIC60, 52). Finally, the Dostoevskian novel presents a narrative model of 'abnegation' that follows the protagonist's journey to his 'utter ruin' (MIC60, 23; *D*, 150).[43]

Dostoevsky undoubtedly provided Gide with an example, but *Les Caves du Vatican* and *Les Faux-Monnayeurs* are not Dostoevskian in tone or technique.[44] Instead, they reveal Gide's own mature conceptualisation of the novel as a critical, ironic form, and his attempt to confront the problem of an unknowable reality by means that inevitably fail. If *Les Faux-Monnayeurs* never achieves coherence or closure this is because Gide intended that the novel end 'by a sort of blurring of its outline'; 'It must not be neatly rounded off', he wrote, 'but rather disperse, disintegrate ...' (*LC*, 49). This formal complexity and especially this preoccupation with ending mapped onto Gide's conceptualisation of the novel as 'the most *lawless*' of genres (*C*, 166), a form aptly suited for a critique of fixed systems, and the disruption of the reader's expectations and beliefs.[45] To borrow from one of Gide's inheritors, Robbe-Grillet, it is in this sense that Gide is a master of contradiction and paradox, and a forerunner of writers like Beckett 'who wish to explore ... insoluble oppositions, fragmentations, diegetic aporias, breaks, voids, etc., because they know that the real begins at the exact moment when meaning falters'.[46]

It should now be clear that Gide's fiction and theory confronted Beckett with a different set of ambitions and problems from those in the work of Joyce or Proust. Gide's continual need to exceed forms of the novel, often by parodying them, and his approach to the novel as a kind of auto-critique which undermines its own foundations, developed out of his struggle with an incommunicable reality. And the concomitant necessity of writing about that reality was always going to lead him toward an art of failure. Even as Proust signalled his ongoing assimilation of the lessons of Symbolism in *À la recherche du temps perdu* (published from 1913 onward), and Joyce followed his own Symbolist inclinations to create the cosmic music of *Finnegans Wake*, Gide's fictional experiments and his absorption of Dostoevsky led him in a different direction. As Beckett put it, Gide was driven by the urge to '*preserv[e] the integrity of incoherence*' in the novel – rather than the need to conceal the unknowable through Naturalistic linearity, or overcome it by a new form of symbolic apprehension and aesthetic mastery (MIC60, 37; Burrows's emphasis).

Following Gide, Beckett would come into conflict with major traditions of the novel – not just its realist or Symbolist exemplars. Specifically, he would have to challenge the form's roots in the masterplot of biography and the arch-paradigm of this plot in the novel, the *Bildungsroman*. These were fights the young Beckett was happy to pick. For, like Gide – that figure of disunity and contradiction – Beckett was not only concerned with the complexity of reality but also of the self. And so when Beckett mocks Goethe's 'pure man' in his first novel ('We live and learn ... like a pure man, and we honour our Father, our Mother, and Goethe' (*DFMW*, 179)), he makes one of his first moves against a major origin of the European novel in the German tradition of self-cultivation. In this tradition, the artwork seeks to shine its light on that inner 'pure Ideal man, whose unchanging oneness it is the great task of his being, in all its changes, to correspond'.[47] Like Gide, Beckett had no use for such unity or purity. In his hands the novel, like the selves that inhabit it, falls under the sway of an unsettling, comic energy which disintegrates unities and activates internal conflicts.

III

Let me reiterate the question posed at the beginning of this introduction: How did Beckett get from his early theoretical notions to the wildly parodic and ironic anti-novel of disintegration that is *Dream*? Let me also add the question: What happened between 1929 (when Beckett wrote 'Dante ... Bruno.Vico ... Joyce') and the spring of 1931, when Beckett began composing his first novel? The answer, in short, is that he took on board the lessons that led Gide toward his greatest experiments in the novel.

We have already seen that aspects of Beckett's aesthetic theory immediately after *Proust* and in the months before *Dream* can be reconstructed by virtue of the lectures he gave in the autumn of 1930. But while the notes taken by Beckett's students have been known to scholars for several years, the importance of the lectures to Beckett's *novels* has not been demonstrated.[48] This is the more unfortunate because Beckett's discussion of literature at this time revolves around his early formulation of a problem that was clearly of abiding significance to him. He confronted it for the first time in his first novel, and it haunted him until his last work, the 1988 poem 'comment dire' ('what is the word'), written in the months before his death. Beckett posed this problem, a paradox, to his students in 1930. We find it recorded in the shorthand of one of his pupils:

Artistic statement – extractive of essential real. Reality – unavailable (MIC60, 105).

CHAPTER I

'The Integrity of Incoherence':
Theory and Dream of Fair to Middling Women

Beckett's focus in his 1930 account of the novel centred on the relationship between the artwork and what he referred to as an 'incoherent', and therefore (for the purposes of the artist) an 'unavailable' reality – an unsurprising emphasis given his valorisation of the 'complexity' of subject and object and their relation in his recently completed *Proust*. In his lectures, Beckett's vision of an incoherent reality remained indebted to his *Proust* (continuing to centre on a novelistic exploration of a 'multiple' subjectivity), but also took on new dimensions and emphases.

Beckett defended Proust in the lectures as a modern writer with crucial insights, but also criticised him for the ultimate 'solution' he provided to the problem of 'indeterminacy' confronted by the artwork.[1] Through the 'miracle' of involuntary memory, Beckett argued, Proust achieved a kind of resolution to the problem of the fragmented, suffering subjectivity at the heart of the novel – a Schopenhauerian vision of a release from suffering through art. Beckett repeatedly emphasised this 'implacable recovery' in Proust's 'equation' for a specific purpose: to illustrate the 'radicality' of other models. These were Gide (who, to a lesser degree than Proust, was also guilty of 'coherence'), and, chiefly, Gide's Dostoevsky.[2] Beckett turned to these exemplars because, in the face of a reality that was ultimately 'unknown', he wished to ask a question unlike that asked by Proust, for whom the '*Whole problem*' of the artwork was '*how to apprehend the real?*' (MIC60, 99; Burrows's emphasis). Rather than this Proustian urge to unite the ideal and the real in a transcendent moment of aesthetic 'apprehension', Beckett described a fundamentally 'different need' from any he had hitherto expressed for the artwork: '*preserving* [the] *integrity of incoherence*' (MIC60, 37; Burrows's emphasis).

Beckett's lectures indicate he found paradigms of indeterminacy and incoherence early in the history of the French novel, specifically in the

17

school of the 'Pre-Naturalists'. Flaubert and Stendhal were his models in this regard, and were given the compliment of being the 'real ancestors of the modern novel' (MIC60, 89). What is most important about these writers is that through engaging with the multiple facets of reality through a number of modes and perspectives, their work leaves 'some material indeterminate' (MIC60, 103). In contrast to Proust's vision of aesthetic consolation and transcendance, there is 'No such solution in Stendhal'. While this lack of solution involves the absence of any 'participation betw[een] ideal & real' (leading to a disjunction in which these poles 'coexist in [a] state of incoherence'), it is also a product of what Beckett terms 'dualism': the engagement with multiple and incommensurable aesthetic approaches or systems within the same work or corpus. In contrast to the Romantics or the Naturalists, who allocated 'absolute value to one system of reference & point of view', having 'only one valid vision of [their] material', Flaubert and Stendhal (while 'both could be called Realists') nevertheless display an 'organic' tension between their romantic heritage and realistic modes. Flaubert's work thus involves '2 different Flauberts' evidenced in *Madame Bovary* and *Salammbô*. While there is an 'implication' of conflicting 'elements' in his work 'merging', 'confusion [is] ineluctable' and in the 'final analysis' the work proves 'incoherent' (MIC60, 89). In a similar fashion, Flaubert combines the tendency to act as a realistic 'photographer' with his use of the 'image' – in the lectures a term connected with the Bergsonian concept of 'intuition' (versus what Beckett terms a Naturalistic 'mechanical intelligence') (MIC60, 3). Stendhal's 'dualism' joins the 'Rom[antic] negation of value' with the 'classicism of [a] psychologist [*sic*]'. The 'psychological real' in Stendhal thus remains 'imperceptible from any point of view'; he 'finds his reality can be satisfied by no value' for 'Only [a] multiplicity of values can satisfy his equation'. In its indeterminacy, his work displays an 'intimate contact with modern thought' (MIC60, 99–101).

Exemplified by Balzac and Zola, the Naturalists present a contrasting 'forced unification' at the level of form and in their portrayal of subjectivity. In place of the psychological complexity demanded by Stendhal's classical realism, Naturalism displays that 'Notetaking', that record of 'surface', which Beckett derided in *Proust* in favour of an 'excavatory' art. The 'Naturalistic and traditional novel seems like nature', Burrows records, 'but is only surface' (MIC60, 47). Beckett also argued that the Naturalists' simplicity is involved with a 'preconceived equation'. This *preconceived* resolution (note the difference here with what Beckett in 1934 termed Proust's 'search' for his own 'equation' (*Dis*, 65)) relates to a major criticism Beckett levied against those artists who 'abdicate' as critics of their own work. While the Naturalists remained in an attitude of self-assured control of their material, in the work of the self-critical writer (Gide) there is a certain 'organic' conflict evident between the artist and the motivations of his characters – the admission of 'antagonism' between writer and creation at the level of composition. The artist thus remains aware of his role and seeks to introduce 'indeterminacy' through limiting this role, even allowing his characters 'free will'. In contrast, the Naturalists see reality and the artwork operating according to predetermined laws. In this view, the 'Material of life [is] a billiard table concerned with [the] impact of balls' and the artist therefore simply 'must set the billiard balls in motion for interest' (MIC60, 5). Beckett similarly described the Naturalistic novelists as involved in a 'Snowball-act', presumably a metaphor to illustrate the inevitability of a foreseeable outcome explicable by rational causes. The 'Snowball-act' 'releases [the] purely mechanical setting' toward the 'Arbitrary direction given to [the] material by [the] artist [, which results in a] constant acceleration to crisis' (MIC60, 40). In Balzac's novels the 'characters can't change their minds or [the] artistic structure crashes – [they] must be consistent' (MIC60, 41). Within such rigid form, the initial 'trajectory' of a character is one which is an 'Irreversible [and] final statement of personality' (MIC60, 40).[3]

As if to turn the Proustian principle on its head, Beckett thus indicated that any 'solution' to the problems posed by the artwork was to be avoided by the writer seeking 'indeterminacy' and 'incoherence'. As becomes evident in the lectures and Beckett's subsequent novel, these terms indicate the failure to arrive at any position from which a value or set of values – including that of the aesthetic – can be conclusively asserted in the artwork. In making such claims, Beckett indicated that he was describing an artistic 'need' foreign not just to Proust, but to what he terms the 'European tradition' (MIC60, 24). This was not yet the 'literature of the unword' which in 1937 Beckett claimed would deploy language against itself (an art which would exploit a 'dissonance between the means and their use'), or the paradoxically 'expressive act' of the 'inexpressive' artist described by 'B.' in *Three Dialogues* (1949), but it was a surprisingly early step toward the internal contradictions of the later theory (*Dis*, 172–3; see *Proust*, 109–126).[4] The 1930 art of 'incoherence' is the attempt to disrupt any 'continuity' of form or content in the novel through addressing the multiple and disjunctive facets of reality – ultimately by allowing incommensurable 'antagonisms' into the work. The subjectivity explored in such a novel would not only be multiple, as in Proust, but divided against itself.

The source of Beckett's 1930 argument for preserving incoherence in art was a text whose importance to Beckett's subsequent work has been hitherto largely unacknowledged: Gide's book *Dostoïevsky* (1923).[5] While Beckett discussed this text in its own right,[6] the remarkable degree to which it undergirds his thought at this point (and anticipates aspects of his later theory) is evident throughout the lectures, not simply his account of the modern novel. Racine's characters, for example, are described as having 'depth' and *'solitary needs'*, while his plays manifest a 'division in [the] minds of antagonists' – qualities Gide contends for in *Dostoïevsky*. Similarly, Stendhal and Flaubert (the 'Pre-Naturalists' in Beckett's terminology) are presented as the 'real ancestors of the modern novel' because of their Dostoevskian 'duality', 'complexity', and 'indeterminacy' (MIC60, 19, 7). Beckett's chief novelistic target in the lectures, and the writer who would become the fall guy of his own novel, hails from the same source: Dostoevsky's foil, the 'Naturalist' Balzac 'with his self-assurance' in the 'perfect consistency of his characters' (*D*, 17).[7] In short, the account of the novel and art given by Beckett in 1930 – a history divided between explorers of complexity (the moderns and the 'Pre-Naturalists') and those seeking 'explanations' and conclusiveness (the 'Naturalists') – falls along the lines of the dichotomy limned in Gide's text between the modern inheritors of Dostoevsky's 'interrogative' art and those following the Western-European exercise of 'mechanical intelligence'.

Dostoevsky is thus introduced in Beckett's lectures as a counterparadigm – again, not simply to French literary tendencies but to what is described as the 'European' novel. This otherness essentially consists in Dostoevsky's treatment of subjectivity. In contrast to the Naturalists, Dostoevsky posits the ultimate incomprehensibility of the actions and personalities of his characters. In Gide's terms, each act is an 'Action gratuite' which has 'no social motive' and evidences a 'secret reason for living' which remains hidden from the individual himself (MIC60, 23). Dostoevsky's 'Rejection of motive' thus denies the fundamental assumption of rational motivation or causality that undergirds Beckett's vision of the Naturalistic novel; his work grants *'no chain'* of cause and effect (MIC60, 23, 29; Burrows's emphasis). Burrows's notes on this subject recall Gide's claim that Dostoevsky's contribution to the novel involves his particularly 'Russian' attention to the 'inner life' rather than 'social connections' (MIC60, 70). It is this attention to his characters' relationships with themselves, or with God, that makes

Dostoevsky's work anathema to what Gide terms 'Western-European logic' (MIC60, 2).

This exploration into the secret areas of the self is accomplished in Dostoevsky's writing through his use of 'light', and most important, 'shadow'. Gide's metaphor is a contrast with Stendhal's figure for the novel as a mirror (though Gide applies this same concept to virtually all novels in the French and English tradition), a plane designed to indiscriminately reflect all the available light of a brightly lit, panoramic world. In contrast, Dostoevsky's novels are works of depth and singular focus, obscuring a portrait, like a single figure set on a stage, within a darkness that the artist does not seek to dispel but rather makes integral to the work (*D, 99*). Beckett paraphrased or quoted the following passage, which I reproduce at length because of its importance to his theory of art in the lectures as a whole.

Between [Dostoevsky's] novels and those of the authors quoted above [Stendhal, Tolstoy, Voltaire, Fielding, Smollett, Lesage, etc.] there is all the difference possible between a picture and a panorama. Dostoevsky composes a picture in which the most important consideration is the question of light. The light proceeds from but one source. In one of Stendhal's novels, the light is constant, steady, and well-diffused. Every object is lit up in the same way, and is visible equally well from all angles; there are no shadow effects. But in Dostoevsky's books, as in a Rembrandt portrait, the shadows are the essential. Dostoevsky groups his characters and happenings, plays a brilliant light upon them, illuminating one aspect only. Each of these characters has a deep setting of shadow, reposes on its own shadow almost (*D, 99*).

While this concept – an art that is a consciously staged portrait in which shadows are the 'essential' – may require some development for its importance to become evident in relation to Beckett's novels, the application to his dramatic work is obvious: stark, painterly images from mature works like *Krapp's Last Tape, Not I, That Time,* or *Ohio Impromptu* immediately spring to mind. But while literal light or shadow is not the issue in the novel, the importance of this principle to Beckett's work in this form is equally significant. Gide indicates that the novelist creates a metaphorical 'shadow' through introducing complexity and irresolution on two interconnected levels: the 'background' and the 'figure' itself.

At the level of background, Dostoevsky follows his 'impulse' to develop as many interrelations as possible between events and elements of the novel, and then, instead of resolving them through an act of artistic mastery, promotes their lack of relation to each other and the work. Again, the notes indicate that Beckett referred to a specific passage in Gide's text:

We notice in Dostoevsky a strange impulse to group, concentrate, centralise: to create between the varied elements of a novel as many cross-connections as possible. With him, events instead of pursuing their calm and measured course, as with Stendhal or Tolstoy, mingle and confuse in turmoil; the elements of the story – moral, psychological, and material – sink and rise in a kind of whirlpool. With him there is no attempt to straighten or simplify lines; he is at his happiest in the complex; he fosters it (*D,* 100).

Second, at the level of character, 'shadow' develops through Dostoevsky's unwillingness to inflict unity upon his characters, choosing instead to display 'divergences' and contradictions in their thoughts, actions, and personalities. To illustrate this point, Gide quotes the French critic Jacques Rivière on the 'two ways of materialising' his character from which an artist must choose. It is a passage that must have gripped Beckett, for its imagery resurfaces in *Dream*:

[The artist] can either insist on its complexity, or emphasise its cohesiveness ... [;] he can deliberately reproduce its absolute darkness, or for the reader he can dispel such darkness by his very description of it; he will either respect the soul's hidden depths, or lay them open. At need, we [novelists of the second order] force things a trifle; we suppress a few small divergencies, and interpret certain obscure details in a sense most useful towards establishing a psychological unity. The ideal we strive towards is the complete closing up of every gulf.[8]

Gide claims that while the urge to 'dispel such darkness' (to reject 'inconséquence') is a tendency within the European novel, it is most characteristically French, for 'what we French require most of all is logic.... We sacrifice truth (that is to say, sincerity) to purity and continuity of line' (*D,* 102). In this sense, Gide argues, Balzac is the archetypal French novelist, and by implication, carries the European novelistic tradition of illumination to its logical end. In contrast, the 'black gulfs [in the novel's characters are precisely what] interested Dostoevsky most, and his whole effort is directed towards suggesting how utterly unreachable they are' (*D,* 100). Burrows's notes also indicate that Beckett contrasted Dostoevsky with Hardy in this regard. Using Gide's metaphor, Beckett criticised Hardy as a 'simplifier' whose 'landscape [was an] animisation of [the] inanimate'. His work thus '[r]eflects shadow + mystery of landscape – not [that of the] character' (MIC60, 53). Borrowing Gide's comparisons, Beckett indicated that Balzac paints like David, and Dostoevsky like Rembrandt.

The notes indicate that Beckett paid particular attention to Gide's delineation of the Dostoevskian incoherence of the figure in its divergence from the Franco-European tradition. For example, Gide states that the Corneillian hero is always recognisable as a rational, coherent entity – although caught in a struggle between the ideal to which he strives to conform and his natural being (Gide terms this situation 'bovaryism'). In Dostoevsky, however, there are 'two distinct personalities in the same body' which manifest themselves in conflict at the same moment: 'Each character never relinquishes consciousness of his dual personality with its inconsistencies' (*D*, 103). Dostoevsky's characters are thus beset by an unsettling 'duality'. For example, in *The Possessed*, we find characters being split between their rational and irrational selves, tortured by the simultaneous manifestation of their twin personalities that drive the 'inconsequential' action of the novel (*D*, 104).

Although Gide claims that 'Dostoevsky seems to recognise a kind of 'stratification' in the self, and that this inner division is indeed a cause of torment, there remains the possibility of a renunciation of self, and thus escape from what might be termed, to borrow from Beckett in *Proust*, the 'suffering of being' (*PTD*, 20). This was apparently an area of interest for Beckett, which he discussed as the attempt at 'abnegation' (MIC60, 23). In a passage that Beckett found compelling, Gide describes

three strata or regions Dostoevsky seems to discern in the human personality: first, the province of intellectual speculation, then the domain of the passions, midway between the former and the third region, a vast realm remote from the play of passion (*D*, 126).

While critics have proposed a number of philosophical and psychological templates for the puzzling tripartite inner division evidenced in Belacqua and Murphy, the preceding quotation indicates that it was in fact Dostoevsky's 'stratification' that provided Beckett with the framework for the 'personality' of his first two protagonists.[9] Murphy and Belacqua also manifest the same Schopenhauerian tendency as Dostoevsky's figures in their gravitation toward the irrational (Belacqua longs for the 'womb-tomb'; Murphy flirts with madness) and their preference for what Gide describes as 'that deeper region, which is not the soul's hell, but its heaven' (*D*, 126). Like Dostoevsky's characters, Beckett's protagonists seek such release through negating that 'Hell, according to Dostoevsky, [which] is the first region [of the self], the realm of mind and reason' (*D*, 127). 'The Kingdom of Heaven' can therefore only be attained by renouncing the self and 'sinking deep in a solidarity that knows no distinctions'. This is

that wider region ... : a region where love is not, nor passion ... : the region Schopenhauer spoke of, the meeting-place of human brotherhood, where the limits of existence fade away, where the notion of the individual and of time is lost, the place wherein Dostoevsky sought ... the secret of happiness (*D*, 125).

Gide himself provided a blueprint for a '*New structure*' of the novel which, like Dostoevsky's use of 'shadow', Beckett later adapted to his own use. Burrows's notes suggest that this new form, as Beckett would write concerning the paintings of Avigdor Arikha in 1982, would need to arise from the 'double awareness' that became so important to Beckett himself: a 'grasp of the past and of the problems that beset continuance' that was to be 'at once transcended and implicit in [the] work' (SB qtd. in Thomas and Coppel, 8). To use Beckett's terminology, this past was the legacy of the Romantic, Pre-Naturalist, and Naturalist traditions in France. As noted, Gide positioned this tradition within that of the 'European' novel – a form for him typified by Western logic and the aesthetic assumptions underpinning Stendhal's realism. For Gide, the 'most self-conscious [and] self-critical of [French] artists', the need to engage with this past thus necessitated the monumental attempt to 'renew [the] traditional structure of [the] novel' (MIC60, 31). Gide thus could accept neither the aesthetic solution provided by the realist novel nor what Beckett termed the modern 'analytical' novel (the latter having been 'killed by Proust' anyway) (MIC60, 31). He 'seeks [a] new narrative form' which is 'analytical without being demonstrative [and] *interrogative not conclusive*' (MIC60, 31; Burrows's emphasis).

For Beckett, Gide's 'new narrative form' is therefore in one sense realist, yet lacks the assumption that the real is simply that which could be reflected by the artwork acting as a Stendhalian mirror of the external world.[10] In fact, in its attempt to portray reality, especially the 'inner life' of a character's relationship to himself, it continually confronts multiplicity and flux. It is analytical, yet in its 'humility' ultimately resists what Beckett termed the 'implacable recovery' and 'conclusiveness' crystallised in Proust's equation (MIC60, 33). The failure to achieve any 'ending' to the narrative (which of course became central for Beckett, as it had been for Gide) is thus highlighted as a primary concern of Beckett's conception of the modern novel as early as the 1930 lectures.

The failure of resolution in this new form of novel occurs at two levels: that of the inner life of the character as he searches for the value of his experience, and in the mind of the novelist as he composes his narrative. It is this *dual failure* to achieve the certainty necessary to conclude that delineates the territory of the modern 'psychological realist'. As one of Beckett's other students, Leslie Daiken, recorded,

The Essential difference between the psychological realist of the 17th and of the twentieth centuries is that [in] the first, the mind … *can* become unified, and *can* attain a state of awareness in consciousness. But Gide's has no end. His novels *don't* end. He cannot see anything seriously, with a sense of finality.[11]

Beckett suggests that Gide partially achieved this inconclusiveness through accepting the division of the self pioneered in Proust and the 'darkness' surrounding the figure in Dostoevsky. In either case, the self could not be depicted in its totality for it is obscured and divided among the 'planes' that compose it, whether through the multiplicity of time, Dostoevskian simultaneity, or, as Beckett seems to suggest was most often the case in Gide, the 'multiplicity' of interpretation possible regarding any action or identity.

Most important, Gide's work contains several innovations in presenting such division at the level of form. Gide's development of a divided or conflicted form is particularly important because in Beckett's view the French novel was essentially the transposition of 'Theatre strictures' imported from French classical drama.[12] According to Beckett, this dramatic emphasis on unity and resolution was one of the primary forces that led to the Naturalistic obsession with closure and resolution, and he argued that Gide resisted this temptation through what Burrows records as an 'interruption' in each of three novels (MIC60, 31). In the light of Beckett's own *Three Novels* (and what he once described as his 'series' extending back to *Murphy*), it is worth noting that the lectures indicate Gide's acknowledgment of a common trajectory among these three works (the *soties Paludes, Le Prométhée mal enchaîné, Les Caves du Vatican*), coupled with the intent to address a 'new problem in each book' (MIC60, 31). Using an analogy recalled in *Dream* (although its origin is almost certainly in *Les Faux-Monnayeurs*), Beckett argued that in *Paludes* the 'Action instead of being treated melodically is treated symphonically – [the] interest [is] in potential, in milieu, unrealised actions' (MIC60, 33). Action in *Paludes* is thus a matter of not only what did happen, but what could happen, or what possibly happened; in this sense, action is deliberately 'subjectivised' as a component of each character's consciousnesses rather than granted as part of an objective stream of events. Thus *'action'* for Gide *'ceased to be interesting* [in contrast to the] *final expansion of personality'*. Recycling a phrase he had used to discuss Dostoevsky's work, Beckett stated that in *Le Prométhée mal enchaîné* such action is further 'devoid of outer motive. E.g., *Action gratuite'* (MIC60, 35).

Les Faux-Monnayeurs, however, was Beckett's concrete example of the formal qualities of the new novel Gide had pioneered. Just as the person and his actions are composed of 'planes' (that is, the person is divided through time, motivation, and so on, just as his actions may be interpreted on a number of levels), so the structure of the novel as a whole is divided into certain levels of internal involvement that results in '[n]o conclusive gesture or judgment' and 'no absolute value' in the work as a whole (MIC60, 35). Burrows recorded that *Les Faux-Monnayeurs* may thus be read as a work involved with each of four increasingly complex and self-reflexive meanings:

1. Objective statement of characters.
2. Intervention of Eduard [*sic*] (author, partly ... Gide) assisting at material to make a novel of it – Journal d'Eduard [*sic*] – comments as spectator.
3. Eduard [*sic*] judged in turn by various characters.
4. Eduard [*sic*] no longer spectator – involved in action by interest in young man (MIC60, 35).

As in Proust's analytical novel, there are many levels on which events may be interpreted, but because 'each plane [is only] provisional [and] potentially true', the whole manifests the structure of the 'Analytic novel refusing to ... make connexions' (MIC60, 37). The multivalent structure of the novel is also indicated in the title, which may be examined in a number of ways: as a title for Edouard's novel within the novel, as referring to the group of schoolboys, the artistic act itself, or as a satiric reference to the Lycée's 'falsification of education' (MIC60, 37). It is the 'incommensurability' – the conflict in the work which echoes the conflict in its characters – between different levels of meaning which results in the '*New* structure' in *Les Faux-Monnayeurs* (MIC60, 37).

The breakdown of levels of meaning in Gide's novel described here does more than indicate different readings that Beckett felt Gide built into the structure of this work; it specifically highlights the importance of Edouard as a liminal figure at once within and detached from the novel. Gide, Beckett pointed out, was interested in just such an exploration of 'liminal consciousness' (MIC60, 42).[13] While the novel may be read on a realist level as an 'objective statement', the 'intervention' of Edouard signals what Beckett would have termed an 'interruption' of any such reading; Edouard becomes a problematic figure for the 'author' who judges his material yet who is nevertheless 'judged ... by various characters'. Indeed, as Edouard claims in his journal, his relationship to his own fictions is a problematic one – while their creator, he nevertheless 'work[s] at their dictation' (*C*, 105). Edouard thus embodies Beckett's claim that in order to engage with complexity, the 'Author must be stated at [the] same time as

[his] material' and the struggle between the artist and his ideas 'must be incorporated in [the] novel' (MIC60, 39). Unlike Balzac, Gide's commitment to the novel as a form of critique meant he refused to be detached from his material as a 'moralist' (MIC60, 39).

Gide's willingness to enter, as it were, into the world of incommensurability and paradox of his novels leads to what Beckett described as 'free will' accorded to his creatures with a resultant, and laudable, 'conflict' between them and the author (MIC60, 40). In *Les Faux-Monnayeurs* this involvement between the writer and characters is evident in 'Parallel planes of sentiment & action' which even involve a paradoxical *'Free will of creator & free will of creature'* (MIC60, 41). While in Balzac's novels the characters can't change their minds or [the] artistic structure crashes', this 'traditional artistic statement [is] broken by Gide' (MIC60, 41). The artist instead '[t]urns to impulse' in his creative work, and determines that an act is 'only interesting [in] suggesting the (multiple) probable – (kinetic) potential' (MIC60, 41). As Edouard claims,

Only this remains – that reality interests me inasmuch as it is plastic, and that I care more ... for what may be than for what has been. I lean with a fearful attraction over the depths of each creature's possibilities and weep for all that lies atrophied under the heavy lid of custom and morality (*C*, 105).

FIGURE AND GROUND: *DREAM, PORTRAIT,* AND *DOSTOÏEVSKY*

Beckett's first novel reveals he was already realising, though perhaps not consciously, that his own path lay not in creating art as an 'expressive vocation', but, as Gide wrote of Dostoevsky, as an exploration of ideas submitted 'in the problematic state, in the form of a question' (*D*, 91). The idea that *Dream* submits in the form of a question, however, is the very possibility of its own emergence under the pressure of Beckett's 1930 criticism of any aesthetic solution to the problem of complexity in the novel. The result is a work that parodies and resists each of the novelistic archetypes – including Gide and his Dostoevsky – with which Beckett had engaged in the immediately preceding years. In spite of all its stylistic correlations with Joyce, or its conceptual debts to Gide and Dostoevsky, *Dream* thus stands apart as a novel of ideas that takes the form of the novel *as* its idea. This tricky position suggests (as Belacqua says of his narrator) that Beckett himself was at this stage still 'a borderman' (*DFMW*, 186). *Dream* charts its author's youthful travels, not just between countries, but paradigms of the novel.

If one were to place Beckett's first novel into any subcategory of the genre, it would be the *Bildungsroman*, and more specifically, the *Künstlerroman*, an account of a young artist's development. *Dream* clearly gestures toward this kind of novel; it is, after all, the story of a young poet and aspiring novelist (Belacqua) who develops a theory of art. Yet while a category will usually relate only to some aspects of a novel's construction, on closer inspection *Dream* suggests a deliberate attempt on the part of the writer to resist and parody the conventions of the *Künstlerroman*, specifically through *Dream*'s engagement with *Portrait*. For example, the depiction of his protagonist's youth in Joyce's novel of education serves as a one-and-a-half page condensation of tensions typical to the genre the hero will confront (social/religious authority and the individual, the creative instinct versus the drive toward conformity, etc.), and closes with the veiled threat of retribution if the hero attempts to step out of the constraints entailed in his origins. Stephen is nevertheless shown beginning to sing 'his song'.[14] In contrast, *Dream*'s introductory section takes Joyce's compression of the dynamics of his hero's origins to a comical extreme (Chapter 'One' takes up only a quarter of a page), and relates as its chief event the artist as an 'overfed child' beholding a 'gush of mard' issuing from a horse (*DFMW*, 1).

Indeed, while *Dream* may be a portrait of an artist as a young man, any education that Belaqua undergoes is closer to that of the disillusionment with ideals and the failure to become an artist charted in Flaubert's anti-Romantic *L'Éducation sentimentale* (which Beckett studied at Trinity) than that provided to Stephen – the much-discussed irony in Joyce's novel notwithstanding.[15] Certainly, the exacerbation, rather than self-defining development, of the protagonist's situation is evident at the close of *Dream*. Perhaps more sceptical than even Flaubert's novel, *Dream* targets not only romantic sentimentality within art and culture, but the very grounds that allow the novel to exist in the first place: like the aesthetic theories of its protagonist, the narrator acknowledges that the hope that *Dream* itself will ever be realised as a work of art remains 'up in the rigging' (*DFMW*, 139). To claim that *Dream* is a novel in the tradition of a post-Romantic education of disillusionment, however, would place a weight of resolution on the work which it will not bear. More as a result of the fact that this novel's 'coherence [has] gone to pieces' than any nihilism, no value, aesthetic or otherwise, seems readily available to the protagonist or the reader as a result of this tale (*DFMW*, 139).

This inconclusiveness is perhaps most significantly due to the fact that Belacqua is never granted the ability to 'make sense' of his own narrative, to achieve that self-assessment crucial for the hero of the *Bildungsroman* that would allow the narrative to achieve a certain closure. Unlike Stephen, who achieves some self-definition, or Flaubert's Frédéric, who at last self-critically beholds his lifelong sentimentality, Belacqua reappears in much the same manner as he did at the beginning – only in a rather worse set of circumstances. Ejected by the second of the 'leading ladies' of the novel, he is seen hobbling alone on his 'ruined feet' through the unrelenting rain on a moonless and starless night with no money for the tram (which is no longer running anyway), in so much pain he is forced to collapse in a foetal position on the pavement 'far from shelter' (*DFMW*, 241). His incredulity at his own body and its (recalcitrant) workings echoes the opening of the novel in 'TWO', as does the command, here given by an unseen policeman, to move along. Like the artist who oversees his narrative, Belacqua at the 'END' still does not 'quite know where [he] is in this story'; like so many of Beckett's heroes yet to come he remains under compulsion, without 'absolution or remission', to go on (*DFMW*, 9, 8).

If Beckett's first novel is pessimistic concerning the very possibility of the novel as a form, this is largely an effect of its subversion of the novel of education at the level of subjectivity. As Thomas Jeffers has recently pointed out, the *Bildungsroman* since Goethe has posed a question that can be succinctly formulated as follows:

Does the life of a young person of sensibility have a purpose, and if so, was that purpose bestowed from without, say by nature or by nature's God, or was it generated from within, by the person's own conscious choices and instinctive impulses? Or could it in some discernible way be the product of both, as in the Protestant concept of cooperative Grace?[16]

Dream unsurprisingly resists both answers (and Goethe's synthesis of Providence and individual choice in *Wilhelm Meister*) because any question like the preceding one presupposes an integral individual essence that *can* be directed or developed, and it is precisely this 'unity' that *Dream* attempts to abolish.[17] Similarly, if there is a Providence in Beckett's novel, it is the capricious, pessimistic voice of the clown Grock whose 'Not likely' subverts any typical trajectory or resolution ('The only unity in this story' the narrator sighs, 'is … an involuntary unity') (*DFMW*, 133). Rather than a question asked of individual experience, *Dream* poses a dilemma to the novel: What is to be done with a character that is 'trine' 'at his simplest' – a protagonist who is 'Centripetal, centrifugal and … not'? (*DFMW*, 120).

There *is* a theory of the novel as a 'portrait' undergirding *Dream*, but it owes less to Joyce than to Gide's Dostoevsky, whose characters are compared to a Rembrandt figure 'repos[ing] in its own shadow' (*D*, 99). Belacqua does not seek to define himself against a world of convention, but to attain a state that can only be described as that of nonbeing in the face of a reality of incoherent values – a state completely without figure and ground, inaccessible to the methods and ends of realism (*DFMW*, 122–3). In this sense, Beckett's caricatural deployment of the conventions of the *Künstlerroman* reveals a parodic rewriting of Stephen's aesthetic theory in *Portrait* through a development of the 'spotlighting' theory in *Dostoïevsky*. Recall Stephen's tripartite exposition of 'the necessary phases of artistic apprehension', the same theory that leads him toward his hope to 'encounter ... the reality of experience' at the novel's close:

your mind first of all separates the basket from the rest of the visible universe which is not the basket. The first phase of apprehension is a bounding line drawn about the object to be apprehended.... temporal or spatial, the esthetic image is first luminously apprehended as selfbounded and selfcontained upon the immeasurable background of space or time which is not it. You apprehend it as one thing. You see it as one whole.... That is integritas (*AP*, 178).

Like Stephen's *integritas, consonantia* and *claritas* arise from a perception of the object as singular and essential, just as his rise toward artistic self-definition against a background of custom and protocol assumes an authentic self which, through the aesthetic act, will be revealed in a 'radiant image' (*AP*, 186).

Rather than simply turning such a system on its head, Beckett's novel endeavours to revel in a complexity and simultaneity of objects by virtue of which aesthetic apprehension would simply fail. Belacqua is dissonant, not 'harmonious'. He is 'trine' rather than 'one thing'. In addition, the confusion of these elements, and the 'disintegration' of the character into the morass of flux and incoherence surrounding him, become the fundamental dynamics of the novel. More radical than even Dostoevsky's presentation of character as described by Gide, *Dream* thus subjects any distinction between background and figure to a principle of disintegration. Lucien, for example, is described with 'his contours in perpetual erosion. Looking at his face', Mr Beckett admits, 'you saw all the features bloom, as in Rembrandt's portrait of his brother.... [H]e was disintegrating bric-à-brac' (*DFMW*, 116–117). As this passage suggests, *Dream*'s fascination with dissolution derives in part from a perverse interest in eliding the 'proper' subject of the artwork (think of Belacqua's aesthetic of inaudibilities) for whatever has lain 'behind' it; in this way, Beckett playfully rejects the impulse to intensify our apprehension of the object (as in Stephen's theory), for the desire to subject it to erasure. Recalling another Gidean metaphor Beckett used in his lectures (the comparison of literature to music), 'Mr Beckett' suggests that it is the *disappearance* of figure into ground (and vice versa) that he hopes to achieve, not its definition – an ambition in which he grudgingly notes he is preceded by Stendhal:

Without going as far as Stendhal, who said ... that the best music (what did he know about music anyway?) was the music that became inaudible after a few bars, we do declare ... that the object that becomes invisible before your eyes is, so to speak, the brightest and best.... The background pushed up as a guarantee ... that tires us. The only perspective worth stating is the site of the unknotting that could be, landscape of a dream of integration, prospective, that of Franciabigio's young Florentine in the Louvre, into which it is pleasant to believe he may, gladly or sadly, no matter, recede, from which he has not necessarily emerged (*DFMW*, 12–13).

THE REJECTION OF UNITY

As this derisive mention of 'background' 'pushed up' as a 'guarantee' (of convincing realistic depiction) suggests, the *Künstlerroman* and Stephen's aesthetic theory are not the only objects of parodic subversion in *Dream*. Predictably, Beckett's overt target is Naturalism. Like Gide in *Dostoïevsky*, or Edouard in *Les Faux-Monnayeurs*, Beckett scorns the 'self-assurance' of the novelist 'whose chief care seems ever to be the perfect consistency of his characters' (*D*, 17). While the great exemplar in this regard is Balzac, Beckett is in fact levelling his critique at Gide's Western-European novel and the effects generated by its philosophical assumptions. To use 'Mr Beckett's' somewhat less reverent description, *Dream* targets that 'Pythagorean chain-chant solo of cause and effect' '[w]hich is more or less ... what one gets from one's favourite novelist' (*DFMW*, 10).

The procédé that seems all falsity, that of Balzac, for example, and the divine Jane and many others, consists in dealing with the vicissitudes, or absence of vicissitudes, of character ... as though that were the whole story. Whereas, in reality, this is so little the story, this nervous recoil into composure, this has so little to do with the story, that one must be excessively concerned with a total precision to allude to it at all (*DFMW*, 119).

Dream attacks this assumption of a rationally demonstrable, integral self in order to critique the stability of values affirmed or denied through it in the novels of Beckett's Balzac and those like him – values which allow the writer to establish 'a stable architecture of sentiment' and achieve a kind of moral resolution (*DFMW*, 101).

To the item thus artificially immobilised in a backwash of composure precise value can be assigned. So all the novelist has to do is to bind his material in a spell, item after item, and juggle politely with irrefragable values, values that can assimilate other values like in kind and be assimilated by them, that can increase and decrease in virtue of an unreal permanence of quality (*DFMW*, 119).

Dream here joins its (learned) critique of the novel's subject matter with an anxious sideswipe at a notion which was attractive and distasteful to the young Beckett in equal measure – the idea of the artist as a transcendent genius. (Conspicuously absent in this jab at 'divine' writers is of course the figure of Joyce, whom *Dream* at times does its best to imitate.) Rather than a transcendent consciousness paring his fingernails over his creation, Beckett's target here is revealed as a mere entertainer; he is a drawing-room magician, even a clown (the image of Balzac or Austen 'juggling politely' is particularly ludic) who has conveniently forgotten 'the [real] story'– the embattled, contradictory realm of the Dostoevskian artist – in favour of 'composure'.

Unlike his strawman, 'Mr Beckett' may be 'without a single Chesnel in [his] whole bag of tricks' (Chesnel is 'one of Balzac's Old Curiosities' from *Le Cabinet des Antiques* (1838) (*DFMW*, 118)), but he does of course have some modern characters at his disposal – whom he describes in terms borrowed from the real Beckett's discussion of *Paludes'* plot (where the 'action instead of being treated melodically is treated symphonically' (MIC60, 33)). Such characters demolish any remnants of the 'novelist's' fantasy of writing 'a little book that would be purely melodic [and] linear' by taking their cue from theories of discordant multiplicity (*DFMW*, 10). For example, 'Mr Beckett' notes that Belacqua's double, Nemo, 'will not for any consideration be condensed' since he is 'not a note at all' but 'a symphonic, not a melodic, unit' (*DFMW*, 10–11). And '[o]n second thoughts' about his hero, 'Mr Beckett' is forced to admit that 'we tend ... to smell the symphonic rat in our principal boy', too (*DFMW*, 11). To use Beckett's own terms, what such characters do – their contribution to the book's (rather negligible) 'action' – is less important than the 'expansion of personality' that they contribute to the repertory of the novel as a form (MIC60, 33). The significance of such characters is therefore largely 'in [their] potential, ... unrealised actions' and the way that they contribute to 'the multiple probable potentials' the book continually throws up (MIC60, 33; 41). Which is 'the real Syra-Cusa'? Will Belacqua end up with the Alba? Will the characters 'do their dope'? The novel plays with the notion that, like us, 'Mr Beckett' cannot know because he does not possess the 'tuning fork' which would 'fix [his characters'] vibrations', enabling him to 'get a line on them' (*DFMW*, 125). But the real author has of course ensured that his characters present at least one calculated effect: a parodic inversion of any fictional paradigm that draws on theories of causation or natural history to bolster its depiction of the real.

The effect or concert of effects, unimportant as it seems to us and dull as ditch-water as we happen to know, that elicited the Smeraldina-Rima, shall not … be stated. Milieu, race, family, structure, temperament, past and present and consequent and antecedent back to the first combination and the papas and mamas and paramours and cicisbei and the morals of Nanny and the nursery wallpapers and the third and fourth generation snuffles.… That tires us (*DFMW*, 13).

Rather than simply leaving such things out, 'Mr Beckett' makes sure he sneeringly lists off the subjects of greatest interest to writers like Zola – whose scientific theories required the novel to focus on 'milieu, race, family, structure, temperament' and so on – only to tell us that he will *not* provide them.

If *Dream* borrows the terms Beckett used to describe Gide's 'symphonic genius' in *Paludes*, it also draws on the related notion of 'simultaneity' he praised in *Dostoïevsky*. Rather than the struggle between his natural being and the ideal toward which the hero strives to conform ('bovary-ism'), or a contest between the individual and the conventions and values of his society, *Dream*'s characters exhibit conflicting natures and values within themselves. For instance, with the traditional background for the Smeraldina-Rima missing, the warring elements within this figure finish off any attempt by the narrator to explain his creature: she is both 'Weib' ('all breasts and buttocks' as Belacqua puts it) *and* ideal spirit, a 'heterogeneous entity' if there ever was one (*DFMW*, 35). This discordance within the character forces the 'novelist' to render his creature 'not demonstrable' within the generic convention that calls for his *premier amour* to represent a stable value in his hero's experience – which would allow the work itself to achieve a 'harmonic' structure (*DFMW*, 13). These characters, 'Mr Beckett' admits, 'epitomise nothing' (*DFMW*, 126).

The most problematic creature in this regard is of course Beckett's protagonist, in whom the principle of a symphonic simultaneity – the rejection of any continuum – is at its most complex. Thus, in line with Gide's argument that the Dostoevskian novelist must concern himself with the 'irrational, the resolute, and often irresponsible nature of his characters', the majority of the chapter titled 'UND' (itself a punctuation of any narrative continuity the novel may have gathered) is dedicated to the attempt to 'pierce the shadows and tangles of Belacqua's behaviour' (an endeavour by which the narrator, in a moment of Gidean 'humility', must 'concede [himself] conquered') (*D*, 14; *DFMW*, 118).[18] Like *Murphy* (whose mind is given a similarly separate treatment in Chapter Six of his novel), Belacqua is revealed to be 'trine' 'at his simplest' – composed of the 'three strata or regions Dostoevsky seems to discern in the human personality' (*DFMW*, 120; *D*, 126). Yet while the 'vast realm remote from the play of passion' in *Dostoïevsky* is salvific and fraternal, Belacqua's 'third being' is paradoxically closer to nonbeing: 'the dark gulf, where the glare of the will and the hammer-strokes of the brain … were expunged' (*DFMW*, 121). Rather than replicate the novelistic 'complete closing up of every gulf' described by Jacques Rivière, *Dream* instead focuses its attention on the dark gulf at the centre of its protagonist, into which he longs to escape. But even Belacqua's longing to free himself from the suffering of willing presents a further 'simultaneity of incoherence' in Beckett's novel – for, as Belacqua realises, 'How could the will be abolished in its own tension?' (*DFMW*, 123). Like Dostoevsky's heroes, Belacqua is actually 'a horrible border-creature' with 'two distinct personalities in the same body': the self that wills and the self that desires only the end of desire (*DFMW*, 123; *D*, 102).

As this suggests, however, there is an important difference between the way that the issue of divided subjectivity in the novel is treated in *Dream*, and in the works of Gide and Dostoevsky. Unlike these writers, Beckett submits his interest in divided subjectivity to yet another parodic caricature. He thereby resists the temptation, as he later wrote of *Murphy*, to take his creatures 'too seriously' (*Dis*, 102). Indeed, the characters' outlandish names and their exaggeratedly schismatic qualities suggest the intent to rewrite Edouard's 'novel of ideas' (or Gide's idea of divided subjectivity and fragmented form) as an idea in its own right – a complex manoeuvre involving *Dream*'s parody of an aesthetic of incoherence within a work of art ostensibly governed by the same principle. In fact, a more fitting analogue for *Dream*'s treatment of Beckett's early theory is *Les Caves du Vatican*, where the characters' farcical names highlight Gide's intent to submit them, and the theories they entertain (including their author's notions of free will in the novel), to ridicule. In a similar manner, Beckett uses the farcical qualities of his book to distance himself from and complicate the unconventional theories that circulate in *Dream*. While Belacqua's postulates on the 'incoherent continuum' may be accepted, to an extent, as Beckett's own, the novel also anticipates the real author's enduring resistance to embracing *any* definition of the aesthetic – even one of incoherence – *qua* definition, favouring instead complex and evasive articulations mediated through caricatural masks (as in *Three Dialogues*) (*DFMW*, 102). In this sense, *Dream* bears witness to Beckett's struggle, as he later put it, to 'get over' the aesthetic paradigms that formed the matrix for his own novel – Gide and his Dostoevsky as well as 'J.J.' (SB to Samuel Putnam, 28/6/32, *LSB 1*, 108).

A (DOUBLED) PORTRAIT OF THE ARTIST AS A STRUGGLING WRITER

Though the Beckett of 1932 could subject his early counteraesthetic to a certain ironic regard even as he deployed it against Balzac's realism and the tradition of the *Bildungsroman*, he remained in the shadow of his French master. For there is of course an additional Gidean 'portrait' in *Dream* looming over its problematic figures and the world in which they exist: a portrait of the artist depicted not as a Romantic surrogate or budding theorist, but as a self-doubting reader/writer of the text, whose difficulties are ironically reflected in the artistic failure of *his* writer-protagonist. *Dream* thus exemplifies a way of thinking about the novel (and one of greater relevance to Beckett's mature work than his protagonist's 'aesthetic of inaudabilities') traceable to Beckett's 1930 account of the new structure of *Les Faux-Monnayeurs*, and the Gidean device of the mise en abyme.[19]

An artwork involved with the complexity of reality cannot simply depict that reality, Beckett argued, but must involve a 'statement' of the author's involvement with the work, dramatising his ultimate *failure* to achieve resolution in the 'struggle [between] artist & idea' (MIC60, 39). In Gide's novel and the *Journal* he published along with it, this struggle takes place on a number of levels, only two of which Beckett co-opted in *Dream*: the struggle of the artist-protagonist with his potential fiction, and that of the novelist-narrator with the fiction in which this protagonist exists. I will first examine this struggle at the level of Gide's protagonist. This is appropriate for two reasons. Most important, it is largely due to the problematic nature of the self as conceived by Edouard in *Les Faux-Monnayeurs* that this struggle must be depicted in the artwork. In addition, when approaching the 'relationship of relationships' that is the mise en abyme, it is perhaps best to give an account of the terms 'from within' before positing their correlation or disjunction with relation to the work itself.

As in *Dream*, it is in line with a view of the self as fragmented, mutable, and nonessential (or ultimately inaccessible) and a view of reality as inherently discordant (composed, like the self, of 'provisional' values and meanings), that Edouard criticises the novel as a genre that has so far only 'clung to reality with ... timidity' and been 'a slave to resemblance' (*C*, 167). His response to this idea of the novel is complex. On one hand, he argues for a removal of every 'realist' component in the interests of realising a 'pure' novel: a work whose success would no longer be judged by the standard of 'get[ting] still nearer to nature' (*C*, 167).

I should like to strip the novel of every element that does not specifically belong to the novel. Just as photography in the past freed painting from its concern for a certain sort of accuracy, so the phonograph will eventually no doubt rid the novel of the kind of dialogue which is drawn from life and which realists take so much pride in. Outward events, accidents, traumatisms, belong to the cinema. The novel should leave them to it (*C*, 71).

Reminiscent of Beckett's criticism in *Proust* of those who 'worship the offal of experience' as well as Gide's early flirtations with Symbolism, Edouard's argument also suggests an autonomous art whose governing principle is that of 'style'. Contrasting his aims with Balzac's (who discovered the proper function of his work in its rivalry with the *état-civil*),[20] Edouard seeks a novel freed from the transcription of 'surface' and given over to a stylizing, *aesthetic* principle – a 'formidable erosion of contours'. To illustrate his point, Edouard holds up ancient Greek drama and seventeenth-century French tragedy as paradigms that exercise 'the deliberate avoidance of life which gave [them the] style' he now seeks for the novel; these are creations that 'don't pride themselves ... on appearing real. They remain works of art' (*C*, 167).

At the same time, however, Edouard desires that his novel should perform a contradictory task: to reveal the complexity of reality in its fullness, without presenting 'life' as cut up by the writer's pen. As he is forced to admit, however, the most obvious problem with this idea is that such a novel cannot have 'a subject'.

Let's say, if you prefer it, it hasn't got *one* subject ... 'a slice of life', the naturalist school said. The great defect of that school is that it always cuts its slice in the same direction; in time, lengthwise. Why not in breadth? Or in depth? As for me I should like not to cut at all. Please understand; I should like to put everything into my novel. I don't want any cut of the scissors to limit its substance at one point rather than at another (*C*, 168).

But if the novel cannot assume its shape through the selective process that gives an artwork its form, the novelist takes on a seemingly impossible obligation: no recognisable subject and no means of formally defining that subject appear to be admissible in this work about 'everything' and 'nothing'. But even if such a novel were realisable as 'the freest, the most *lawless*' of literary genres (*C*, 167), what about Edouard's other, oppositional urge: to create a novel that is not concerned with 'appearing real' but with achieving a 'pure' form governed by 'style'?

Edouard's nonsolution (the very object of this theory being in one sense to avoid aesthetic solutions) is a profoundly interesting one in relation to *Dream* and Beckett's later novels. Edouard's novel does end up being written, but only as a perpetually unfinished record of his struggle to produce it as taken down in his diary along with the multitude of events and thoughts that occur to its writer. Edouard theorises that it is the very labour of creating an artwork within impossible parameters and with impossible material that will become the substance of his work.

I invent the character of a novelist, whom I make my central figure; and the subject of the book, if you must have one, is just that very struggle between what reality offers him and what he himself desires to make of it (*C*, 169).

It is this struggle 'to represent reality on one hand' and the oppositional 'effort to stylize it into art' – 'the struggle between the facts presented by reality and the ideal reality' – that will become the novel's true subject. This struggle, dramatised in the figure of the writer, is inherently paradoxical for it is the conflict between irreconcilable ends: the formal arrangement toward which the aesthetic endeavour must gravitate through the selective process that brings it into existence, and the desire to present a complexity, lawlessness, and freedom that is at odds with any such process (*C*, 168–9). The result is a work perpetually becoming in a process of forming and unforming itself; the novel becomes a metafictional and diaristic record in which Edouard takes down 'the state of the novel in [his] mind' as his thinking about it changes day by day. Instead of resolving difficulties in his 'story', he articulates and studies them. The 'novel' is thus extant *only in the journal's account of its author's struggle to create it*. In this sense it presents not only what Edouard terms a 'running criticism' of its own emergence, but levels its critique at 'the novel in general' (*C*, 170). (Remember that in Edouard's reading the novel hides the artifice of its own construction.)

But of course Gide's novel does not present Edouard's project as ultimately successful, for his project is only a theory of a novel to be titled

Les Faux-Monnayeurs and he remains a character within a fiction of that name; only the 'novelist' of *Les Faux-Monnayeurs* has ostensibly created the work that recalls its own genesis, and behind him stands the writer Gide who published the account of *that* fiction's emergence in the *Journal des Faux-Monnayeurs*. Here I only wish to highlight the importance of the second term in this series in relation to *Dream*: the relationship between the 'novelist' and Edouard. Just as Edouard's approach is fraught with contradiction, so the 'novelist's' relationship to him is ambivalent. On one hand, much is done to suggest a correspondence between the 'novelist' and his writer-protagonist (both have an authorial relationship, 'real' or virtual, to a novel called *Les Faux-Monnayeurs*; they share similar aesthetic concepts; etc.). Yet Gide also purposefully institutes important differences between these writers. For example, the 'novelist' criticises Edouard's ambitions as idealistic, inflexible, illogical, and naïve; unlike Edouard, the 'novelist' is not above putting 'facts' such as news items (and, with regard to Boris, ones that Edouard is particularly uneasy about) into his *Les Faux-Monnayeurs*. As Lucien Dällenbach has pointed out, the ambiguity that Gide develops in this relationship is deliberate and productive in that it allows Gide to play a 'double game' that distributes responsibilities within the novel. Via the mise en abyme, he could put forward *and* critique an incoherent theory of art that seeks to unite a 'pure' artistic form devoid of Naturalistic detail and contrivance with the impure flux of existence (Dällenbach, 33).

Though in a less complex fashion, Beckett appropriated the Gidean device of the novelist within the novel to similar effect in *Dream*.[21] Like Edouard, Belacqua is patronised by the narrator as naïve and idealistic, but he is also given a certain status as the most complex character in the novel. Likewise, parallels are developed between Belacqua and the narrator, though *Dream* also suggests that it is *not* the work that Belacqua would have written, if his theory is anything to go by.[22] In these ways, Beckett uses the mise en abyme technique to complicate any relationship between himself and his own counter-theory, and to avoid assigning his protagonist an unambiguous value within a fiction that claims to reflect 'complexity'.

One of the more interesting ways that he did this was through rewriting Edouard's failure to accept the ramifications of his theory of a pure and incoherent art. In effect, what this amounts to is a critique of Belacqua's concern with incoherence as *another* form of idealism that itself cannot confront the confusion of reality. This critique largely takes place in Belacqua's conversation with the Mandarin at the end of 'TWO', a passage that probably reflects something of a self-criticism (Beckett drew it up in terms borrowed from his *Proust*), though it also parodies Stephen's exposition of his aesthetic theory to Cranly in *Portrait*. Unlike Stephen, who emerges triumphant from his own discussion of art (and woman), Beckett's hero is cowed by his *eiron* in an exchange redolent of that most Gidean of moments in the novel: 'the delicate moment when [the protagonist's] thoughts become disordered'.[23] Here Beckett demonstrates that Belacqua's theory of art cannot itself accommodate an incoherent reality, for incoherence must be limited to a certain sector that he can oversee and control, namely, that of art. This disintegration of Belacqua's theory of disintegration recalls two consecutive entries in Edouard's journal (26 and 28 October) that also discuss the same subjects (aesthetics and relations between men and women) with relation to the self's lack of 'continuity' (*C*, 68). Interestingly, it seems that Beckett modelled his hero's experience on the 'slow *decrystallization*' of love that Edouard anticipates as the subject of *his* novel in these entries: 'What an admirable subject for a novel', Gide's hero muses, 'So long as he loves and desires to be loved, the lover cannot show himself as he really is, and moreover he does not see the beloved – but instead, an idol whom he decks out, a divinity whom he creates' (*C*, 69). More naïve than Edouard, Belacqua does not recognise such a topic as a subject for art (especially not the artwork in which he himself exists), though he inevitably undergoes such a process of 'decrystallization' with the Smeraldina. His model of the beloved is Beatrice, though the Mandarin tries to disabuse him: 'You simplify and dramatise the whole thing with your literary mathematics. I don't waste any words with the argument of experience, the inward *decrystallization* of experience, because your type never accepts experience' (*DFMW*, 101).

Ironically, Belacqua, like Edouard, is in fact a literary idealist who cannot live up to his own theory. Like the Naturalists they abhor, both characters desire to project order onto the confusion of experience. For all Edouard's consideration of the novel as a 'lawless' genre, he ultimately desires a 'poetical' order in the world and the artwork;[24] and his inability to 'make use of' Boris's suicide in his novel is finally less about his rejection of 'outward events, accidents, [and] traumatisms' than his need, like the crassest Naturalist, to only include those occurrences 'accounted for by a sufficiency of motive' (*C*, 343). Similarly, the Mandarin can see that in spite of Belacqua's theorising about the 'incoherent reality and its authentic extrinsecation' he remains committed to a romantic conception of individual essence which, like the conventions of the novel that rely upon it, is revealed as comically naïve (*DFMW*, 102).

Like Edouard's virtual novel, though, *Dream* may finally be less about its protagonist than its author. Borrowing another Gidean self-reflexive device (which he would return to in *Watt*), Beckett's narrator is also a 'Mr Beckett' who, as Laura warns Edouard, 'won't be able to help painting [him]self' in his struggle to write (*DFMW*, 169). Like Gide's 'novelist', 'Mr Beckett' occupies a dual role. He is at once the writer and, by virtue of his incomprehension, a *reader* of this novel: he seems both inside and outside the fiction. The narrator reflects upon this painful duty in the chapter 'UND', which is modelled on Gide's chapter 'The Author Reviews His Characters'. Although Gide's narrator is less sardonic than 'Mr Beckett', he is similar in several regards, most importantly in his uncertainty about his creation and his lack of control over it. Like 'Mr Beckett', he describes himself as an unwitting and unlucky individual who by some mischance has become responsible for his irritating and recalcitrant creatures. Both narrators position themselves as the 'undiscerning author [who] stops awhile to regain his breath, and wonders with some anxiety where his tale will take him' (*C*, 195). The narrator's puzzlement and distress, his complicit tone with the reader, his disappointment and even anger at his characters, and his irritation with the novelist who has a secure set of values and predictable creatures to work with, all suggest the attempt to confront what Beckett described in his lectures as free will and indeterminacy.

But do such techniques, and especially this inclusion of the embattled narrator, achieve the aims that Beckett was apparently striving for – to allow a lawlessness and freedom into the form that would erode the tired conventions of the novel? Recall that Beckett argued that even in Gide's books there remains a residual 'coherence' 'that in spite of [his] humility he can't avoid' (MIC60, 25). Indeed, the title of *Les Faux-Monnayeurs* indicates that each attempt to achieve the authentic complexity of reality in art must involve another fiction, another form of contrivance and representation. And it quickly becomes clear that the novel's counterfeiting proliferates not only at the level of the characters, but at the level of narration. To appropriate Albert Sonnenfeld's comments on *La Porte Étroite*, 'the semblance of spontaneity' in the interjections of Gide's or Beckett's narrator, though suggestive of the *un*formed flux of reality, is actually 'a literary and psychological stratagem' at one with the *in*forming task of the traditional novelist.[25] Though more self-conscious than the novels Gide's Lafcadio despises, *Dream* and *Les Faux-Monnayeurs* are of course similarly calculated, *revised* utterances at the opposite pole to an inscrutable, happenstance reality. As Walker has pointed out of Gide's novel, although the 'novelist's' interjections fragment the narrative at the level of action and inhibit the reader's immersion in a uniform diegetic world, they also serve to provide a continuous experience at the level of reading. By means of his interjections, the 'novelist' is in fact maintaining contact with the reader through colluding with him in a shared experience of bewilderment, drawing him along from one episode to the next. The narrator thus dispenses with traditional time sequences only to replace them with alternative kinds of transitions (Walker, 'Challenging the Novel', 207).

One could take this argument further by considering *Dream*'s formal integrity. Despite 'Mr Beckett's' talk of 'dehiscence' and 'discord', his book is carefully patterned according to these very ideas. While retaining the traces of a chronology roughly based on Beckett's own youthful experiences, the novel is also subject to Gide's notion of the work as a composition: an arrangement of interacting elements that stage the contingency of the real even as they assume their place within an artificial order. This means that even as the theory that Belacqua ponders under the night sky finds its formal analogue in the structure of the novel itself – here, too, 'the terms appear crazily spaced' – the work is fragmented *and* united through the gaps and voids that proliferate at every level of its construction (*DFMW*, 125). To take one example, *Dream*'s obsession with bridges, while reflecting a real aspect of Dublin's topography, inevitably recalls Belacqua's theory of a work of 'intervals' preoccupied with 'the dumb-bell's bar' and the 'hyphen of passion' – though the bridge is also a fitting analogue for the many dashes and conjunctions that both break up and link together this book at the levels of chapter (as in 'UND') and syntax (*DFMW*, 27). The notion of the bridge is also important at the level of narrative: it serves as a *topos* that figures the real author's Gidean preoccupation with complicating endings. It is not an accident that Belacqua's double, Nemo (whose name means 'no one' and whose 'most valued possession is a suberb aboulia of the very first water' (*DFMW*, 184)) meets his end by falling off a bridge, nor is it a mistake that the novel itself closes with its protagonist 'marooned on [a] bridge' – neither in one place nor the other but 'between the statements' in a chapter fittingly titled 'AND' (*DFMW*, 241).

Finally, the narrators of these novels and their authors cannot escape from the circle of artifice in the novel because there is no escape from the circle of representation in language. As Gide's Strouvilhou realises, those 'promissory notes which go by the name of words', like the conventions on which the artist builds his work, may seem to 'pass current', yet they 'ring as false as counters' when tested (*C*, 291). In this view, reality, which art strives to express in its most essential form, can only appear through an inevitably misleading representation; even worse, as in the grim teaching of Schopenhauer (whose shadow falls over both *Dream* and *Les Faux-Monnayeurs*), reality may turn out to be nothing *but* representation. Freedom from artifice in the novel, like freedom of will in Schopenhauer's cosmos, predictably begins to appear as just another false coin in a currency of illusion.

Dream draws on and affirms Beckett's 1930 argument that the novel cannot resolve but only restate the problem that confronted it in the modern age. It suggests that, though the novelist must attempt to dissolve conventions to approach an essential reality, he must ultimately admit failure in the face of an irreducibly complex, incoherent universe. Beckett was still almost two decades away from accepting this failure and setting it at the core of his artistic theory. But by following in Gide's footsteps, he had already started down the path toward a fiction governed by a radical scepticism, and which continually erodes its own foundations.

CHAPTER 2

'An Ironical Radiance':
Murphy *and the Modern Novel*

The relevance of Beckett's early theory of the novel to his fiction might seem to have faded quickly after *Dream*. For example, Gide does not appear in C. J. Ackerley's recent and exhaustively annotated companion to *Murphy*, and to my knowledge any allusions to him in this fiction have yet to be identified. Yet Beckett had not left his theory or his early master behind. In the months before he started his second novel, he made the last of at least three frustrated attempts to compose his monograph on Gide.

This book seems to have come tantalizingly close to realisation. In early February of 1932, Beckett suggested to Prentice that he write a book on Gide, but the idea was turned down (*DF*, n78, 733). By August, Beckett was again considering the project, this time for *New Statesman*, and during this summer the book seems to have developed a certain shape and focus; Beckett told McGreevy that he was considering a subtitle ('*paralysed in ubiquity*') (*DF*, 165). He was frustrated with his inability to write up at this point, however; he 'made a desperate effort to get something started on Gide but failed again', despite having progressed to the stage that he had collated all the quotations he wished to use by September of 1932 (SB qtd. in *DF*, n116, 735).[1] In early August of 1934, Beckett again wrote to McGreevy, telling him he had proposed an essay on either Gide or Rimbaud to *The Bookman* (*DF*, 189). This last proposal was turned down in favour of a piece on 'the "wicked" Censorship in Ireland' – a commission Beckett accepted 'without enthusiasm' (*DF*, 189).[2]

Nevertheless, Gide's influence did make its way into Beckett's next novel – most apparently in his handling of character. Murphy's divided mind and Schopenhauerian retreat from willing have long fascinated commentators, yet this character's oddities play an important part in the modern attempt to resist novelistic Naturalism and its ally, coherence. As in *Dream*, Beckett appropriates Gide's tripartite scheme for the irrational and conflicted modern character. And although Murphy's much-discussed

43

mind – composed of 'the three zones, light, half light, dark, each with its specialty' – does not feature *Dostoïevsky*'s content for the first two zones, Beckett did cull the most important, third division from Gide's plan.[3] As *Dostoïevsky* prescribes, this is the dark area 'remote from the play of passion' and the *ratio* – a 'deeper region, which is not the soul's hell, but its heaven' (*D*, 144, 126):

a region where love is not, nor passion … : the region Schopenhauer spoke of … where the limits of existence fade away, where the notion of the individual and of time is lost, the place wherein Dostoevsky sought … the secret of happiness (*D*, 125).

Murphy's chair is of course the vehicle by which he abnegates the willing Schopenhauer deplores and thereby enters a Dostoevskian dark – a 'solidarity that knows no distinctions' (*D*, 127). Note how, as in Gide's text, time and individual consciousness fade as Murphy enters the third zone:

the dark [was] nothing but forms becoming and crumbling into the fragments of a new becoming, without love or hate or any intelligible principle of change. Here there was nothing but commotion and the purest forms of commotion. Here he was not free, but a mote in the dark of absolute freedom (*M*, 65–6).

Murphy's tripartite *mind*, however, is not as important as his divided *self* – which is not tripartite but dual. In fact, sidetracked by analyses of Murphy's mind as 'it felt and pictured itself to be', Beckett's commentators have neglected the crucial schism in this hero that is intended to playfully subvert the 'realist' novel at the level of character: Murphy is less a Spinozan, Schopenhauerian, or a Cartesian creature than a parodic type of the 'dual personality' Gide valorised in *The Possessed* – which Beckett read at Trinity, in French, after studying Gide's theory. In contrast to the 'bovarysm' of characters by European writers (like Corneille) – 'the tendency of certain human beings towards complementing their real life by a purely imaginary existence' (*D*, 102) – Dostoevsky presents

a second personality … grafted upon the original, the one alternating with the other and two groups of sensations and associations of ideas being formed, the one unknown to the other, so that before long we have two distinct personalities sharing the one fleshly tenement…. [I]n Dostoevsky the most disconcerting feature is the simultaneity of such phenomena (*D*, 103).

Beckett drew up the first half of what the 'novelist' terms Murphy's 'unredeemed split self' (*M*, 106) by grouping Gide's first two Schopenhauerian 'strata' of the subject (intellect; passions) – the components he had *not* used in Chapter Six's account of Murphy's mind. Thus the *first* Murphy is given to the 'steady activity of the mind' and is prey to his bodily urges ('his deplorable susceptibility to Celia, ginger, and so on' (*M*, 102)) while the *second* Murphy longs for the 'third zone's' realm of 'abnegation'. This duality will not be collapsed; as Gide writes of Dostoevsky's characters, Murphy never 'relinquishes consciousness of his dual personality with its inconsistencies' (*D*, 103). In fact, the drama of the novel largely consists of the intensifying struggle between his 'simultaneous' selves: 'the self whom [Murphy] loved' and 'the self whom he hated' (*M*, 109) – a conflict that continues right up to Murphy's final attempt to return to Celia after his encounter with Endon, and culminates in his literal explosion.

MURPHY'S IRONIC 'NOVELIST'

Beckett's comic re-deployment of *Dostoïevsky*'s discussion of character suggests that *Murphy* should be read as another subversion of the European tradition of novelistic realism, but Beckett's commentators have long been divided over this point. In fact, the majority understand *Murphy* in an opposite manner: as an example of 'Beckett's early realism' (Hugh Kenner, Andrew Gibson) and a retreat from the self-reflexivity and narrative experiments of *Dream of Fair to Middling Women*.[4] A very few readers have suggested that *Murphy* is either an ironic metafiction presenting 'a parody of the traditional novel' (John Fletcher) or that it plays a complex game with narrative authority that targets the very 'rules' and 'codes' of the Novel (J. M. Coetzee), but such approaches have gone largely unheeded.[5] More is at stake here than a reading of one of Beckett's early novels; how we understand *Murphy* plays an integral part in how the story of Beckett's artistic development is told. In the first reading, *Murphy* is a 'sole exercise, and an anomalous one' that Beckett had to abandon for a 'turn away from realism after *Murphy*' and the complexity of the postwar fictions (Kenner, *Samuel Beckett*, 75–6; Gibson, 142). In the second, *Murphy*'s unsettling narrative technique anticipates the inner workings of Beckett's masterpieces of the forties and fifties; its 'attitude of reserve toward the Novel' 'grows, and by the time of *The Unnamable* (1953) has become ... the subject of Beckett's work' (Coetzee, 'The Comedy', 37).

In the following, I will show that Beckett's readers have misread his second novel as a work of realism because almost without exception they have neglected the role of the key figure in this book's ironic meta-fictional strategy: *Murphy*'s narrator. This speaker reveals that in line with his *Dream*, the Beckett of *Murphy* was not only concerned with disturbing the 'coherent' realist subject but also intent on complicating narrative linearity and authority in the novel.

Because he remains nameless and his gaze roams over his world from on high, there is perhaps a temptation to pass over Beckett's speaker as a conventional convenience – a version of the realist omniscient narrator transported from the work of the 'divine Jane [Austen]' or Balzac (*DFMW*, 119). But unlike Austen's or Balzac's narrators, Beckett's speaker frequently interferes with the diegesis, using a mixture of deliberate clichés, ironic reflections on literary texts and devices, and references to censors, the reader, or other novels to emphasize *Murphy*'s status as textual construct:

> The ceiling was lost in the shadows, yes, really lost in the shadows (*M*, 40).
> It was an aposiopesis of the purest kind (*M*, 94).
> He tried with the men, women, children and animals that belong to even worse stories than this (*M*, 141).
> The above passage is carefully calculated to deprave the cultivated reader (*M*, 69).
> The cackle of a nightingale would have been most welcome, to explode his spirit towards its nightingaleless night. But the season seemed over (*M*, 134).
> His body being too active with its fatigue to permit of this, he submitted to sleep, Sleep son of Erebus and Night, Sleep half-brother to the Furies (*M*, 100).

Aspects of this ironic technique – especially the use of allusion in the last two quotations – might initially suggest a debt to Joyce, and one can usefully compare the irony in *Murphy* to that of *Ulysses*, especially from 'Wandering Rocks' onward. As David Hayman and Hugh Kenner have pointed out, in this episode a narrating consciousness seems to emerge behind Joyce's novel 'like a giant ... slowly coming awake'.[6] This consciousness at times stresses 'the artifice of [the novel's] surfaces' and exposes style as a 'game [he] is playing' (*U*, 64, 63). And this 'Arranger' of the text is not playing an innocent game. He is 'capable of a great deal of malice, of deliberate Schadenfreude' in his tracking of the characters and in his commentary on their actions and thoughts; in his regard of the reader, too, the Arranger possesses a '*seriatim* accuracy of observation that hovers just this side of being malicious' (Hayman qtd. in *U*, 65; *U*, 67). An important result of the Arranger's interference is that it alters the nature of the irony in the text. Irony in *Ulysses* is not 'objective' as Kenner argues it is in *Dubliners* or *Portrait*, but is generated by our sense of the giant's knowing gaze as he manipulates the novel's carefully wrought style and order (*U*, 71). Similarly, *Murphy*'s allusions serve to reveal an individual who hovers over the novel and reflects on it. And, in a manner somewhat reminiscent of Joyce's giant, this figure's arch gaze is not only directed at the story's textuality.

It is hard to say where the fault lies in the case of Ticklepenny … but certainly the quality of his speech is most wretched. Celia's confidence to Mr Kelly, Neary's to Wylie, had to be given for the most part obliquely. With all the more reason now, Ticklepenny's to Murphy. It will not take many moments (*M*, 53).

Yet there is a sardonic obtrusiveness to this speaker's comments which is not Joycean, or is more than Joycean. (We can even be somewhat specific about this narrator's personality: unlike the dutiful workman of *Ulysses*, Beckett's narrator's archly confidential tone ('It is hard to say where the fault lies'), and his world-weary air suggest he has something of the aesthete about him.) Unlike the Arranger, who does not use 'the voice of the storyteller' for he is 'not a voice at all, since [he] does not address us, does not even speak', *Murphy*'s narrator rehearses *Dream*'s Gidean mirroring of the writer within his own fiction. Joyce's tale may not be 'in the old sense … "told"; it is mimed in words arranged on pages in space' but Beckett's story *is*, by a figure who has the power to control his narrative techniques (and as we shall see, the plot itself) in accordance with his whims (*U*, 65). In the passage that follows the quotation above, for example, *Murphy*'s narrator refuses to allow Ticklepenny to speak for himself; instead, the narrator paraphrases the discussion with Murphy in order to avoid listening to any more of his character's 'wretched' speech (*M*, 53). This figure is more than a narrator, then; he is what *The Unnamable* calls the 'ventriloquist' of the text.[7] With perhaps the exception of Murphy (an important exception), he controls the novel's characters with impunity.

All the puppets in this book whinge sooner or later, except Murphy, who is not a puppet (*M*, 71).

Unlike Joyce's giant – who 'exists side-by-side with a colourless primary narrator who sees to the thousand little bits of novelistic housekeeping no one is meant to notice' – Beckett's narrator has no helper (*U*, 67). And it is precisely the Beckettian narrator's resentment toward his tasks and his creatures that spurs him into showing his hand.

It is most unfortunate, but the point of this story has been reached where a justification of the expression 'Murphy's mind' has to be attempted. Happily we need not concern ourselves with this apparatus as it really was – that would be an extravagance and an impertinence.... A short section to itself at this stage will relieve us from the necessity of apologizing for it further (*M*, 63).

In short, this speaker is a figure for the *novelist*, and in this sense, as Frederik Smith and C. J. Ackerley have recently suggested, there is a parallel between *Murphy*'s narrative technique and Thackeray's 'puppet-mastery'[8] and the storytelling machinations of writers like Fielding (Smith, 75–6). Yet this comparison breaks down when we take a harder look at the role of *Murphy*'s 'puppeteer'. *Murphy*'s 'novelist' not only suggests the textuality of his world and refers to his characters as 'puppets', but (in a way that Thackeray never does) he dominates and ironically regards them as they fail to recognise their status *as* characters within that world. The ironic stance of this 'novelist' reveals a modern view of art and the artist behind *Murphy* that is alien to Thackeray's jovial puppeteer, and distinct from the types of irony one finds in Sterne or Swift. It is an irony that represents one response to what Beckett considered the crucial problem facing the modern writer after Proust.

'AUTHENTIC INCOHERENCE AND THE COHERENCE OF RACINIC STATEMENT'?

As in *Dream*, the Beckett of *Murphy* targets not only the artificial unification of character in the Naturalist novel, but its contrived narrative trajectory – which inevitably moves toward closure and the affirmation of a hierarchy of values. And if *Dream*'s 'Mr Beckett' was his author's initial response to Gide's attempt to disrupt the novel in chapters like 'The Author Reviews His Characters', *Murphy*'s 'novelist' rehearses a version of this metafictional gesture in his Chapter Six (quoted earlier). Here, as in 'UND', the 'novelist' sketches the problematic divisions in his tripartite Dostoevskian character with a sardonic flourish, literally breaking up the diegesis and showing his hands.

Yet as we have seen in *Dream*, Beckett knew that such attempts to critique the novel by destabilizing its centre of narrative authority are inevitably contrived counterfeits in their own right. That is, everything in the work is of course *controlled* and ordered – and even the 'novelist's' staged struggle with his characters, and his unorthodox use of form and chance events, move the story toward the type of narrative closure decided upon by the real author. As Beckett acknowledges, there is thus a 'Coherence in Gide that ... he can't avoid' (MIC60, 25); 'language' he concludes, 'can't express confusion' (MIC60, 16–17). In one sense, the argument for the modern novel terminates here in an impasse: the novelist can never adequately express an incoherent reality by means of a form that forces that reality into coherence.

But if Gide's work presents no solution to this problem, it does suggest the possibility of an ironic reflection on this dilemma at the level of form – a complex double manoeuvre through which both randomness and its opposite are ironically *staged* by the 'novelist' within the fiction. Using Bergson as a signpost for modernity, and Racine (in this instance) as an example of a writer whose form fatalistically proceeds toward an inevitable closure, Beckett argues that with the exception of the Surrealists,

> Gide alone ... insists on [a] reconciliation between [the] authentic incoherence of post Bergsonian thought & [the] coherence of Racinic statement (MIC60, 16–17).

In other words, Gide joins the modern attempt (at portraying the irreducible complexity of experience) with an overtly 'coherent' structure by which the characters are, as Ackerley puts it regarding Racine and *Murphy*, 'brought to a preordained ending' (*DP*, 38).[9] Gide's ironic conjunction between a form that deploys the inevitable coherence of narrative in the interest of exposing the author as a puppet-master who can only *play at* presenting reality – *especially* the reality of incoherence. This 'reconciliation' was revealed not primarily through Gide's 'thought' but his 'quality of expression' and his 'style' (MIC60, 17).

For several reasons I think that in discussing this 'reconciliation' via a certain 'style' Beckett was thinking primarily of the way authorship is dramatised in the *sotie* Gide completed immediately before *Les Faux-Monnayeurs*: *Les Caves du Vatican*.[10] This fiction is the obvious point of reference since it has been received as an exploration of the way that 'chance' events in the novel ironically reveal their 'preordained' position in an ordered structure, and it appears that Beckett read it in a similar way given his focus on Gide's treatment of the unmotivated crime (which is the event around which Gide's investigation of chance turns). This supposition is also supported by the fact that Beckett's statement concerning the joining of 'authentic incoherence' with coherence took place immediately after his account of *Les Caves du Vatican* in his discussion on Gide as the modern inheritor of Racine. Most important, I will show that Beckett's novel reveals an appropriation of *Les Caves du Vatican*'s ironic narrative techniques.

TIME SEQUENCES

As Peter Broome has argued, *Les Caves du Vatican* represents an important transition in Gide's writing away from the spirituality and nuanced sentiment of his *récits* toward the 'drier, more elliptical', and perhaps more overtly ironical and 'critical' type of fiction that culminated in *Les Faux-Monnayeurs*. Gide also shifted from a first to a third-person narrator and used restricted characterization, the devices of the puppet-theatre, and knockabout farce to explore his notions of 'l'accidentel' and 'inconséquence' in fiction, concepts that led him toward the cultivation of strategies intended to disrupt any kind of fixed sequence in the novel by the introduction of the unexpected (Broome, 11–12). *Les Caves du Vatican* also marks Gide's interest at this time in the adventure novel and a subset of this genre, the detective novel, because they are ideally suited to this purpose. Motifs such as the search and the elaborate chain of circumstance, for instance, provide opportunities for creating situations in which events appear to occur unpredictably or by chance, disrupting the Balzacian model of the novel. *Les Caves du Vatican*, Broome has argued, 'is a breeding ground for all that upsets sequences and predictable progressions' (Broome, 49). Protos and Lafcadio are themselves agents of disturbance, problematizing any straightforward plot: the latter seeks an act that will be free from plausible motivation and the former runs a secret organisation that manipulates the other characters. But it is Lafcadio around whom the most poignant chance events cluster, just as it may appear that his attempt to achieve a free action defies notions of causality.

Lafcadio's attempt at a free action is of course his murder of Fleurissoire. Gide goes out of his way to point up the ways that this meeting is the result of a highly improbable intersection of arbitrary and comic circumstances. Equally, in responding to it Lafcadio's only motivation appears to be the paradoxical desire to act without motivation, and even seems to rely on events outside his control to dictate his actions. For example, considering whether he should murder the man whom he will later realize is actually his half-brother, Lafcadio appears to surrender the onus of the decision to an arbitrary time-space relation: 'If I can count up to 12, without hurrying, before I see a light in the country-side, [Fleurissoire] is saved'.[11]

But all of Lafcadio's actions, even his attempt to break out of consequence via a free act, are framed within a self-reflexive narrative. And just as *Les Caves du Vatican* raises the possibility of Lafcadio's freedom, it also calls that freedom into question. In fact, though Gide succeeds in presenting an unpredictable novel that avoids a mechanistic sequence of events, he does so to such an extreme that the wildly artificial quality of his narrative is also ironically exposed as part of an inevitable, preordained progression. This exposure of artifice actually only provokes questions of possibility, even as it ironically suggests that the novel cannot present inconséquence or freedom. By revealing the fabricated nature of the fiction's narrative structure, Gide's *time sequences* reveal ironic perspectives in the novel that are unavailable to his characters:

> The structural devices chosen by Gide [such as] the juxtaposition, then sudden convergence in time, of unrelated series of events ... emphasise and highlight some aspect of the relation of time sequences to consequence. Gide's literary ordering of time opens into his world perspectives which are not those of the characters involved in the story. These perspectives are different in nature from those the ordering of time introduces into the world of Proust or Joyce (Brée, 'On Time Sequences', 47).

These perspectives are alien to those encountered in Beckett's other great novelistic masters because, raised above the limited view of the protagonists, the reader encounters the knowing gaze of a colluding individual: Gide's ironic puppeteer, playing a 'double game' of chance *and* determinism in the same text.

Gide achieves this elevation partly through sheer overdetermination of the conditions governing chance in the novel (thereby indicating a relation of these conditions to an overarching design), but in *Les Caves du Vatican* the novelist's continually obtrusive presence and his omnipotent role are also highlighted in the mise en abyme of the Millipede. This is a hidden organisation that manipulates characters in the manner of a novelistic plot, and even revises Lafcadio's spontaneous crime for its own ends.[12] In this way, the Millipede functions as an inner mirror, holding up to us the fact that the novel's plot is only a form of play with the idea of chance conducted by the ironic novelist.[13] It is for this reason that the precise timing of the multiple plotlines is extremely important. A gesture at the unknowable complexity of reality, they are also part of a fictional strategy that reveals the limitations of the novel in communicating inconséquence – once again by exposing the novelist as its master.

Ironically, the same aspect of *Murphy*'s construction, the apparent ineluctability with which the ending is brought to pass by the 'machinery of the plot' (*DP*, 38), has been used by Beckett's readers to describe its structure as that of a realist or traditional novel, or as evidence of a sceptically anti-novelistic approach.[14] Yet once the source of this technique is understood, *Murphy* reveals itself as a text that only borrows the modes and means of realism to energetically expose itself as the construct of a cunning personality. Like the novelist figure of *Les Caves du Vatican*, *Murphy's* speaker ironically plays with the 'plausible concatenation[s]' of the detective genre to present an elaborately farcical plot in which carefully timed chance occurrences only *appear* to converge to determine events (*PTD*, 82).

One such sequence occurs in Chapter Seven, where we learn how Beckett's unwilling protagonist was found and lost by Neary's man, Cooper. The twin factors of Cooper's alcoholism and the presence of a gin palace 'superior to any he had ever seen' right on the corner of the mews where Murphy lives lead to the first delay in contacting Neary (*M*, 70). Murphy's collapse 'in the appalling position described in section three' seconds before Cooper finally enters the room (and which suggest to him that 'a murder had been bungled' (*M*, 71)) result in his second. The third delay is caused by the destruction of the mews precisely at the time Cooper goes looking for a drink in Wapping, eventually returning him to Neary with no idea as to Murphy's whereabouts. But these chance events also fatefully bring together Neary, Counihan, and Wylie with Celia by virtue of another chain of coincidence. The fact that Cooper glimpses Celia as she slips into Murphy's at the exact moment he is leaving seems to be the initial event here; but remember that in Chapter Three we learned that Celia's presence there in the first place has also been carefully predicated on chance and unlikely timing. Seconds before glimpsing Cooper, she is racked with indecision as to whether to abandon Murphy; unable to choose, she flips a coin and, based on its verdict, decides to leave. At that very moment, Murphy falls and cries out and Celia decides to rush in after all, running past Cooper.

There is no mise en abyme in *Murphy* for the figure of the novelist, but like Gide, Beckett does not need one to remove any doubt that such coincidences are not actually random after all. One could easily argue that all of the convergences and divergences in *Murphy* (Celia's delivery of the horoscope and Murphy's encounter with Ticklepenny excepted) have little or no effect on what actually happens in the end. This alone grants the reader an ironic perspective and the suspicion – as each opportunity just misses its mark or suddenly falls into convenient alignment with what 'has to happen'– that the novel is actually an extended knockabout farce inevitably leading to a preordained dénouement. Like Cooper's shuttered-up gin palace, *Murphy's* entire plot is 'bathed ... in an ironical radiance' 'by ... striking coincidence' (*M*, 70). For instance, recall that having waited at home day and night, Celia eventually misses Murphy by just five minutes when she goes for a walk, just as Murphy goes to his doom. Or consider Celia's glimpse of Murphy's birthmark after he falls over in the chair, a sign that allows her to identify him after he has been immolated. To borrow Walker's contention about Gide's development of this technique in *Les Faux-Monnayeurs*, 'each coincidence … marks the point at which the narrative advances via an articulation which is essentially self-contradictory, being so obviously unforeseeable as an event, so flagrantly purposive as a structuring device' (Walker, *Gide*, 159).

Instead of quelling our suspicions about the 'purposive' nature of these events, the 'novelist' does his best to *cultivate* them. The most obvious example of this is his favorite refrain: 'It was Sunday, October the 20th, Murphy's night of duty had come. *So all things limp together for the only possible*' (*M*, 131; my emphasis).

'Despite all these coincidences', *Murphy*'s 'novelist' seems to say here, 'there will be only one outcome: that of my choosing'. And let us not forget the *deus ex machina* that triggers this awaited end: Murphy's breakdown and recourse to the chair coincident with the unexplained influx of gas that had earlier stymied the resourceful Ticklepenny. Given the 'novelist's' disgust with his protagonist – never more evident than in his pleasure at the *ironic fulfilment* of Murphy's desires (for his body to be quiet, for heat, for 'chaos') – can we doubt *who* turned on the gas and applied the spark in this parody of 'Racinian lightning'?[15]

The gas went on in the WC, *excellent* gas, *superfine chaos*.
Soon his body was quiet (*M*, 142; my emphasis).

THE CRITIQUE OF SYSTEMS

It is becoming clear that Gide's and Beckett's exposure of the novel as an artificial system also reveals a common view of the 'novelist'. He is not only a counterfeiter, but an almost malign being that creates, thwarts and disposes of his characters virtually at will. As we shall see, he does so as part of a joke (which he finds tiresome) at the expense of systems *per se*.

This attempt to parody and undermine systems is central to Gide's *soties*, and especially to *Les Caves du Vatican*. Wolfgang Holdheim has argued that the novel is primarily a 'critique of systems' while Alain Goulet has suggested that its focus is subverting fixed notions of being;[16] but whatever Gide's specific targets in *Les Caves du Vatican*, critics agree that 'the characters have some unquestioning way of knowing that [he] seeks to disrupt'.[17] To borrow from Jonathan Culler, *Les Caves du Vatican* anticipates the kinds of modern fiction that do not present the novel as mimesis but 'the novel as a structure which plays with different modes of ordering' and creating meaning.[18] The novel's self-reflexivity thus parodies the need to make sense of an illogical and problematic situation by means of inevitably self-serving beliefs. To use Germaine Brée's analogy, this disjunction between reality and belief is the comedy of an absurd game in which the players do not know the rules but think they do, a game that 'emphasises the ironical incongruity of an inner coherence when it is transferred outwards and attributed to a world moving at random' (Brée, 'On Time Sequences', 47).

Les Caves du Vatican is full of characters that stubbornly commit to various 'closed systems' (*M*, 36); some represent specific targets, but Gide's attack is more broadly aimed at the human need to simplify complexity in a system. Anthime, for example (a scientific atheist who is converted to Catholicism and then reconverted to atheism at the end of the novel), is perhaps the most obvious example of the need for truth.

Organic matter was obviously governed by the same involuntary impulses as those which turn the flower of heliotrope to face the sun (a fact which is easily to be explained by a few simple laws of physics and thermochemistry). The order of the universe could at last be hailed as reassuringly benign. In all the motions of life, however surprising, a perfect obedience to the agent could be universally recognised (*L*, 13–14).

Once he has converted to Christianity, Anthime behaves just like the rats that he has been experimenting on, repeating automatically, 'Whatever is done in the Lord's name is well done' even as he is fleeced and abandoned by the Church (*L*, 136). Two other obvious representatives of 'closed systems' are Julius, the novelistic Naturalist who fails to comprehend the anti-hero Lafcadio (he tries to study Lafcadio through a Naturalistic 'background' investigation of Lafcadio's room but fails to understand what he finds), and Blafaphas, the representative of bourgeois commercial enterprise (he wants to know how the Italians make the hole in the macaroni). Fleurissoire is of course the grand example of the way that even '[f]act, instead of correcting, can give credence to fiction' (Broome, 35). Fitting each event into his fantasy a heroic destiny (which positions him as the unlikely saviour of the Pope), Fleurissoire inevitably sees support for his theory everywhere – for example, in the suspicious formalities of the Castel Sant' Angelo, and even in the press cutting Protos shows him that exposes Fleurissoire's delusion as one of the Millipede's scams.

Like *Les Caves du Vatican*, *Murphy*'s ironical incongruity consists in the characters' projections of coherence onto an incoherent situation. The most obvious examples are Murphy's attempt to gain a self-sufficient freedom in his elaborate conception of his mind (which is increasingly coupled with his astrological destiny); Neary's Pythagorean mysticism (*The Doctrine of the Limit*); and Wylie's vision of the 'quantum of wantum'.[19]

The advantage of this view', said Wylie, is, that while one may not look forward to things getting any better, a least one need not fear their getting any worse. They will always be the same as they always were'.
'Until the system is dismantled', said Neary.
'Supposing that to be permitted', said Wylie (*M*, 36).

Like Anthime's, Wylie's construct is a self-serving delusion whose excesses are fundamentally comic: the 'system' has been designed to dampen his anxieties, but in order for it to work, he must also give up hope (and not least the hope that the 'system' itself may one day be 'dismantled').

Murphy is perhaps the worst offender, persisting in his 'lovingly simplified and perverted' delusions with all the fervour of a Fleurissoire until he too is disposed of for his impertinence (*M*, 112). By the time he has begun work at the Magdalen Mental Mercyseat, 'Nothing remained but to see what [Murphy] wanted to see' (*M*, 101). 'Any fool can turn the blind eye,' the novelist acknowledges, but Murphy's resistance to reality outstrips even that of a Wylie: 'but who knows what the ostrich sees in the sand?' (*M*, 100).[20]

Of course, these worlds are *not* governed by Murphy's stars, Wylie's system, or Fleurissoire's destiny, nor do they revolve at random. And the disjunction between the reality the characters cannot grasp and their systems reveals a Gidean irony at work in Beckett's novel. This irony appears most poignant when the novelist, enjoying being pedantic, habitually uses Murphy's own astrological system to describe events that Murphy believes are leading him to freedom, but are actually tending toward his doom:

Celia's triumph over Murphy, following her confidence to her grandfather, was gained about the middle of September, Thursday the 12th to be pedantic, a little before the Ember Days, the sun being still in the Virgin. Wylie rescued Neary, consoled and advised him, a week later, as the sun with a sigh of relief passed over into the Balance. The encounter, *on which so much unhinges*, between Murphy and Ticklepenny, took place on Friday, October the 11th (*though Murphy did not know that*), the moon being full again, but not nearly so near the earth as when last in opposition.
Let us now take Time that old fornicator ... back to Monday, October the 7th (*M*, 67; my emphasis).

The novelist is clearly controlling the arrangement of events as easily as he manipulates the diegesis. He is arranging his figures like pieces on a chessboard, an analogy that both novels use as an inner mirror for their characters' behaviour. Though Lafcadio claims that in life one should have 'no more right to take back one's move than at chess,' the reader can see what Lafcadio realises only later: that Lafcadio's move is actually part of a larger game whose rules he does not understand (*L*, 216). In the same way, each of Gide's and Beckett's characters is caught in the maze constructed by the final system-builder, the novelist. As in Murphy's final match with Endon, the apparent choices the characters make, and the apparently random moves they observe, lead to an inevitable 'fool's mate' at the hands of the scornful chessmaster who waits to brush them from his board (*M*, 138). As Beckett's narrator says of the unctuous Ticklepenny, there will be no chance for these pieces to take back a move; if they do return, it will be in a rather less serious match of his devising. There is only one destiny operating in this cosmos:

This creature does not merit any particular description. The merest pawn in the game between Murphy and his stars, he makes his little move, engages an issue and is swept from the board. Further use may conceivably be found for Austin Ticklepenny in a child's halma or a book-reviewer's snakes and ladders, but his chess days are over. There is no return game between a man and his stars (*M*, 51).

Like the two chimps 'playing chess' in the photograph that Beckett desired for the cover of *Murphy,* the characters in these novels cannot understand the complexities they are faced with; like monkeys in an experiment, they are pawns rather than players.

MUTATIONS

Beckett's novelist also borrows another test procedure from Gide's laboratory: while subverting his characters' systems and desires he subjects them to startling 'mutations'.[21] This parodic technique was the result of Gide's reading in evolutionary theory; unlike Beckett,[22] he seems to have embraced evolution because it could serve as a justification of his view of chance, contingency and inconséquence:

[Evolution] denies the existence of a teleological design within nature and suggests that nature develops through the disordered exploration of multiple possibilities. Natural selection operates upon the products of contingency (Walker, *Gide*, 84).

But Gide's reaction to evolution was not one of wholehearted acceptance. He remained troubled by Darwinian notions of linear development, which were too closely connected with an idea of unbroken causality for Gide's liking. In his reading of Bergson's *L'Évolution créatrice,* however, Gide learned of the Dutch botanist Hugo de Vries, who argued that Darwin's notion of gradual transformation was incorrect and that previously unknown species can come into being through the sudden appearance of new characteristics. By the early thirties, Gide had excitedly allied himself with the views of such so-called saltationists, whose theories provided his concern with unforeseen occurrences and discontinuities with a new theoretical justification. Typically, Gide then burlesqued this concept in his developing fiction about inconséquence. De Vries's sudden 'leaps' appear in *Les Caves du Vatican* as the startling 'mutations' of Anthime and the novelist Julius – both, as we have seen, arch-systematisers. Such parodic inconséquence, as Beckett pointed out to his students in 1930, is of course a deliberate subversion of the Naturalistic idea of character depiction in the novel. It is a comic upset on two levels, resulting in a disruption of the reader's expectations, and the characters' ideas of themselves.

Anthime's physical inability to kneel parodically reflects his unyielding stance as a defiant atheist, but after his comic standoff with the Madonna, a bizarre spiritual and physical transformation takes place in his sleep. In what Broome aptly terms a 'comic swap', the Madonna's loss of a hand results in Anthime's gain of a leg. The 'novelist' predictably expresses his disingenuous incredulity at the results.

He was not sitting; he was not standing; the top of his head was on a level with the table and in the full light of the candle, which he had placed upon it; Anthime, the learned man of science, Anthime the atheist, who for many a long year had bowed neither his stiff knee nor his stubborn will (for it was remarkable how in his case body and soul kept pace with one another) – Anthime was kneeling! (*L*, 41).

Like his brother-in-law Anthime, Julius undergoes a startling mutation. Initially the respectable, religious, and restrained proponent of the argument against inconséquence ('There is no such thing as inconsequence – in psychology any more than in physics' (*L*, 98)), Julius becomes the excitable and reckless character scarcely recognisable to himself, showing signs of materialism, critiquing the Church, and obsessed with the notion of writing a novel about a creature whose 'very reason for committing [a crime] is just to commit it without any reason' (*L*, 229).

Whether or not he understood the Darwinian influence, Beckett certainly grasped the significance of Gide's burlesque approach to the 'unforeseen' in the novel, and he appropriated this technique for some of his own characters, the most obvious being Cooper.[23] Cooper's physical rigidity is matched by his laconic personality and his mechanical reliability in performing certain tasks (to drink when the possibility arises, to obey authority, etc). Wylie considers him virtually subhuman: 'Do not be alarmed, my dear' he assures Counihan when Cooper inopportunely walks in on their amours, 'This is Cooper, Neary's man. He never knocks, nor sits, nor takes his hat off'.

It was true that Cooper are never sat, his acathisia was deep-seated and of long-standing. It was indifferent to him whether he stood or lay, but sit he could not. From Euston to Holyhead he had stood, from Holyhead to Dun Laoghaire, lain. Now he stood again, bolt upright in the centre of the room, his bowler hat on his head (*M*, 69).

The narrator's multiple puns, like his depiction of his rigid Chaplinesque victim (complete with bowler hat), sets the stage for his character's transformation through the kind of comic swap undergone by Anthime. Murphy's death in his rocker miraculously coincides with Cooper's new lease on life (and, in another fitting swap, Cooper gains the ability to sit). And though Cooper 'did not know what had happened' (*M*, 153), it is clear who has brought this miraculous event about. Beckett's narrator not only imitates Gide's idea of a character whose rigid body and soul 'kept pace with one another', but also adopts the false surprise of the Gidean 'novelist' at such a miracle: 'Cooper sat – *sat!* – beside the driver ...' (*M*, 143).

Cooper's is not the only striking 'mutation' that occurs as a result of Murphy's demise. At the same time Murphy is being burnt, Neary, too undergoes a death and rebirth. Like Cooper's, Neary's physical transformation signifies a deep-seated change in feeling.

A curious feeling had come over Neary, namely that he would not get through the night. He had felt that this before, but never quite so strongly. In particular he felt that to move a muscle or utter a syllable would certainly prove fatal. He breathed with heavy caution through the long hours of darkness, trembled uncontrollably and clutched the chair-arms. *He did not feel cold, far from it*, nor unwell, nor in pain; he simply had this alarming conviction that every second was going to announce itself the first of his last ten minutes or a quarter of an hour on earth.

When Wylie called the following afternoon, four or five hours late, Neary's hair was white as snow, but *he felt better in himself* (*M*, 125; my emphasis).

Though Neary can only guess at what has happened, the novelist makes sure that we can see the strings he is pulling. Neary's 'sense [in *his* chair] that he would not get through the night', like the comments that he 'did not feel cold, far from it', and he 'felt better in himself', evokes Murphy's experience as he approaches his own transformation into a charred corpse in the rocker at the same time. But if Murphy's first mutation into a body without a mind (his second being into a bag of ash) is the unpredictable event on which others like it hinge, what might be the significance of Neary's experience of the unforeseen? A clue appears in his conversation earlier that fateful night when he speaks of 'the repudiation of the known' (*M*, 124). In the events leading up to Murphy's doom, Neary loses not only the fervour of his former desires, but the certainties of his former convictions – theories which we have seen allowed him to conceive of the novel's world as a balanced 'closed system' corresponding to arcane laws of mathematics (*M*, 36).[24] By the time he emerges from the MMM, Neary has been thwarted and transformed by the 'novelist's' *own* system, which is rather closer to Murphy's vision of a 'matrix of surds' than a universe of Pythagorean harmonies. 'Life', he admonishes Killiecrankie when the latter protests at his 'irregular' arrangements for Murphy's disposal, 'is all rather irregular' (*M*, 152).[25]

THE QUESTION OF FREEDOM

The novelist may control the final system but Beckett was interested in following Gide in contesting this inevitable determinism through a struggle between the free will of one exceptional character and the system of the novel. In *Les Caves du Vatican* this character is of course Lafcadio, a figure obsessed with the Gidean desire to subvert conventions. Gide allows him to 'struggle' through his resistance to being wholly appropriated by the three rival 'novelists' in the work who seek to absorb him into their constructs. The first of these is the Naturalistic novelist Julius; the second, Protos, is a type of the anti-novelist; the third is the 'novelist' of *Les Caves du Vatican*. This last 'novelist' demonstrates his dominance by placing Protos in a *roman policier* that leads to his capture by the authorities, just as Protos (unsuccessfully) tries to reprimand Lafcadio by forcing him to play a role for the secret organisation of the 'slim' (*L*, 252).

But though he manages to evade Julius and to narrowly fly Protos's net, Lafcadio's freedom in the novel remains ambiguous. Has he, by the end, managed to escape the novelist's control? As Babcock notes, there is 'a certain air of ambiguity about the conclusion of *Les Caves du Vatican*'. The unlikely ending, in which Lafcadio is let off scot-free and welcomed back into society, coupled with the novelist's closing intrusions and his commencement of a 'new book' seem to suggest that his 'playful domination of his character' is again present (Babcock, 83). On the other hand, now that the 'night' of fiction has passed with the 'phantoms' of the 'novelist's' brain, it also seems possible that Lafcadio is preparing to do something *truly* unexpected. His gaze 'through the wide open window, at the coming of dawn', his harking to a bugle's cry, and the final question of the 'novelist' (revealing his uncertainty as to his character's actions?), suggest Lafcadio has achieved a certain freedom. But, as is typical of Gide, there is also another, contradictory reading inscribed in the text. The 'novelist' has been careful to associate Lafcadio's last bid for freedom as *inherently fictive*. His contemplation of Paris in the dawn light ironically recalls the actions of another novelistic character, Balzac's Rastignac (Babcock, 84). Beckett was less concerned with the complexity that Gide painstakingly introduced into his novel on this score, but he too designed a protagonist who falls outside of the dominant systems. Most obviously, Celia disastrously fails in assimilating Murphy into her mercantile gehenna, and (though much more pacifically than Lafcadio) Beckett's anti-hero resists the social order. Neary's mathematical and philosophical system, and his technique for inner 'apmonia' also fail to accommodate Murphy (he remains a 'surd'), and Murphy seems to find Wylie's quantum unconvincing. Like Dostoevsky's figures, Murphy's taste for madness and idleness reveals his desire for 'an invitation, as it were, to rebel against the psychology and the ethics of the common herd' in a decidedly un-Gidean (and un-Dostoevskian manner) (*D*, 109).[26] Most important, though, Murphy remains something of an unpredictable element in the system of the novelist: 'All the puppets in this book whinge sooner or later, except Murphy, who is not a puppet' (*M*, 71). In spite of the animosity between Murphy and the novelist, this rather grudging acknowledgment of Murphy's uniqueness adds another dimension to their relationship and raises him, if not to the level of a would-be novel-destroyer like Lafcadio, to something of a rival 'author'. Believing '*he* was the prior system', Murphy assumes the events of the novel are of his own devising when, in his 'chance' meeting with Ticklepenny, the fulfilment of Suk's predictions seem to vindicate his belief in his destiny: 'Thus the sixpence worth of sky, from the ludicrous broadsheet that Murphy had called his life-warrant ... changed into the poem *that he alone of all the living could write*' (*M*, 56; my emphasis). At this moment, when the situation 'appeared as finally correlated in all its parts as the system from which it purported to come', Murphy pulls out the horoscope to destroy it in a moment of Lafcadian pride. In a move more typical of Beckett's comic fundamental unheroic than Gide's temper of passionate indecision, however, Murphy holds back, 'mindful of his memory, and that he was not alone' (*M*, 56).

As we have seen of other events in the novel, this chance meeting reveals an ironic perspective unavailable to Murphy: the encounter as a pre-planned move by the novelist as he arranges his piece's 'fool's mate' on his Racinian chessboard (*M*, 138). Here the artifice behind this 'chance' (as well as its fatal repercussions) is highlighted by the pattern weaving Ticklepenny's offhanded reference to Romeo ('Wotanope!') with the famous (and ill-fated) *defiance* of the stars that appears as the epigram to Murphy's (ironically titled) 'life-warrant' (*M*, 52). Such relations and patterns are in themselves obvious aspects of the novel's construction to the seasoned Beckett reader, and extend well beyond those described here. But once Beckett's modern perspective on the novel and its limits is reestablished as a governing theoretical frame *for* these relations we can begin to see *Murphy* as a work of fictional critique. Like *Dream*, Beckett's second novel arises from his efforts to erode the illusion of 'plausible concatenation' in the novel and expose 'the grotesque fallacy of a realistic art' (*PTD*, 82; 76).

CHAPTER 3

'The Creative Consciousness': The Watt Notebooks

Beckett's careful construction of his novels as (to borrow his description of *Work in Progress*) self-destructive 'machine[s]' had allowed him to ironically complicate the form with a certain success (*Dis*, 31). But this approach had also led him toward a rather schematic, if pointedly unorthodox, treatment of the form. To be sure, *Dream* and *Murphy* are not as carefully composed as their Gidean models, but a reader attentive to Beckett's self-conscious manipulation of the form's 'architectonics' might be excused for feeling that, like Gide's creative process, the young Beckett's seemed to work in reverse – with his imagination *following* his ideas.[1] Yet Beckett had long felt uncomfortable with art that appeared to arise from a highly cognitive, willed effort. And while his third novel, *Watt* (1941–45; pub. 1953), has been widely understood as a philosophical parody (a reading that would link *Watt* with the critical trajectory of *Dream* and *Murphy*), the record of the *Watt* manuscripts indicate that this novel owes as much to Beckett's reconsideration of the act of *writing* as to any critique of reason.[2] As we shall see, in *Watt*, Beckett was forced into a fresh deliberation over his compositional process that prepared the ground for the art of 'ignorance' after the war. And this struggle – which specifically impacted the novel's treatment of narration – also left its mark on the final shape of Beckett's book: the habitual questioning that typifies Watt and largely determines his story's form can, in part, be traced to his author's reconsideration of voice and narrative authority in his novel even as he struggled to compose it.

Self-reflexivity in Beckett's writing was not new, but several factors contributed to its formative significance in *Watt*. Perhaps most important, for the first time Beckett wrote a novel without deliberately collecting components for it from external sources (*Dream*) or attempting to plan his novel's structure beforehand (*Murphy*). Writing 'blindly' in the *Watt* notebooks, he deployed approaches to the novel and narration that he had used in the thirties, but soon found his work was developing in a number of seemingly irreconcilable directions. In May of 1942, after well over a hundred pages, a frustrated Beckett paused to assess his progress. He then composed one of the most important yet obscure of his theoretical writings: a conceptualisation of what he termed his 'creative consciousness'. In this passage, he sketched out the categories he would later deploy in the most famous of his theoretical writings – *Three Dialogues* (1949) – and, for the first time, accepted 'folly' as a mode of artistic praxis that could unchain his creative daemon.

THE POET AND THE PROFESSOR

As John Pilling reminds us, Beckett put his first creative impulses into his poetry, and it was as a poet that the young Beckett wished to be known.[3] Beckett had a penchant for antithesis, and from his student days at Trinity into the mid-thirties he repeatedly made use of this device to draw a distinction between the real poets and artists (the company to whom he deeply wished to belong) and the counterfeits.[4] We find this contrast worked up for the first time, with the help of a strawman, in one of Beckett's student essays on Giosuè Carducci. Beckett attacks the Italian on several other occasions, but his later critiques only reinforce the dichotomy set up in this early piece: Carducci is 'an excellent university professor but an excessively bad poet'.[5] Carducci's verse is for Beckett the type of forced, intellectual effort one might expect from a learned man; he is a 'verse manufacturer' whose 'erudition + complicated metres' inevitably 'stamped' his work 'with a desperate self-conscious effort'. (In 1934 Beckett described Carducci's 'Satan' as one of the 'great pharisee poems' – a piece that makes a great 'taratantara' yet wants the humble 'prayer' of authentic verse (*Dis*, 68).) With his fall guy down, Beckett uses Leopardi and Shelley to set up his ideal: 'the highest poetry has been written in simple language and with a simply constructed system'. Carducci's verse was 'produced … by sheer force of intellect', he concludes, while Rimbaud, Racine, and Baudelaire wrote 'what they could not help saying and they said it with that direct + inevitable simplicity of language'.[6]

This early rejection of self-consciously learned works for a 'simple' writing born of 'need' and 'feeling' is telling, as is the distinction between the true poet and the academic. Beckett targeted the 'professors' several other times in the thirties, yet as the decade wore on, the force of such convictions increasingly haunted him with the dread of a self-betrayal.[7] It is well known that Beckett disliked and even feared the idea of becoming an academic (recall Estragon's ultimate insult: 'Crritic!'),[8] but the truth about his artistic dependency on techniques drawn from his academic practice, and the relation of his creative writing to the intellectual persona he developed as a young critic, is assuredly more complex than has been commonly recognized. Two markers – Beckett's resignation from his lectureship at Trinity College Dublin (TCD) in January of 1932 for the life of a writer (he began his first novel in earnest that February) and his half-hearted application for a lectureship in Italian at the University of Cape Town five years later – mark off a formative period during which the tension between what we might term Beckett's poetic and professorial selves issued in a series of oppositions in his writing. The schism between the learned, sardonic mask Beckett donned in his criticism and reviews, and the introspective, tormented voices of his poetry is obvious. Yet each of Beckett's writerly personas in the thirties – including that of the young critic – also reveals similar contradictions *within* itself. The now-famous opening of Beckett's 1929 apologetic on *Work in Progress* ('The danger is in the neatness of identifications'; 'Literary criticism is not book-keeping') sounds like the poet's avowal of academe's limits (*Dis*, 19). But those who have sat through the ensuing lecture (on Vico's 'scientific'/mythic treatment of the origin and function of poetry: 'Croce opposes him to the reformative materialistic school of Ugo Grozio, and absolves him from the utilitarian preoccupations of Hobbes, Spinoza, Locke, Bayle and Machiavelli' (*Dis*, 19)) may feel that *Beckett's* style sits uneasily with his defence of poetry as a mode of 'direct expression'. 'Here form *is* content'? (*Dis*, 27).

The young Beckett considered 'prose as a kind of poetry' in theory if not always in practice (Pilling, 'Beckett's *Letters*', 180), but this meant that his approach to the novel, too, was rather like 'the young thought of Belacqua': 'confused in a way that was opposed to its real interests' (*DFMW*, 35). The novels up to 1937 are hardly the products of a manufacturer like Carducci, yet they do indulge an interest in the orchestration of complex systems, rely on and display the author's (considerable) erudition and intellect, and cannot conceal his self-conscious effort. This is partly because Beckett's novelistic practice, and the narrator-personality he adopted in his fiction, grew out of a view of the *novelist* more closely allied to Beckett's idea of the *critic* than his notion of the *poet*. Like his early master Gide, even as he hungered for an art of sincerity Beckett conceptualized the novel as a form of ironic critique, arming himself in 1930 with a Gidean commitment never 'to abdicate as a critic even in [the] novel' (*MIC60*, 41). This critical drive manifests itself in the essays, reviews, and novels of this period in a common attempt: Beckett's speaker exposes the conventions and limitations of the mode he is (reluctantly) engaged in, while simultaneously demonstrating a virtuosic mastery of its means. (As he scorns the technique of 'one's favourite novelist', the 'Mr Beckett' of *Dream* even cultivates the ironically detached 'we' of the smug young academic who performed the same service on behalf of 'Mr Joyce' in 1929 – to the extent that one could be forgiven for mistaking one of Beckett's didactic speakers for the other.)[9]

Not surprisingly, the narrators who oversee the critique of the novel Beckett was engaged in from the early to mid-thirties are ill at ease with the poetic selves who appear *in* the fiction – where they are subjected to their narrators' pedantic irony. 'Don't be too hard on him', says 'Mr Beckett' of Belacqua, 'he was studying to be a professor'; yet if Belacqua's own writing is anything to go by (unlike 'Mr Beckett', Belacqua is a *poet* not a novelist) he hopes to become anything but (*DFMW*, 48). The doubled, contrasting portraits of the author that segregate Beckett's novels of the thirties at the level of form thus betray a deeply felt tension within their author's psyche. That is, if the narrators of these novels represent an approach to fiction grounded in an ironic critique of form and convention (the task Beckett the critic undertook in his essays and reviews), Belacqua and Murphy represent their author's oppositional urge to explore ignorance, suffering, and what he later termed 'folly'. As we shall see, it therefore makes sense that it was only by eliding this division between the suffering subject of the fiction and his narrator – by subjugating the sardonic critic of his novels to an *experience* of ignorance and folly – that Beckett was able to 'get over' what in the *Watt* drafts he termed his own inner 'Pharisees'.[10]

But the intrusive, ironically authoritative speakers who preside over Beckett's early novels would not be easy to dismiss. For their critique was complemented by and in some senses 'built in' to the fiction through the schematic, academic working methods that Beckett relied on to give structure and substance to his novels at this time. It is often acknowledged that *Dream* and *Murphy* draw heavily on external sources, but what this meant in practice was that these novels evolved from a large body of prefictional writing (including notes, plans, and theoretical writing) that Beckett composed while wearing his academic hat.[11] For example, in spite of Beckett's suggestion that his first novel was an impulsive affair, we should be wary of crediting *Dream* as a spontaneous or 'unplanned' fiction.[12] As I have shown, this novel relies heavily on the complex artistic theory Beckett delivered in his 1930 lectures at TCD; the characters are drawn up according to the tripartite schema of the self that Beckett cribbed from Gide, and the novel's fragmented form is largely a parodic rehearsal of the new structure for the novel Beckett dismantled in his lectures on *Les Faux-Monnayeurs*. In short, *Dream* as we know it could never have existed without Beckett's lectures and his notes for his Gide monograph – that is, it could never have existed without Beckett the academic.

As for *Murphy*, the *Whoroscope* Notebook clearly indicates that by the mid-thirties its author was approaching the task of novel writing methodically and systematically. Beckett's second novel was developed from and for some time progressed alongside a body of discursive writing that helped Beckett to organise the raw material gathered from his notes, and allowed him to draw up various trajectories, frameworks, or 'principles'. The *Whoroscope* Notebook (one blueprint for *Murphy*'s eventual design) contains masses of material taken from various sources accompanied by 'propositions' marked off by solid lines and tabulated by number. From such beginnings, it is not surprising that the ironic narrating personality who eventually appears in the fiction continues to recall the young academic who drew together the raw material for his novel. Chapter Six's pseudo-philosophical 'justification' (headed with an epigram cribbed from Spinoza, retaining the Latin for effect) is perhaps the most glaring example of this speaker's knowingly critical treatment of the task of writing.

If the Beckett of the thirties was sceptical of his own poetic abilities,[13] then, he had some cause – especially with regard to the form that consumed most of his efforts. Still closely following his greatest exemplars in the novel by imitating the professorial 'notesnatching' of 'Mr Joyce' and miming the supreme theorist and critic of the novel who dominates Beckett's 1930 lectures – André Gide – Beckett could have comforted himself that he, too, was a technical 'innovator' (*Dis*, 20). But even as a modern novelist – that is, to use Beckett's early analogy, an *engineer* of intricate and ironically self-destructive 'machines' – this would hardly have made up for his failure to achieve an 'inevitably' 'direct' and 'simple' form of expression that he could call his own.[14] By the mid-thirties, Beckett felt he was not only failing to grow out of his influences but was also exercising aspects of his own psyche that he increasingly considered inauthentic. Even as the young critic airily dismisses the 'thermolaters' and their 'academic' interest in 'scenery' rather than 'self-perception' ('Recent Irish Poetry', 1934), the poet wearily admits how an authentic statement on 'the existence of the author' in *his* work has been strangled by 'years of learning' (*Dis*, 70–1, 76).

Spend the years of learning squandering
Courage for the years of wandering
Through a world politely turning
From the loutishness of learning[15]

In 'Gnome', Beckett the would-be academic appears dangerously similar to the Carducci of his Trinity days. Both are stunted creative selves sheltering behind their erudition, shying from the courage required of the true artist and the call to 'wander' into the unknown.

By the summer of 1937, this tension between the poet and the professor had worsened – to the point that Beckett at this time distinguishes between what he calls the 'real consciousness' and the false one preoccupied with 'understanding' (SB to MM, 30/8/37, *LSB 1*, 30). Recently returned from his German tour, Beckett was distressed and unsure of which direction to take. He felt that his travels had been aimless and had failed to produce good writing. Even as he half-heartedly gestured toward reassuming the academic role he had tried to leave behind in his years of wandering (applying for the post of lecturer in Italian at Cape Town in late July)[16] he made a vigorous attempt to resuscitate his creative process through his old academic methods, hoping that long days in Dublin's National Library would provide him with enough fodder for his Johnson play (*BC*, 68).[17]

One index of Beckett's need for succour at this time is his turn to one of his old favourites on suffering – Schopenhauer – as early as the first week of July (he arrived back in Foxrock in mid-April), an encounter that helped him to further distinguish between what he called different 'consciousnesses'. During a bout of gastric influenza in early September he immersed himself in the philosopher, writing to McGreevy on 21 September that 'the only thing I could read was Schopenhauer', 'I always knew he was one of the ones that mattered most to me, and it is a pleasure more real than any pleasure for a long time to begin to understand now why it is so' (SB to TM, 21/9/37, *LSB 1*, 548). The insight that Schopenhauer offered to Beckett at this vulnerable time and, Beckett indicates, undergirded his interest in the philosopher throughout the thirties, is suggested in an earlier letter to Mary Manning on 30 August. Here he describes the disconnection between what he terms 'the chaos' and the labour of rational thought and 'work' – surely an allusion to his labours for the Johnson play (the play had stalled by this time and was eventually abandoned until the spring of 1940).[18] Deploying Schopenhauer's vocabulary ('willless') Beckett describes an urge to reach 'an end of making up [his] mind', and to escape 'the temptation of light, its polite scorching & considerations' for the 'real consciousness' (SB to MM, 30/8/37, *LSB 1*, 546).

There is an ecstasy of <u>accidia</u> – willless in a grey tumult of <u>idées obscures</u>.... The real consciousness is the chaos, a grey commotion of mind, with *no premises or conclusions or problems or solutions or cases or judgments*. I lie for days on the floor, or in the woods, accompanied & unaccompanied, in a coenaesthesia of mind, a fullness of mental self-aesthesia that is entirely useless. The monad without the conflict, lightless and darkless. I used to pretend to work, I do so no longer. I used to dig about in the mental sand for the lugworms of likes and dislikes, I do so no longer. The lugworms of *understanding* (SB to MM, 30/8/37, *LSB 1*, 546; Beckett's underlining, my italics).

Once again, the Beckett of the thirties reveals himself as a divided figure seeking a self 'without the conflict' between rational 'work' (here allied with Schopenhauer's despised will) and, as he put it later, the 'things [he] feel[s]' (qtd. in *DF*, 352) – here a sense of willlessness that Beckett was then able to express (without the professor's crushing irony) only in his poetry. '[T]he state that suits me best', he admits, is the one in which 'I do nothing' but 'write the odd poem when it is there'; writing poetry, he goes on, is 'the only thing worth doing' (SB to MM, 30/8/37, *LSB 1*, 30). This dichotomy between writing that is poetic (arising from feeling) and that which arises from 'premises' backed up by 'judgments' reappears in his September letter to McGreevy; Beckett's enduring pleasure in Schopenhauer is inseparable from the fact that the philosopher 'can be read like a poet, with an entire indifference to the apriori forms of verification' (SB to TM, 21/9/37, *LSB 1*, 548). But if the Beckett of the late thirties reaffirms the poetic self he had hoped to nurture early in his career, he also admits the feelings of inauthenticity that had dogged him for almost a decade – to the point that he momentarily considers abandoning the processes that had nurtured his fiction altogether: 'I used to pretend to work, I do so no longer' (*LSB 1*, 30).

The choices which the Beckett of 1937 perceived suggested that there was no outlet for his authentic, creative self in prose: he could dig for more 'mental lugworms' or explore his 'real consciousness' but this 'consciousness', for all its legitimacy, could only issue in 'the odd poem'. As we shall see, though, one key to Beckett's escape from this impasse is present in these very letters: a practice of self-examination and self-reflection that issued, in part, from Beckett's doubts concerning the way he was heading as a writer. Such anxieties encouraged Beckett to experiment with forms of self-inscription, a tendency most apparently reflected in his changing note-taking practice. In contrast to the academic manner of recording material adopted in the *Whoroscope* Notebook (1932–7), Beckett's notebooks from the summer of 1936 to the summer of 1937 are personal diaries. The 'Clare-Street' Notebook (inscribed '13/7/36') and the subsequent German diaries (1936–7) reflect a shift in Beckett's nonfictional writing that Mark Nixon has described as the effort 'to move away from erudition toward a poetics based more directly on the emotional dimension of the self'.[19] But Beckett was unable to incorporate these more personal modes into his creative practice in the late thirties, and he returned to his note-taking methods as he prepared for the Johnson play in 1936–7.[20] By 1940, however, he had failed to produce anything more than a fragment in which Johnson never appears – an outcome that surely fostered doubts in Beckett's mind about not only the feasibility of his project on the 'Great Cham', but the methods that had not produced results.[21] As we shall see, such doubts reappear in the manuscript of his third novel: Johnson's spectre and the memory of the massive amounts of research Beckett sank into the project continued to haunt him as he composed *Watt*.

Beckett himself suggested that the way that he approached his new novel was different. *Watt*, he pointed out, was written 'as it came, without pre-established plan' (SB qtd. in *OLSK*, 12). Clearly, external circumstances played a significant part in the way that Beckett chose or was forced to compose this work, but *Watt*'s curious, even 'unsatisfactory shape' cannot be solely attributed to its wartime composition.[22] Other important factors hampered Beckett's technique. Without a body of notes, theoretical writing, or a critique of the novel to structure his new book, Beckett lacked the preparation that had given form and content to his previous novels. Consequently, he was forced to sketch out his fiction at the same time he wrote it, calling up texts and quotations even as he generated and revised his imaginary world and its characters. This unplanned approach to composition issued in some remarkable results.

BECKETT'S NARRATOR IN NOTEBOOKS 1 AND 2

Beckett's attempts to begin his third novel on the 'evening of Tuesday 11/2/41' are marked by an intensity of revision that was unlike anything he would face in initiating a major work of prose fiction in the next eight or so years (NB1, 3). The struggle to find out what and whom his novel was going to involve was not confined to the first few pages, but extends in competing narrative trajectories through Notebooks 1, 2, and part of 3 for over a hundred pages. Beckett's uncertainty about how to proceed is clear: although he begins by attempting to conjure a protagonist, he quickly turns his attention to the preliminary task of developing a narrator.

Beckett's initial attempts to start the novel each renew the same effort: to move from the interrogative mode initiated by his rather banal opening (the scholastic *memoria technica* of 'who, what, where, by what means, why, in what way, when') to a descriptive mode. By the time he had covered the first page of his notebook with false starts and begun on the verso, however, Beckett had little more than a 'man' as his subject. Yet if his protagonist remained vague, Beckett *had* quickened a certain narrative voice through toying with his emerging hero:

For our part, if <without wishing to anticipate here + now,> we venture to speak of the old, and withhold the exact, age of this old man, it is simply (NB1, 4).

Beckett never finished the sentence, but this is the birth of the narrator who will 'tell the tale of the old man' and vie with Beckett's protagonist proper (the old man who anticipates Knott, and in Notebooks 1 and 2 is named Quin) for the role of the dominant personality in the story until the appearance of Watt in Notebook 3. (The narrator remains an unnamed 'we' until, approximately halfway through Notebook 2, he appears as a character in the text known as 'Johnny'.) Further essays into the attempt to 'venture to speak' about the protagonist are carried over to page 5, and Beckett's method here begins to gather its own momentum. On page 12, a rough version of the narrator's (and Beckett's) intention appears.

To endeavour to formulate a modest demand as to of whom it is question; to simply try to frankly postulate of what & to essay a tentative outline or rough sketch of mind, so to speak, of time, supposing there to be a same, and of body, so to say, & of same again, the supposition being taken for granted for the sake of convenience at the moment of goose-chase; to make so bold as to hasard a manner of enquiry into possible relations as well as with other persons, as the saying is, as with other things; to throw out a cautious ~~interrogation~~ <feeler> as to the nature of the position no less in time (if one may say so) than in space (if one may have said so); to face <moot> not entirely without trembling: the vexed question with regard to <the> possession; the knotty problem of the subject of the act; the famous old ~~question~~ <teaser> apropos the suffering (NB1, 12).

OLD APPROACHES TO WRITING METAFICTION: THE PROFESSOR IN THE UR-*WATT*

Who is this verbose orator? David Hayman, who has examined the early stages of the manuscript in detail, suggests that Beckett's early narrator imitates the 'coy and ponderous circumlocutions' of *Ulysses'* Ithaca chapter, but this comparison ultimately breaks down.[23] Joyce's narrative mode is modelled on the question and answer format of the catechism (or perhaps a scientific examination) while Beckett's persona here is the figure of the man of letters self-consciously outlining a 'vexed' intellectual problem. Joyce's approach results in an extreme form of realistic documentation (recording the movements of characters as if they are bodies in a physics experiment, for example) while Beckett's narrator spends his effort undercutting the attempt to explore his subject in 'tentative outline[s]' made up of unjustifiable 'suppositions'. This is a figure who mimics Beckett's own concerns as a *writer* (NB1, 12).

This narrator is in fact cut from a familiar cloth. Struggling to get his new novel started, Beckett calls on the novelist-professor to revamp one of his old lectures. Predictably, this speaker is 'not entirely without trembling' as he starts again into the 'literature of saving clauses' that had him quaking at verb conjugations in Beckett's first novel.

> We find that we have written *he is* when of course we mean *he was*. For a postpicassian man with a pen in his fist, doomed to a literature of saving clauses, it is frankly out of the question, it would seem to be an impertinence – perhaps we should rather say an excess, an indiscretion – stolidly to conjugate *to be* without a shudder (*DFMW*, 46).

Periphrastically ironic, Beckett's new speaker once again dramatises the task of narration – though his comic difficulties at the beginning of the ur-*Watt* stem from his struggle to *piece together*, rather than manipulate, his 'puppets'. All the same, for a third time Beckett considers a certain type of fiction: one in which the narrator critiques the novel and exposes its limits through ironic protestations of irritation, personal confusion or inadequacy.[24]

Thematic parallels with Beckett's first two novels in Notebook 1 also suggest the attempt to draw up another ironic anti-novel. As in *Dream* and *Murphy*, Beckett develops themes of nothingness or limbo as central to the experience of his protagonist: a reclusive, eccentric old man who seems to stand between the heroes of Beckett's youth and the solitary derelicts that appear in his postwar fiction. On page 47, for example, the narrator describes a 'feeling of weakness' that follows his hero's ruminations on his preferred manner of death. The exhaustion the old man feels as a result of these considerations dissuades him from leaving his house or garden; like Murphy or Belacqua, he then seeks cover from the sun. Beckett even considers using Geulincx's Occasionalism (which he used as a governing principle for Murphy's 'dark') as a possible point of reference in discussing his new protagonist's ills.

The feeling of weakness + fatigue, insofar as it was a matter at all, was as dark a matter as what has <sometimes> been called the occasional kind (NB1, 47).

Formally, too, Beckett sketches familiar structures traceable to his early encounter with *Dostoïevsky*'s tripartite stratification of character and *Dream*'s imitation of Gide's chapter 'The Author Reviews His Characters' in *Les Faux-Monnayeurs*. Like Belacqua's personality (as explained in 'UND') or Murphy's mind (treated in Chapter Six), Quin's experience of internal vacancy is addressed by his irritated narrator in an ironic, faux-scholarly 'Chapter': 'The ~~Isolation~~ Nothingness'. And, like his early heroes, Beckett's new character is a mechanism built out of Dostoevskian 'antag-onisms' that are 'resolved in three parts or elements' – '(1) The ~~Isolation~~ Nothingness, (2) The Sky, (3) The Waste, in alphabetical order' (NB1, 69). In another similarity with his predecessors, the old man exhibits the Schopenhauerian drive toward abnegation that Beckett also cribbed from *Dostoïevsky*: the 'irrational' hero's attempt to escape into an experience of the third region, the 'null':

To leave this feeling of blessedness which it was so seldom Quin's good fortune to enjoy, and to return to the feeling of nothingness from which he suffered without intermission, if what is without intermission may be called a suffering, this latter may perhaps be defined as the resultant of two equal, wellnigh paral-lel and approximately opposite emotional forces, between whose warring pres-sures the soul of Quin would certainly have been pressed, as in a press, had not Nature, by a most beautiful and merciful provision, suffered them to be replaced by the lesser diagonal of the exceedingly flat ensuing parralelogram, the exceed-ingly flat ensuing parallelogram indeed.

The two forces that thus threatened to grind Quin's soul into its component atoms, were: on the one hand the sense of kinship with, on the other that of an estrangement from, the All.

Thus Quin, rather than feel himself at one time and the same time, one thing and all things, which would have been fatal to his immortal soul, had no choice but to feel himself no thing, in the midst of some thing, and this at all times.

In other words, Quin felt himself null, in order to continue in his being (WTS, 57–59; NB1, 69–77).

The purpose of bracketing off this apologia in a 'bulletin' (to use the 'nov-elist's' term in *Murphy*) remained the same. As Beckett pointed out in a letter to George Reavey in 1936, he wanted to keep such material at a dis-tance to avoid the 'difficulty and danger' of treating what he now termed 'the famous old ... <teaser> apropos the suffering' 'too seriously' (*Dis*, 102). Still thinking as a parodist of the novel in Gide's modern tradition, Beckett lets the professor lay on the irony; *he* will not assign his suffering subject a serious position within what *Dream* calls a system of 'irrefragable values' (*DFMW*, 119). To borrow Beckett's comments on *Murphy*, the narrator's sympathy for the protagonist of Notebooks 1 and 2 goes 'so far and no further (then [he] los[es] patience)' (*Dis*, 102). It is therefore appropriate that the professor's new disquisition closes with a flourish of disgust recalling his parting shaft in *Murphy* after the 'discharge' of his 'painful duty' in that novel's Chapter Six ('no further bulletins will be issued' (*M*, 66)): 'So much for the Nothingness' (NB1, 12).

One of *Watt*'s first recognisable narrative trajectories, then, is a meta-fictional approach that allows Beckett/his narrator to ironically regard the task of writing and his emerging protagonist. Once again, the fiction is driven by the urge to acknowledge 'the existence of the author' – a figure that coaxes his recalcitrant material, mocks his absurd characters, and derides the conventions he cannot satisfy (*Dis*, 76). Yet though he will not be silenced, Beckett's critic-novelist does not have the stage to himself; the ur-*Watt* is a cacophony of narrative modes. Two other strands are worth noting here. The first of these is an increasingly intense realistic style that is virtually dominant by the end of Notebook 2. This 'research' mode met Beckett's new need for a more objective, investigative voice by which he could document the developing world of his protagonist's home.[25] This mode exists in tension with another narrative trajectory that gathers momentum from page 27 of Notebook 1: the attempt to develop Quin's house as a place of mystery and obscurity. The result of this approach is that the house begins to take on an uncanny atmosphere already suggestive of the shifting stairs which so torment Watt during the initial stages of his sojourn.[26] As John Pilling points out, 'the latter pages of the first *Watt* Notebook are an attempt to do two contradictory things: to make Quin both more and less of an enigma' (*BBG*, 173).

FICTIONALIZING HIS WRITERLY CONCERNS:
THE THEME OF CONTINUAL REVISION

Beckett's dual struggle in the ur-*Watt* – to sketch out ideas, and create fictional text from these ideas – also led him to experiment with more self-reflexive approaches to composition. At times he seems to have generated material by fictionalising his own concerns with the very task of writing, a tactic he used especially when he felt he was stuck or the narrative was stagnating. The effects of Beckett's contemplation of his own struggle to compose survive as several minor incidents in the final text. Far more importantly, however, one of the novel's central considerations also seems to have been partly derived from this response to writing blindly: the theme of potentially endless 'revision'. We can trace this theme to Beckett's own struggle to traverse the difficult terrain he was forced to map out and narrate in Notebook 1.

Here we find a significant number of passages like the one that follows. It is heavily reworked and self-consciously redundant; the passage is itself also a rewrite of several earlier passages, and would itself continue to be rewritten.

A man, [~~illegible~~] an old, it is <perhaps not premature to say here> old man. To say here the age of this old man, were premature perhaps. ~~Perhaps~~Per-haps ~~Perhaps not however Perhaps not. A case may then be made out for, and against~~ Arguments for and against the <u>prematureness</u> prematureness of saying here + now, the age of this old man, could we are <well> aware, ~~each~~ well be made out by those versed in ~~making out arguments~~ that ~~difficult arduous act operation~~ <difficult> operation. Even by some sane person if we are to believe what we hear, and we ~~tend to~~ <do our best> ~~difficult~~, in successive ~~operations of the mind~~ acts of intellection (NB1, 7).

What is most interesting about this passage is the way that Beckett's revisions (his many strikeouts and insertions) become a topic of narrative interest in themselves and are eventually staged as a product of his narrator's tiresome reasoning. 'We's' subject may initially be the old man, but, playing with the idea of what is and is not 'premature to say here', he quickly becomes entangled in 'arguments for and against' which bring *his* verbose personality to the fore ('we's' prolixity is such that he even enjoys extending his favourite word: 'per-haps'). As noted, unlike his predecessors in *Dream* or *Murphy*, this frustrated pedant does not yet *have* a world to describe; in passages like this one, he therefore finds himself reflecting less on his creatures than on the revisions that compose and frame his narration. And if all this self-awareness makes 'we' sound somewhat deranged, Beckett apparently thought so too: playfully deploying his reconsiderations of the evolving text as his *surrogate's* 'successive acts of intellection', Beckett begins to broach the notion of his narrator's mental instability (the 'prematur[ity]' of telling the 'old man's' age could be debated 'Even by some sane person', to say nothing of 'we' (NB1, 7)).

Beckett returns to the theme of potentially endless revision later in Notebook 1 where he strengthens the link with insanity and deterioration. Here Beckett regards his struggle to write from a further ironic remove – transferring an experience of futile reasoning from his narrator to his protagonist, Quin. Quin's 'meditations' do not revolve around telling a story but the ideal manner of death. In his earliest thoughts of death Quin arrives at the conclusion that it would be best to die in his sleep – a notion that, on more mature reflection at the age of forty, gives way to the argument that one is perhaps better off passing away fully conscious (NB1, 47). After numerous revisions to his original conclusion, Quin later decides (again) that it would be best of all to die peacefully and quietly in his sleep, without warning (NB1, 47). The content of this passage may not have survived, but it was Quin's process of rethinking (described as his taste for 'tripe') that Beckett found important: as if to secure this dynamic for later use in the novel, he has 'we' point out that such useless 'revision' to an earlier judgment was typical of this character (NB1, 47). 'We' then suggests the dire effects that this habit will entail: Quin is confined to his bed, finds himself unable to leave his house and garden, and feels compelled to hide in darkness.

Even if Beckett may at times have felt that the revisions *he* was performing were useless, one of the chief games that *Watt* will play – a game that to an extent determines its narrative – begins to swim into view here. Like Quin, Beckett's narrator 'we' and his final protagonist Watt undergo an experience of traumatic collapse following their reflections and revisions on 'the old man' (who becomes Knott) in this mysterious house – a collapse that of course leads Watt to the asylum, where he meets Beckett's revised narrator-surrogate, Sam.

But as Beckett squared up to start his third notebook in the early May of 1942, these important stages in the text's evolution lay in the future. At this time he was thinking less about his characters (whom he found tiresome) than the dynamics of his own creative drive – which had produced over a hundred pages without a clear end in sight.

'WHO ENDURES CONQUERS': NOTEBOOK 3'S 'CREATIVE CONSCIOUSNESS'

In a highly unusual passage which opens Notebook 3, we find Beckett exploring a form of diaristic writing, reflecting on the creative process I have been following. The result is one of the most interesting and obscure of his theoretical writings and is of no small importance to his later theory. Because of its length (until now, this passage has never been printed in full), I have divided it into parts. I have retained its order, however, leaving nothing out, including the line breaks that Beckett scored on the manuscript to signify a halt in composition or the end of a thought.

5–5–42

The creative consciousness is driven & obscure. Obscure and obscene when it acts, terrible and driven when it receives.

Its action is a receiving, its receiving an acting.

When it acts it receives its own act, when it receives it acts on the act of another.

God said that it was good. Paul de Kock also.

My consciousness that it could be improved is an act. Smith's consciousness that it might be is an understanding, but mine is an act. Endless acts.

Yesterday I saw the latest pictures of Georges Rouault. Small, few, well presented.

Smith saw them at the same time. And now Smith knows, & Smith's friends know, why it is they are good, or why it is they might be improved.

Shut in one samples a new act set free. Set loose. Simply!

Two, four, eight, sixteen, thirty-two – a new concern.

Smith judges.

I am judged.

Smith at rest.

I am ~~in torment~~ <not>.

~~Smith is one kind of fool.~~ <Smith's sorrow is one kind.>

I am another kind. <Mine another.>

Perhaps the most striking aspect of this passage is its gnomic style: structured according to a series of equivalences and contrasts, it begins (as it will end) in a mock-biblical mode (note the chiastic structure of line 2, and the ludic conflation of two rather different acts of creative approval in line 4). This playfully cryptic tone is appropriate, since the passage is concerned with the mystery and caprice of artistic creation, and specifically the link between 'obscure' and 'driven' forces in the mind of the artist. These attributes correspond to the two reciprocal functions of the 'creative consciousness': aesthetically productive acts of reading and writing.

The relationship between these terms emerges in Beckett's example of two kinds of reading in his description of the encounter with Rouault. The key point here is the distinction made between 'understanding' (non-creative reading) and 'act'. The critic/observer Smith gains only critical understanding (pronouncing 'why it is [artworks] are good'), passes judgment ('why it is they might be improved') and finds himself 'at rest'. But Beckett's response entails being somehow judged *by* the artwork in a way that leads to a productive 'torment': the artist's confrontation with the new ultimately results in 'a new [creative] concern'. But if we have now arrived at the rather commonplace notion that the artist, unlike the critic, produces work through turning extant texts into creative occasions, the nature of this creative act or, more accurately, *acts* (like the structure of the passage itself, the process described entails stages) is not as clear: What might it mean, for instance, for the artist to be judged *by* a text so as to forego his *own* judgment?

The 'creative consciousness' is not only uninterested in the appraisal of existing works (both de Kock and God are capable of pronouncing something good or not, but this does not – Sartre would agree – make either of them artists); it is finally unconcerned with other texts per se ('receiv[ing and] act[ing] on the act of another'). Creativity here occurs within a self-reflexive process; 'receiving' may initiate its work, but when the artist's consciousness 'acts it receives its *own* act' (my emphasis). This is why Beckett describes the writing process as functionally hermetic. It is in the process of being 'shut in' that the artist *acts* as an artist, setting his creativity 'free' and responding to his emerging text in a manner that exponentially multiplies it ('Two, four, eight, sixteen, thirty-two') until 'a new concern' is born.

When it acts it receives its own act.
    It accepts & suffers it.
    It is its own ~~acceptation~~ <accepting> & its own suffering.

As this makes clear, the creative consciousness figures a dynamic of *self-writing* ('when it acts') through *self-reading* ('receiv[ing]' its own act) that is potentially perpetual. And as with the artist's act of reading another's text (his 'torment' with the Rouault paintings), so in the act of creatively reading his own text: the artist's consciousness 'suffers' by permitting (accepting) such acts to remain *without subjecting them to critical scrutiny*. The creative consciousness, then, is the irreverent ('obscene') stifling of the *critical* consciousness. As Beckett's opening statements illustrate, the acts of reading and writing that drive the creative consciousness are also necessarily 'obscure' – that is, opposed to the Smith-like tendency to 'understand' – and must remain so in the interests of *preserving the conditions for artistic success*.

Each act is the accepting & in its continuance the suffering.
    In the creation is the cross.
    Vincit qui patitur.
    With a Pyrrhic victory.

Here Beckett at last formulates the thought that he has been groping for in the previous lines, collapsing his thinking about the interlocking

processes of the creative consciousness into a series of equivalences (acting is accepting is suffering is creation). At the same time, he conjoins
the language of Genesis with the imagery of crucifixion (imagery that
is prevalent, of course, in Rouault's painting) to present the redemptive
conclusion to all this suffering: *vincit qui patitur* means 'who endures
conquers'. But as with Christ's victory, this triumph will come at a cost.
That cost, and the repercussions of this new conceptualisation of artistic
praxis, begin to flicker into view in Beckett's closing thoughts.

> For example, I write: 'With a Pyrrhic victory' or: 'Walking in his garden Quin
> had an encounter'.
> 11–5-42
> Accepted as soon as ~~sai~~ <done> (~~written~~ <written down>), not accepted &
> then done, not done & then accepted, but accepted in the doing & done in the
> acceptance.
> written in the reading.
> Then suffered to stand, suffered to engender.
> Because it had once been ~~good~~ <tolerable>. For an instant, once, not a shame.

Referring to an episode in Notebook 1 where Quin goes walking in his
garden and meets an old man (NB1, 21–5) Beckett considers that, if 'suffered to stand', even his earliest and least promising efforts in the ur-*Watt*
can 'engender' 'a new concern'.[27] The creative consciousness passage thus
reveals Beckett's theorisation of an approach to writing that does not
seem to have arisen out of his knowledge of other writers (Gide; Joyce;
Dostoevsky), but from his own experience of writing 'blindly' in the
Watt text itself. This process is governed by an autonomous inner logic
of 'accepting' and responding to what has been written – crucially, as
he points out here, in the very moment of the writing itself ('accepted in
the doing & done in the acceptance'). The cheering implications of this
theory are obvious for a writer beginning without the theoretical scaffold-
ing and various types of fodder (the material in the *Dream* notebook, for
example) he had relied on in his first two novels; the new book will be
'written in the reading' of its own writing: a process that of course proceeds without the need for a predetermined closure or purpose.

Yet Beckett's reflections on his creative process here did not arise solely
out of his contemplation of the messiness and apparent lack of direction in
the ur-*Watt*. The way that the terms of this passage come together (specifically, Beckett's differentiation between judgment and action, and foolishness
and suffering) are the culmination of a longer process or self-evaluation.
Most apparently, Beckett here effectively rejects the Gidean dictum he had
accepted in 1930 and had followed in his fiction and criticism ever since: 'not

to abdicate as [a] critic even in [the] novel' (MIC60, 41). His new rule – at least with regard to the task of composition – was to allow what had been written to interact with other elements in order to 'engender' a new situation: no longer would his imagination follow his intelligence. But in other ways as well, the passage looks backward. For instance, the opposition between artistic 'acts', and 'knowing' and 'understanding' is new, but it also recalls the conflict between Beckett's poetic and critical/academic selves in the thirties in important ways. Once this is recognised, the implications of this passage for Beckett's 'mature' theory begin to surface.

We have seen that the Beckett of the late thirties described a conflict between what he considered his real consciousness and his work, but the experience then seemed useless – an immersion in a realm of inner chaos incapable of producing any acts at all. It was only in Beckett's next attempt at the novel that he could transform his 'obscure' intuitions into a theory of creative praxis. As in the 1937 letter to Manning, two visions of consciousness are juxtaposed in the 1942 creative consciousness passage. But in Beckett's new formulation a series of 'endless acts' now follows from the experience of being 'shut in' himself (a situation that evokes his earlier 'coenaesthesia of mind'). Rediscovering his real consciousness as a *creative* consciousness, Beckett again despises the work of understanding – now the quotidian critic Smith's job: 'My consciousness that it could be improved is an *act*. Smith's consciousness that it might be is an *understanding*' (NB3, 1–2; my emphasis).

But being 'shut in' is not without its price. In contrast to Schopenhauer's theory – according to which the aesthetic raises the genius above the torment and folly of willing – artistic creation immerses the Beckett of 1942 *in* suffering. For him, the artist's task is far from consolatory; in fact, it entails accepting the 'shame' of being another kind of 'fool'. Beckett's linkage of folly and artistic failure (writing will be for him 'a Pyrrhic victory') also alerts us that if his revelations about his creative consciousness can be traced back to his struggle between his poetic and professorial selves in the thirties, they also look ahead to the theory of the forties and his most famous writing on aesthetics. *Three Dialogues* – a piece that also uses a modern painter as a springboard for a theoretical foray – clearly develops the antithesis I have been tracing; once again Beckett sets up a straw man's *understanding* (now the unfortunate Duthuit's assigned position) versus the 'obscure' situation of the artist who will acknowledge 'a certain situation [of failure] and ... consent to a certain *act*' (Bram Van Velde) (*PTD*, 119; my emphasis).[28] Beckett also recycles the emphasis he had placed on 'accepting' seven years earlier: Van Velde's insight consists in being 'the first to *accept* a certain situation' (*PTD*, 119; my emphasis). The hated idea of 'work', too, reappears in *Three Dialogues* as 'straining to enlarge the statement of a compromise' along 'the plane of the feasible' (the process that typifies all artists before Bram Van Velde), and the need to 'establish the data of a problem to be solved, the Problem at last' (Masson) (*PTD*, 109, 111). In this light, *Three Dialogues* reveals itself as a hard-won riposte to the sense of failure and paralysis Beckett suffered in the late summer of 1937, and as a revisitation of the 'Pyrrhic victory' of his revelation in 1942. The insight that sets Van Velde apart from the entire history of painting (though 'utterly useless' from Duthuit's perspective) is the same acknowledgment that Beckett had come to through an experience of near mental collapse in the late thirties: that he 'cannot act'.

An important, intermediary stage between these three markers (August 1937, February 1942, March–December 1949) should also be noted. In the summer of 1945, Beckett connected 'folly' with major changes in the way he conceived of writing and which he linked to the production of his masterworks.[29] Speaking of the revelation that he had in his mother's room, Beckett claimed that 'Molloy and the others came to me the day I became aware of my own folly'; 'Only then did I begin to write the things I feel' (qtd. in *DF*, 352).

I realised that Joyce had gone as far as one could in the direction of knowing more, [being] in control of one's material. He was always adding to it; you only have to look at his proofs to see that. I realised that my own way was in impoverishment, in lack of knowledge and in taking away, in subtracting rather than in adding (qtd. in *DF*, 352).

The Beckett of *Watt* did not yet know that his path lay in erasure and attrition, and he could not have known that his (struck-out) intimation that he was a 'kind of fool' would so impact his use of the accretive and schematic methods that had underpinned his novels of the thirties. Yet in 1942 he does celebrate a mode of writing at odds with 'knowing more, [being] in control of one's material', and valorises each act of his 'obscure' compositional process as a form of necessary failure.[30]

If there *is* a connection between Beckett's approaches to composition and the narrative modes that he favoured in the thirties, we should expect that the changes in the way that Beckett conceived of the act of writing in 1942 had an important effect on his new novel. Specifically, the role of Beckett's narrator must shift from a perspective primarily concerned with passing judgment from a safe remove (*Dream*'s and *Murphy*'s narrators;

'we') to one that somehow accommodates the obscure processes his author now acknowledges as his creative animus. And for this to happen, the critical space between the narrator and the fiction's 'suffering subject' must be considerably narrowed. In the playful conclusion to the creative consciousness passage, Beckett anticipates doing this through deploying the crucifixion narrative: joining the artist, his narrator (who appears here as Pilate in a contest against the high priests of revision and irony), and the suffering subject of the fiction (a Christ surrogate) in a common *agon*. 'In the [act of] *creation*', Beckett claims, 'is the cross' (NB3, 1–2; my emphasis).

> Because it had once been ~~good~~ <tolerable>. For an instant, once, not a shame.
>   Jesus of Nazareth the King of the Jews
>   No, Jesus of Nazareth 'the King of the Jews'.
>   <Jaysus the King of the Jews written without inverted commas.>
>   Prefer one's Pilate to one's high priests (NB3, 1–2).

Pilate's statement ('Jaysus the King of the Jews') rebuts the overt and absolute critique of the Pharisee's inverted commas, but not without retaining a certain irony in its deliberate misspelling. And Pilate's famous final remark ('what I have written, I have written', John 19:22 (*KJV*, 121)) surely underlines Beckett's emphasis on a prose that is allowed to stand without the meddling of the critics – who *had* been allowed to craft the pharasaical statements presiding over Belacqua's and Murphy's 'crucifixions'.[31]

'SENSING A CHANGE': *WATT*'S NOTEBOOK 3

Beckett's theorisation of a new approach to composition is only one reason the narrator of Notebooks 1 and 2 transforms in Notebook 3: a series of strikeouts in Notebook 2 suggests Beckett's own increasing frustration with his tale and the direction 'we' was taking the novel. So it is likely that Beckett approached Notebook 3 with change on his mind. If so he accomplished it – by imposing the experience of a traumatic 'change' on his characters.

Beckett initially takes up the thread he had left dangling at the end of Notebook 2: his narrator-protagonist 'we' (also called 'Johnny' (NB2, 53–98)) urges one of Quin's servants, Arsene, to frantically sing and dance. Beckett could not disapprove of such *commedia dell'arte* buffoonery from the safe remove of the novelist-narrator (he had surrendered that position to map out Quin's world from the perspective of the documentary researcher) but he was unable or unwilling to go along with this clowning any longer.[32] 'We's' cavortings at the beginning of Notebook 3 are

repeatedly struck-out and aborted, and Arsene experiences a newfound
fatigue that suggests Beckett's own resistance to any more of 'we's' dictation. In the pages that follow, Beckett alters the trajectory and focus of
the narrative in several important ways. First, he subjects Arsene to the
feeling of exhaustion that 'we' has ironically described as the main experience of Quin's life in Notebook 1 (NB1, 47); shortly after, Arsene collapses
(NB3, 5).

Second, 'we's' own frolics do not last long. Night falls and, for the first
time in his fiction, Beckett begins to expose his *narrator* to an experience
of silence, ignorance, and darkness (previously these were merely topics of
ironic discussion for 'we' in his analysis of Quin). A widening disjunction
then begins to appear between Arsene and 'we', who have been hitherto
indistinguishable comic doubles (in Notebook 2 'we' had even claimed
that he somehow 'was' his counterpart). Beckett then redeploys a theme
he had developed in relation to the old man of Notebook 1: after his collapse, Arsene undergoes a mysterious transformation and grows silent.[33]
In the weird darkness that so troubles Quin in Notebook 1, he becomes
an enigmatic figure for the first time anticipating his 'mirthless' descendant in the *Watt* text: "'You find me changed", said Arsene. "You too are
changed. I was not always, I shall not always be, the man I am. But I shall
do my duty.... And take the consequences'" (NB3, 15).

The change here, which Arsene prophetically points out will continue to affect 'we' as well, not only anticipates the theme of 'doing one's
duty' that leads to Arsene's and then Watt's respective breakdowns, but
it suggests Beckett's awareness that his narrative had reached a crucial
point: metamorphoses and 'consequences' lie ahead. This altered Arsene
(note the newly cryptic, laconic quality of his speech) gradually assumes
the centre of narrative interest and becomes the figure in control of the
dialogue. This change unsettles 'we'; he desires to leave the house, but
finds himself compelled to stay by Arsene's disquieting silence. But to
his repeated inquiries regarding the dark and the night, 'we' receives no
reply. When Arsene does break his silence, it is to ask 'we' if he can feel
a 'brink' on which they are hovering and have been on the verge of all
evening. 'We' uneasily denies feeling any such thing. 'There is nothing
to be ashamed of', Arsene says knowingly to an uncharacteristically flus-
tered 'we', 'The best of us feel brinks from time to time.... Let me linger
a little on the brink' (NB3, 17).

As this statement suggests, Beckett had virtually turned the task of
directing the plot over to Arsene at this stage. Appropriating the role of
'we' (note Arsene's use of 'us') in commenting on the tale and serving as

his author's narrator-surrogate, Arsene hints that the novel itself is also lingering on the threshold of a change. The importance of the developing conversation between Arsene and 'we' is suggested by Beckett's revision and extension of it well beyond the halfway point of Notebook 3. (He was still adding to it on page 79 after he had to stop writing because of the flight to Roussillon.) As he continued writing and redrafting this passage, Beckett stressed the obscurity his narrator has fallen into – a manoeuvre that suggests a critical reflection on 'we's' attempt at narration in the previous notebooks.

This criticism becomes clear when, following Arsene's comments on the 'brink', 'we' reasserts his purpose to record the events of his stay at the house in a text to be titled 'A Clean Old Man'. Arsene, however, laughs 'mirthlessly' at such an idea, derisively inquiring whether the project will be written 'in form, with a beginning, a middle and an end, [with] stiff boards and a cover to keep off the dust'.[34] The dianoetic laughter in *Watt* was thus initially directed at the attempt at writing a conventional account of the old man (Arsene's stressing of the narrative simplicity and crude materiality of the book emphasises his point about the subject's obscurity and ineffability). This account would presumably be completed in a realist mode governed by an omniscient narrator – the endeavour that Beckett himself had been engaged in, on and off, for well over a hundred pages through 'we'. That such a self-reflexive criticism is intended is made clear when 'we' recalls that before he came to Quin's house he was in the National Portrait Gallery among the portraits and busts of Dr Johnson, doing research. Arsene then menacingly suggests that after a week in Quin's mysterious house, the narrator's laugh, too, will be 'purged' – evacuated to the point that it may become a laugh laughing at its own unhappiness (WTS, 211; NB3, 29).

As Beckett allows 'we' to experience Arsene's doubt and sceptical laughter, the ironic, self-satisfied detachment the narrator maintained throughout both his omniscient and 'researcher' roles erodes. Beckett then begins to exploit the comic potential in his (newly) confounded narrator's attempt to record and *interpret* Quin's strange world.

'SUFFERED TO ENGENDER': QUIN'S POSS AND THE FAMISHED DOG SEQUENCE

Beckett had already developed the narrator's descriptive role into a comic mode of narration in Notebook 2. In this mode, the narrator's exhaustive enumeration of objects allows the examination of an object to 'engender' further investigations that uncover a series of (satiric) narratives. For instance, Beckett took advantage of 'we's' 'consideration' of the paintings of Quin's father and mother to generate a discourse covering (among other things) lengthy comic biopics of the painters Art Conn O'Connery and 'the Master of the Leopardstown Halflengths', Matthew David McGilligan. A description of two paintings thus expands to reveal a series of comic narratives satirising Irish history and identity (either a surfeit of corned beef and cabbage or the unmasking of Parnell occasioned the death of O'Connery), the Catholic priesthood (McGilligan's meditations include the question of the rat and the consecrated wafer), and Stephen Dedalus's moment of aesthetic apprehension with the wading girl (McGilligan's life-changing revelation before 'the celebrated painting by Gerald of the Nights of a girl in her nightdress catching a flea by candlelight' is the reason he renounces the priesthood to become an artist (NB2, 7)).[35]

In Notebook 3 Beckett returns to this technique for generating a dizzying and comic multiplication of concerns and joins it with the new emphasis on the limitation of the narrator's knowledge. As a result, the narrator's intellect, when faced with the need to give an account of the enigmatic Quin and his mysterious house, begins to take on the 'thoroughly concussed' status so familiar to Watt (NB3, 31). In this way, Beckett discovered that he might *deepen* the enigma of Quin's household precisely *through* a process of documentary investigation, *while* exploring the themes of nothingness, aporia, and the failure of intellection from a first-person perspective. Well before the appearance of Watt, then, Beckett managed to develop central concerns of the novel: a debilitating experience of nothingness (Quin's experience, then Arsene's, then 'we's'), the failure of the trope of the journey ('Johnny's' journey to Quin's home), and the futility of rational investigation ('we's' attempt to explore the house and write his account).

The passages Beckett then composed are not surprisingly some of the most entertaining in *Watt*, and, alongside the short statement (developed from the conversation between Arsene and 'we' noted earlier), are the first large tracts of material to survive almost intact: Knott's poss, and the famished dog sequence. In contrast to previous sequences (like those concerning the paintings) the exhaustive description of Quin's poss or the wild speculations/history concerning the famished dog do not direct their satiric attention on much other than the process of intellection or the possibility of knowledge itself. The narrator's tone, while preserving a playful tenor, now incorporates a new sense of uncertainty that directs the investigations away from a complete and exhaustive account toward termination in aporia. In addition to several comic back-stories, the description of Quin's poss is also followed by a series of speculations regarding its origins. These speculations inevitably lead to an admission of tenuous understanding and limited knowledge: 'Further than this', the narrator claims, 'no man can go in the present state of ~~our~~his knowledge' (NB3, 75). Beckett here anticipates the ways that continual reasoning and revision comically bump up against the limits of knowledge in *Watt*, always making sure he allows his narrator to retain a (dangerous) hope that this 'present state' may yet give way to another (which would allow him to change his mind and begin revising his opinion again).

Notebook 3's exhaustive speculations regarding the origins of the famished dog[36] are of particular interest because this sequence immediately precedes and in a sense gives rise to Watt's appearance. Indeed, the transition from the narrator's extravagantly speculative conjectures in this passage and Watt's emergence is practically seamless. As Beckett works out this incredible paradigm (which straddles pages 86–157 of Notebook 3), he perfects the dominant mode by which the *Watt* narrative will proceed.

In the poss speculations the narrator had been forced to concede doubt and defeat at the end of his exhaustive reasoning. By the time Beckett started the famished dog 'Quin-Lynch spectacle', he knew enough to riddle his paradigm with instability much earlier on. In spite of the titanic proportions of the enterprise (at its height an international phenomenon), and the herculean efforts of the narrator to recapture its significance and scope, the narrator concedes that little information was to be attained even as he launches into an exposition of the Lynch millennium (NB3, 151). The narrator's process of reasoning hence imparts a sense of endlessness to his task. The original object (the 'spectacle') *recedes* from view as, after each appeal to reason or evidence, the narrator's (and the reader's) understanding is further confounded by another history, chart, or truth table. Sixty-five pages into the 'history', Beckett's narrator pauses to acknowledge that his attempts will end in failure. (As if musing on his newfound theme, Beckett traced over 'incomplete' several times in the passage below.)

the time comes, for every trace, when it must disappear and leave ~~illegible~~ <no> trace behind, ~~and not~~ to tell where it had been. <For ~~illegible~~ as ~~illegible~~ things vanish, so much traces vanish, and the traces of traces as the traces of things.> And the accounts are notoriously **incomplete** (NB3, 151).

Watt's rhythms are already in evidence here: the delight in repetition and redundancy, the eager application of the comma, the continual expression of uncertainty. Following this passage, Beckett presses the difficulty of deriving any 'conclusions' from these 'accounts', speculating, as he had near the beginnings of the project, on the need to make statements in the absence of information.

Various conclusions have been drawn from the various facts, preponderantly by persons in whom the need to conclude was highly developed (NB3, 151).

Still using the passive constructions that recall the academic arguments of previous narrators ('various conclusions have been drawn from the various facts'), Beckett hints at the character traits and the conditions that will become central to his new novel: he needs a character who has a 'highly developed' 'need to conclude' in the face of the 'notoriously incomplete'.

After two further pages of trying to determine the geographical and genetic 'cradle' of the spectacle, the narrator's interrogations become less concerned with the possibility of understanding the spectacle's true origins and lapse into a series of 'perhaps' statements circling around the 'unknown' – an area that now expands to include Quin's possible knowledge of the spectacle and his habitually satisfied appearance. The nature of Quin's feeling of contentment then becomes a new subject of speculation. The sentence 'Quin was content' (NB3, 151) is juxtaposed with the shortest verse in the King James Bible, 'Jesus wept' (John 11:35, 111), to comically emphasise the profound inscrutability of Quin's appearance and the limitations of the narrator's reason: Christ's grief before the crucifixion cannot be fathomed, and like Quin's contentment, it is best acknowledged as briefly as possible. (The narrator has of course come to this revelation through a lengthy process of reasoning.)

Beckett realised that in this new narrative mode of questioning and reasoning he did not need the ironic detachment or omniscience of his old narrator. In fact, the process of thwarted investigation he had now established was itself far more important than a narrative personality. If anything, the investigative researcher 'Johnny' 'we' now stood in the way. Beckett therefore elides him and instates a new character: Watt. With Watt, Beckett disposes of 'we' *and* continues to develop the fruitful speculative and investigatory modes his narrator uses earlier. In other words, Watt explores Knott's world from a position of ignorance no longer burdened with the task of narrating the text at hand. The text can therefore be given over much more fully to the narrative trajectory Beckett now desires to explore: a persistent (and 'concussed') 'seeker's' continual attempts to reason in the face of the incomprehensible.

On page 157, Beckett realises that the time is ripe for the crucial shift he had been preparing for since he began to immerse his narrator in darkness and ignorance at the beginning of Notebook 3. Continuing without a break or a change in his handwriting, he shifts the narrative perspective to focus on a new personality who seems to have been 'sitting doing nothing' in his author's mind as Beckett finished the 'Quin-Lynch spectacle'. This new figure then takes up the investigative concerns of the narrator who, Beckett realised, could come 'thus far and no further'.

Quin was content. Jesus wept. Thus far and no further. Thus near and no nearer. For the time being. For some reason or another.

Erskine came <running> down the stairs and along the passage, into the kitchen where Watt was sitting doing nothing + said:

'Did you see Mr Quin?'
'Whom?' said Watt.
'Mr Quin' said Erskine.
Erskine was forever going up the stairs and coming down them again
    (NB3, 157).

In the passages that follow, Beckett applies what he has so recently learned. Watt's ignorance (he has not seen Quin) and Erskine's continual movement up and down the stairs are all that is needed. The pre-formed mechanism of Watt's thought process does the rest.

Watt did not care to inquire into the meaning of all this, for he said to himself, All this will be revealed to me Watt in due time, meaning when Erskine went and another came. But knowing that a hypothesis was all he risked, he ventured within himself to make inquiry, concerning these strange movements of Erskine, with the pleasing result of that after quite a short time he had quite a new subject of conversation with himself, and sitting quietly in the kitchen, at the chimney-corner, would say, Watt, what do you make of all this? Then Watt would say, after a little pressing, Perhaps Quin sends him now downstairs, and now up ... (NB3, 157).

To use Beckett's terminology, Watt here needs only to 'shut [himself] in', fixate on the obscure (the 'strange'), and his own tendencies will create 'a new subject of conversation' – 'a new [creative] concern'. An isolated act of reading thus results in multiple rereadings and acts of revision. Following this passage, the now nameless narrator (later simply 'N' then 'Sam') proceeds to establish Watt's character in the bell investigation and his encounter with the painting in Erskine's room (both passages are virtually identical to their final versions). And this new hero's origins in Beckett's own concern with revision reappear for a moment before they too vanish in a text now governed by the experience of the 'notoriously incomplete'. Faced with the painting in Erskine's room, Watt's considerations recall Quin's taste for 'tripe' even as they evoke Beckett's early fictionalisation of his *own* 'successive acts of intellection' – the process by which 'each additional act of reflexion' now results in 'But a very little further reflexion, and so on, and so on, [causing] Watt to change his mind, and adopt again as true what he had rejected as false' (WTS, 321).

CHAPTER 4

'Telling the Tale': Narrators and Narration (1943–1946)

Beckett's struggle to compose and revise *Watt* 'as it came' is an important point of origin for the disorienting questioning that largely determines this novel's form. But if *Watt* represents a departure from the schematic and theoretical compositional approaches that shaped *Dream* and *Murphy*, it nevertheless returns to and develops Beckett's key strategy in the thirties for cultivating tension within the novel: troubling the relationship between the narrator and the world he creates. In this sense, *Watt* poses a significantly more disquieting set of problems for the reader than Beckett's earlier fictions, largely through its confusion of voices and its related use of textual apparatuses that frame the narration proper, such as its footnotes and addenda. Just as important, it was in *Watt* that Beckett first began to experiment with monologue, a narrative approach he returned to with powerful effect in 'Suite', *Mercier and Camier,* and *Three Novels*.

WATT'S VOICES

Much valuable space has been saved, in this work, that would otherwise have been lost, by avoidance of the plethoric reflexive pronoun after *say* (*W*, 6).

This is *Watt*'s first footnote, a faux-scholarly reference that may initially seem trivial – until we consider that it suggests the hand of a playful creative writer (in the mould of *Dream*'s professor-novelist), rather than the reporter Sam claims to be. On the basis of this note Matthew Winston argued in 1971 that the entire text of Beckett's third novel should be understood as Sam's creation, a claim Ackerley recently dismissed as 'excessive' and 'dubious' (*OLSK*, 29).[1] But though Winston does not do enough to substantiate his argument, which is admittedly too simple, we should not quickly disregard the way he highlights *Watt*'s narrative complexity and the unsettling game it plays with the reader. In spite of the widely held view that *Watt* exemplifies a parody of reason, its philosophical 'message' is not, I think, the most perplexing aspect of this novel. Far more unsettling is the reader's sense that behind *Watt*'s truth tables and logic games there is another game afoot, a game with narrative that seems to be conducted by *several* voices, and whose rules we – readers of the novel – are unable to grasp.

This narrative game comes into clearer focus when we compare Beckett's novel with a work that uses similar narrative devices but plays by rules the reader can follow. Frederik Smith has argued convincingly that Beckett's use of devices like the footnotes, 'Hiatus in MS', 'MS illegible', and the lacunae in the text (advertised by question marks) can be traced to Swift's *A Tale of a Tub* (1704). Yet despite Smith's considerable insights, he misses a fundamental difference between the ways narrative works in *A Tale* and *Watt*. Importantly, the lacunae, 'hiatuses', and footnotes in *A Tale*'s 'manuscript' are part of a coherent narrative strategy; Swift's text sets itself up as an *objet trouvé* that has been read by 'the bookseller' who writes the 'Apology', and the 'several gentlemen' whom 'the bookseller' has contracted 'to write some explanatory notes' on it.[2] Thus, when one of these editing gentlemen notes that the 'Hiatus in MS' on page 29 of the text, like the other gaps in the manuscript, is only a 'pretended' 'defect' intended to mask the 'author's' inability to write something interesting, we recognise a complex, yet internally coherent ironic narrative stratagem at work (Swift, 29). This stratagem is intended by the real author to critique 'the egocentric dishonesty of the modern writer' (Smith, 41).

But in Beckett's text, devices like the footnotes, addenda, various lacunae, and the written-in 'Hiatus in MS' operate together in a different way. Unlike *A Tale* – or *Dream* and *Murphy* – *Watt* disorients the reader instead of providing him with recognisable ironic perspectives. (As stated, in Swift's text these ironic perspectives can be ascribed to our co-readers, the gentlemen editing the manuscript.) At times *Watt* seems to suggest the presence of an unaccounted for and unnamed 'editor', or even – if we take Kenner's description of the footnote as a 'ventriloqual gadget' for all it's worth – a 'novelist' who uses Sam like a puppet (Kenner, *Samuel Beckett*, 40). For how can we ascribe to Sam passages like the following?

Haemophilia is, like enlargement of the prostate, an exclusively male disorder. But not in this work (*W*, 100).

Simply, *A Tale of a Tub* – like the other novels in the eighteenth-century English tradition that Smith calls on to account for Beckett's narrative technique – never attempts to discomfort and disorient the reader in the ways that *Watt*'s narration can and does.

Beckett's readers have dealt with *Watt*'s problematic narration in a number of ways. At times, they have sidestepped this issue by describing the footnotes, addenda, and hiatuses as 'Beckett's' notes, or as elements that reveal 'Beckett's' hand.[3] Others have acknowledged *Watt*'s troubling narration but have not argued for a specific narrator or strategy behind Beckett's technique. For Coetzee, Beckett's troubling of the novel results in a complex 'antigrammar' that is of 'tentative and of questionable consistency' at this time.

> *Watt* is narrated by one Sam, who takes down Watt's words in his little notebook and pieces his story together in a fragmentary book. Because Sam belongs both inside the fiction – literally walking the grounds of an asylum with Watt – and, as its nominal author, outside it, there is generally only one box within the box that is *Watt*. A third and outermost box is, however, occasionally slipped over *Watt* for a moment … proclaiming the fictiveness of the fiction (Coetzee, 'The Comedy', 37).

Rather more ambitiously (and risking a version of what Ackerley describes as a 'perhaps fallacious argument from design') Ann Beer suggests that *Watt* may be narrated by a 'plural self' that animates Sam and the novel's other creatures.[4] But caution is needed. For several reasons – not least of which is Ackerley's argument that the 'inconsistencies' of Beckett's novel are the result of a complex, unplanned, and prolonged act of composition – we would do well to recall Coetzee's warning about *Murphy*:

> Sometimes … what poses as a problem for the reader of choosing rationally among [narrative] authorities may be a false problem, a problem designed to yield no solution, or only arbitrary solutions (Coetzee, 'The Comedy', 31).

We have seen that this 'false problem' in *Murphy* should be understood with relation to Beckett's emulation of texts like *Les Caves du Vatican*, and in the following I suggest that such modern techniques remained important to the writer of *Watt*. Crucially, however, they were imposed on the novel at a late stage of its composition, and do not form a fully developed narrative strategy. These techniques were also not made to 'fit' with another important change to the novel's narration initiated at the time of the early typescript: the attempt to reestablish a nominal 'author' narrator. And because this narrator's (Sam's) account of the text's narration was only added in the late drafts (in the second half of Notebook 4), it does not 'match' with significant portions of previously existing text that Beckett re-drafted in this same notebook. As a result, devices like the footnotes, addenda, lacunae, and 'Hiatus in MS', which Beckett imposed on the novel in its late stages, imply a 'third frame' – but no specific narrative personality – that seems to preside over Sam's (already dubious) account of the text's narration. Further, in line with his new interest in the 'obscure', it seems that Beckett was aware of the effects of (further) destabilising *Watt*'s narration by means of these devices, and sought to strengthen the discomforting power of the multiple 'voices' in *Watt* in the late drafts.

By the stage of the early typescript (which Ackerley indicates pre-dates the second half of Notebook 4), Beckett had effectively dispensed with his problematic narrator 'we', transferred to Watt crucial aspects of 'we's' thought processes (as developed in Notebook 3), and set up Knott's house as a mystery to confound Watt. At some stage when he was reviewing the material he had typed up, Beckett sought to impose his new character over passages previously centring on his old narrator-protagonist 'we'. In the early typescript we thus find Beckett crossing out 'we' and putting in 'Watt' and 'he' (WTS, 227–29) – a move that resulted in some 'narrative confusion' that was only later resolved in a rewrite of this material in Notebook 5 (*OLSK*, 250; see NB5, 11). In the same typescript, though, Beckett began pondering his need for a new narrator, and we find 'we' crossed out and a cipher narrator ('N') inserted (WTS, 311–13). It is only in Ackerley's 'late draft' (the portions written after the early typescript, beginning on page 93 of Notebook 4), however, that Beckett reinstates a specific narrator. In the first draft of the asylum scenes of Watt's section III (NB4, 97), Beckett ponders who this first-person singular narrator might be, first using 'me' but then crossing it out and writing in 'Sam'. For some time after Beckett began to use this mirroring technique, however, Sam remains somewhat undeveloped as a character. For example, the passage where Sam reveals himself as the story's narrator for the first time (*W*, 76) does not appear in the late drafts (NB5 25–7).[5] As Ackerley points out, Sam's absence at this point indicates that it was very late in the ur-*Watt* when Beckett decided to deploy Sam as the narrator of passages that Beckett had initially penned for 'we'. The late drafts are thus

indicative of the surprisingly late decision by Beckett to render retrospectively, and only gradually, the narrative of part II as (perhaps) having been presented through the mediation of Sam (*OLSK*, 97).

Even as he gradually imposed Sam on the text, Beckett left lacunae in the new material he was writing. We can be relatively certain that Beckett intended to fill in several of these gaps. For example, the lacuna that appears on *Watt*'s page 167 as 'the faculties so-called of ????' appears this way in the galleys (after the final typescript). But in the late draft (NB4, 138), a reference to John 'LOCKE' is indicated by Beckett, almost certainly a note to himself to fill in the space later. At other times, we cannot be so sure about Beckett's intentions, and it is possible that by Notebook 4 Beckett had begun to leave gaps that he did not intend to fill. For instance, Beckett left no note to himself regarding the 'deficient in ?' lacuna that appears on *Watt*'s page 30, and according to Ackerley, Beckett's mark here ('?') suggests that the gap was intended from the beginning (*OLSK*, 53). But even in Notebook 6, it seems likely that Beckett still intended to fill in similar spaces. The '?' that appears after 'Mr Case read:' (*W*, 227), for example, is indicated with the note '(Quotation)' (NB6, 53).

Later in Notebook 6, though, Beckett complicates the text's narration by imposing blank spaces on the text that he did not intend to fill and that cannot have been left by Sam. The 'Hiatus in MS' on *Watt*'s page 238 appears in Notebook 6, page 100, and on page 105 Beckett inserts the 'locus illegibilitis' that appears in *Watt* as 'MS. illegible' (*W*, 240). As I have already mentioned, by the stage of the galleys Beckett insists that his editors 'Respecter la disposition du manuscrit' by maintaining 'un point d' interrogation au milieu d'un espace' in various places – some of which had *not* featured lacunae in earlier drafts (SB qtd. in *OLSK*, 51).[6]

Is Beckett simply toying with various narrative approaches at this late stage, sticking Swiftian devices into an already profoundly ludic novel? We can be relatively sure of how he conceptualises the novel's narration only at certain points in the ur-*Watt* (for example, when he begins to elide 'we' and insert 'Sam'), and I do not wish to argue that Beckett had a clear narrative design in mind at the time of the late drafts. But it is impossible that Beckett was unaware that the material he developed after the early typescript troubles Sam's account of the text's narration. After all, Beckett had recently paid considerable attention to establishing this point of view in the first place. In the early typescript, Beckett spent a substantial amount of effort changing over the narrator from 'we', to 'I' and 'me', and inserting a significant body of new material to justify the new first-person singular narrative perspective. After he introduced Sam in Notebook 4, he also tried to develop his new narrator by detailing how Sam came to hear Watt's story. In the same notebook, however, Beckett rearranged material that he wrote earlier (such as the Hackett episode in Notebook 2) in ways that undermine the version of events he had so recently related through Sam. In the final text, this material is even more perplexing than the lacunae or the 'Hiatus in MS' Beckett went on to insert in the novel in Notebook 6.

Watt's opening section was put together near the end of Notebook 4 (after the early typescript) and the beginning of Notebook 5 from earlier fragments. As several commentators have noted, this section presents the most obvious and problematic examples of events that can only with great difficulty be ascribed to Watt and his 'mouthpiece'.[7] Regarding such mysteries, Sam supplies this explanation in Part II:

And so always, when the impossibility of my knowing, of Watt's having known, what I know, what Watt knew, seems absolute, and insurmountable, and undeniable, and uncoercible, it could be shown that I know, because Watt told me, and that Watt knew, because someone told him, or because he found out for himself. For I know nothing, in this connection, but what Watt told me. And Watt knew nothing, on this subject, but what he was told, or found out for himself, in one way or in another (*W*, 126).

We may now see that the incommensurability of the Hackett material with Sam's account can partly be explained by the fact that it was only late in the novel's composition that Beckett decided to deploy Sam as the narrator of passages he had initially penned for an omniscient narrator in Notebooks 1 and 2: 'we'. Likewise, the 'explanation' was not originally given by Sam, but by an unnamed speaker at a time when Beckett was still casting around for a new narrative personality. This speaker appears late in Notebook 3 and is described only as 'we'. Not surprisingly, this late 'we' retains his earlier manifestation's annoyingly self-reflexive and omniscient manner – hence the playful gesture at suspending the reader's disbelief (NB3, 157).[8] At the time that Beckett was trying to get rid of the first 'we' in the early typescript, he crossed out this late 'we' and inserted 'I' and 'me', then 'N', Sam's cipher precursor. In this way, Beckett's late 'reporter' narrator inherits his earlier narrators' ironic and playful modes.

But there are other unusual aspects of *Watt*'s opening section that cannot be explained by Beckett's deciding to narrate existing material with his new speaker. And these elements suggest that a deliberate effort to complicate the novel's narration informed Beckett's decisions in the late drafts. Very late in the novel's composition, Beckett went out of his way to deploy techniques that are already familiar to us from Gide – techniques that reveal a 'novelist' showing his hands in playful ignorance at his own tale.

One noticed [Evans's] cap, perhaps because of the snow-white forehead and damp black curly hair on which it sat. The eye came always in the end to the scowling mouth and from there on up to the rest. His moustache, handsome in itself, *was for obscure reasons unimportant*. But one thought of him as the man who, among other things, never left off his cap, a plain blue cloth cap, with a peak and knob (*W*, 24; my emphasis).

Evans does not appear in the late drafts (NB4, 221) and seems to have been part of Beckett's attempt – clearly in evidence by Notebook 6 – to appropriate self-reflexive techniques from writers like Swift and, here, Gide. Who is this 'one' who knows Evans well enough to think of him as 'the man, who, among other things, never left off his cap'? Not Sam, surely.

The part of *Watt* that concerns Mr Hackett also gives clues that Beckett sought to problematise Sam's version of the text's narration by indicating an extra-diegetic narrator 'over' Sam – a narrator who is a playful 'novelist'. Consider that in some odd way, the narration of the Mr Hackett section not only follows Hackett as its centre of interest, but is restricted to his point of view – as if an 'ignorant' narrator were listening in on Hackett's conversation with the Nixons. This becomes apparent when, like Mr Hackett, the narrator only begins to call Goff and Tetty by these names when they themselves mention them (previously they are the 'gentleman' and the 'lady'). The same thing occurs again after Mr Hackett learns the surnames of his fellow characters, at which stage the narrator begins to refer to Goff and Tetty as Mr and Mrs Nixon. (Hackett initially thinks of them as Mr and Mrs Nesbit, but the narrator does not follow him in this error (*W*, 15).) As a result, the reader may hear an echo in the text – that of the narrator eavesdropping and playfully following his character's lead. Beckett here puts into practice Gide's dictum in the *Journal des Faux-Monnayeurs* (which he had read in the early thirties) that

The poor novelist constructs his characters; he controls them and makes them speak. The true novelist listens to them and watches them function; he eavesdrops on them even before he knows them. It is only according to what he hears them say that he begins to understand who they are (LC, 44; my emphasis).

The addenda are the most extended examples of Beckett's attempts late in the novel's composition to impose elements on the text that imply this 'author' in *Watt* who cannot be Sam. For instance, we cannot in good faith accept that Sam is the author of a section that contains such entries as 'change all the names' or 'no symbols where none intended' (*W*, 254; 255). On one hand, these are clearly the notes of a writer of fiction (which Sam claims he is not), recalling Beckett's earlier imitation of the Gidean 'novelist's' appearance in his text in chapters like 'UND' or *Murphy*'s

Chapter Six. On the other, we cannot consider this section to be simply attributable to 'Beckett' – as if, abandoning his narrator, the Beckett of the title page somehow emerges to reveal a selection of fossils from the ur-*Watt*. (The section is also signposted as the work of the pedantic guiding consciousness that has overseen the rest of the novel. And to make things even more ambiguous, the very title 'ADDENDA' is footnoted in the same faux-scholarly style as the text ostensibly narrated by Sam.)[9]

Here the ur-*Watt* is of little help. As I have already pointed out, several of the addenda items appear on the inside back cover of Notebook 5 (182), but these notes are only arranged *as* the addenda to the novel in the final typescript. The entire section is clearly a gesture toward the limitations of the author, but which author? And if we could answer this question we would need to ask several others: What is the relation of the addenda's author to the author of the text proper? Who *is* the author of the text proper? To exacerbate this situation, Beckett sees to it that there is at least one undeniable connection between the two apparatuses that already bear an uneasy relation to the text proper – the addenda and *Watt*'s footnotes. Addenda items 35 and 36 'answer' the question posed by *Watt*'s 'author' in the footnote on page 32:

What, it may be inquired, was the music of this threne? What at least, it may be demanded, did the soprano sing? (*W*, 32).

As if to imply that *Watt* is a puzzle that even the 'author' of the footnotes has not managed to solve, the music for the missing soprano's part is presented in the addenda (but by whom?).

But if the addenda provide no answers to our questions, the way that these clues play *with* questions and answers also fleetingly reveals a familiar tension at work in *Watt*, though in a way that betokens a new approach to the novel. The addenda's author's 'lack of control' (his potential insanity and assured 'fatigue and disgust') here becomes a part of a textual game we do know – a game that the 'novelist' plays with his reader: 'We stole that one. Guess where' (*DFMW*, 191). But unlike *Dream*'s allusive fragments, or *Whoroscope*'s parody of Eliot's notes to *The Waste Land*, *Watt*'s closing materials do not encourage the reader to search outside of the work itself for keys. These fragments are the first indicators in Beckett's novels that his fiction will play a different game after the war from the one staged by the novelist-professor. The addenda, like the narratives that make up *Molloy*, *Malone Dies* and *The Unnamable*, suggest that the voices that narrate Watt's story, and even at times seem to create its world, do not understand the order of this world. And in creating various cross-connections within and between such texts, Beckett does not suggest a knowing author behind the fiction, or a cosmic ordering principle (for example, Vico's cycles, or Dante's cosmology), as much as an inscrutable and hidden order order*ing* the text. *Watt* hints that its text is the product of a consciousness that has tried, and failed, to assemble a narrative under pressures it cannot fully comprehend.

Beckett made no attempt to finally reconcile the various narrative approaches he had deployed in different stages of *Watt*'s development. As a result, *Watt*'s potentially confusing narration is partly the result of a late effort to complicate the account of a new type of narrator in Beckett's fiction – a figure who is not a 'novelist', but a reporter. And this is why the parts of the text that trouble Sam's account of *Watt*'s narration appear in footnotes, the addenda, breaks in the text, and *Watt*'s opening section: these aspects of the text were added later, and broadly constitute Beckett's urge to incorporate existing material while 'layering' the novel with various ventriloqual devices. In doing so, Beckett performed an additional operation: cultivating the kinds of perplexing connections within the novel that we have seen between addenda items 35–6 and the footnote on page 32. These connections seem to hint at a hidden order in *Watt*'s world.

The perceptive reader who senses these connections in the finished novel might be excused for feeling as Ann Beer does: that the text often implies that it is the product of a 'plural self' or a fragmented consciousness. And we now know that there is a theoretical approach to the novel behind this type of order. By the time of *Watt*, Beckett had long been a devotee of Gide's dictum that the modern author should indulge a 'strange impulse to group, concentrate, centralise: to create between the varied elements of a novel as many cross-connections as possible' without resolving them or governing them by means of a master plan or meaning (*D*, 99).

Just as Sam is a mirror-image of his own author, Sam beholds himself as a mirror-image of Watt, his fellow-witness. Watt is in some obscure way linked to Mr Hackett, even as Arsene, Knott, and Sam are linked to Watt by means of the strange serialising tendency they all manifest.[10] Hackett joins 'hack' (a bad writer) with 'Beckett', even as Watt and Hackett are joined by their common problem of whether to 'go on'. To erase any doubt about this last relationship (Hackett has never seen Watt before but, atypically for Hackett, is intrigued by him), Mr Nixon points out that when he thinks of one, he thinks of the other.

The curious thing is, my dear fellow, I tell you quite frankly, that when I see him, or think of him, I think of you, and that when I see you, or think of you, I think of him. I have no idea why this is so (*W*, 17).

Like Fleurissoire or Neary, Nixon is a Gidean creature who begins to sense the strange order of the world in which he exists, but cannot understand the nature of that order.

If Beckett's 'novelist' is present in *Watt*, he has retreated into the background to the point that he is often invisible. Yet this does not indicate that by the forties Beckett was losing interest in complicating the novel with speakers who trespass its various narrative 'estates', or characters who resist their authors. Transformed, the 'novelist' reappears in the postwar fiction at the very centre of *Three Novels*. And here Beckett's preoccupations with '[f]iction [as] the only subject of fiction', and the view that 'fictions are closed systems, prisons' become the fundamental subject of his work (Coetzee, 'The Comedy', 38). *Watt*'s compositional process is important from this perspective because it reveals a gesture – Beckett's attempt to complicate one mode of narration with additional 'frames' – that we will see rehearsed on a much larger scale and with greater deliberation and effect when, in *The Unnamable*, Beckett 'frames' all of his previous *novels* as the fictions of a plural voice. (Remember that the Unnamable considers himself *Watt*'s 'ventriloquist', too (*T*, 348).) Beckett's attempt to deploy mise en abyme across a range of fictions will be the subject of this book's final chapter, but first we must turn to his exploration of a strange new voice in the Novellas – a voice drawn from *Watt* and born of Beckett's practice of writing in the dark.

'NOTHING CHANGED': STYLE AND MONOLOGUE IN *WATT, LA NAUSÉE*, AND 'SUITE'

The period from February 1946 (when he began his next fiction, later titled 'Suite et Fin') and May 1947 (when he started *Molloy*) saw Beckett feeling for new approaches to narration to express what he then described as 'the terms in which our condition is to be thought again' and 'a vision ... of humanity in ruins'.[11] But rather than attempting to complicate narrative structure (through the use of footnotes or multiple narratorial voices, for example), Beckett focuses on developing a new type of voice that he deploys and further develops in *Three Novels*. This voice marks an important shift in Beckett's approach to the task of narration. Rather than ironically commenting upon the suffering of a protagonist in the past tense, this voice speaks from and of its *own* ongoing decrepitude and ignorance. But, as Beckett's readers have often noted, there is a troubling gap in our understanding of how exactly Beckett began to channel the first-person speakers who make the postwar fiction so distinct, a situation not made any simpler because the manuscript evidence for 'Suite' seems to support the notion of a radical, spontaneous change. In stark contrast to the struggle that marked the composition of his last fiction, Beckett begins the first page of the 'Suite' manuscript with his protagonist and narrator fully formed. Consider, for instance, the relatively superficial amount of revision Beckett conducted on the story's opening five sentences and their proximity to the 1967 Grove version, several revisions and decades later:[12]

February 17th 1946
They dressed me and gave me money. I knew what the money was for, it was to ~~pay costs~~ pay my way. When that was finished, they said, I could ~~earn~~ <procure> some more, if I wished to continue. It was the same for my boots, when they were worn out I could have them repaired, or procure another pair, or continue my way barefoot, if I wished to continue, so they said. The same ~~was true for my~~ remarks applied to my coat and trousers, I ~~did~~ did not need to be told that, ~~though~~ though I could pursue my way very well if necessary in my shirt sleeves, especially in warm weather, if I chose to do so.[13]

They clothed me and gave me money. I knew what the money was for, it was to get me started. When it was gone I would have to get more, if I wanted to go on. The same for the shoes, when they were worn out I would have to get them mended, or get myself another pair, or go barefoot, if I wanted to go on. The same for the coat and trousers, needless to say, with this difference, that I could go on in my shirt sleeves, if I wanted.[14]

The apparent lack of an intermediary stage between *Watt* and 'Suite' has encouraged Beckett's commentators to follow red herrings. For instance, it is often noted that 'Suite' is Beckett's first French fiction (he began composing in French on page 28 of the manuscript) and from Kenner onwards Beckett's readers have referred to the story's 'composition in French' to answer questions about the provenance of Beckett's new style and use of first-person narration after the war.[15] Beckett's use of a foreign language, so the argument goes, compelled him to shed the clever narrators of his early fictions as well as the convoluted logic games of *Watt*; French provided a space where Beckett was free to construct himself anew and narrate his stories in the first person. But we should be wary of such accounts. While it is true that Beckett stated that he wrote in French 'pour avoir moins de style', what he meant by this is not altogether clear. It is clear that (as the English half of 'Suite' reveals) Beckett's use of the first person was fully established before the shift into French. Just as important, the manuscript and typescript record of the Novellas demonstrate that the relative brevity of the sentences and the simplicity of their syntax and vocabulary were in evidence in the English half.

In fact, some stylistic elements that mark the Novellas' style for English readers were actually made at the much later stage of the English typescript. To take one example, it was in the English typescript – not the French half of the manuscript or even the French *Temps* text (July 1946) – that Beckett began to cut many of the commas that riddle early versions of the story and are a lingering vestige of his prolific use of this punctuation mark in *Watt*. Consider a passage from the *Temps* text compared with Beckett's revision of the English typescript version, where he marked his deletions in the margin with a slash:

Mon aspect prêtait toujours à rire, de ce rire robuste et sans méchanceté qui est si bon pour la santé. A force de garder le côté rouge du ciel autant que possible à ma droite j'arrivai enfin au fleuve. Ici tout semblait, à première vue, plus or moins comme je l'avais laissé. Mais à y regarder de plus près j'aurais découvert bien des changements, sans doute.[16]

/My appearance <still> made people laugh,/ with
/that hearty,/ jovial laugh so good for the health. By keep-
/ing the red part of the sky as much is possible my right,/
/I came at last to the river. Here all seemed,/
/at first sight,/ more or less as I had left it. But if I had looked
/more closely,/ I would doubtless have discovered many changes.[17]

This deletion of commas is by far the most common revision Beckett conducted on 'Suite's' English typescript – a relatively minute modification, but one that has an important impact on the way the text reads. Here, the period or the unpunctuated sentence predominates, slowing the narration to an even, lulling rhythm, as if the speaker pauses to breathe before each sentence. This syntax evokes the speaker's state in a 'stillness of eddies' (*N*, 28). With regard to punctuation, at least, the grammatical 'simplicity' of the Novellas cannot be said to result from Beckett's working back from French. Rather, at each stage of the writing process Beckett *continued* to craft his style in order to more closely approach his original idea of how his derelict should sound. As the English half of the 'Suite' manuscript has it, this is a man who must speak slowly and 'be very careful if [he] want[s] to be understood' (MS 91–1, 10).

To repeat the question, then: If Beckett had worked his way into a new way of thinking about narration by the late forties – a shift that he himself acknowledged was of major importance to his thinking about fiction – why is there no record of the struggle? One partial answer is that the apparent ease with which Beckett changed his approach to narration in the 'Suite' manuscript is misleading. For the shift into what Beckett called 'monologue' took place years before 1946 and was indeed born of trial and error. Just as important, at the time of these experiments Beckett was emulating and borrowing from at least one major exemplar.

'Suite's' narrator is not the first of Beckett's speakers to recall an earlier life from a present position of uncertainty, anxiety, and dereliction. Such an approach first appears in Arsene's short statement, a passage indicating that this character is a 'border-creature' who helps make sense of the apparent gulf between Beckett's prewar novelist narrators and his derelict speakers in the Novellas and *Three Novels* (*DFMW*, 123). Arsene combines in himself traits of these different types of narrators. His speech carries striking echoes of the ironic, know-it-all novelist narrators of *Dream* and *Murphy* ('I speak well, do I not, for a man in my situation?', he coyly acknowledges (*W*, 57)); and like the young critic whose persona Beckett's early speakers often borrow, Arsene indulges himself in a learned avowal of learning's limits ('quite useless wisdom so dearly won' (*W*, 61)). As *Dream*'s 'Mr Beckett' with his Belacqua, Arsene is another 'intellectual sort of chap' who describes and critiques the wanderings of a university man (a Mr Watt) from a sardonic remove (*W*, 48). But like the narrators of the Novellas and *Three Novels*, Arsene also suffers under a cloud of profound uncertainty, anxiety, and even terror that is foreign to Beckett's narrators prior to *Watt*. This aspect of Arsene's monologue – the tale of an educated man struggling with a sense of uncertain menace triggered by an ineffable 'change' – adds a new dimension to Beckett's narrative repertory. It also has roots in a novel he read and admired several years earlier: Sartre's *La Nausée*.[18]

At the centre of Arsene's short statement lies his account of a discomforting 'change', an experience of estrangement from the world of objects and from himself. The change itself ultimately remains 'ineffable' though it obliterates Arsene's sense of purpose and *nostos* at Mr Knott's and returns him to a fallen state in which the world is no longer an 'accommodating' place. 'This I am happy to inform you', Arsene claims, 'is the reversed metamorphosis. The Laurel into Daphne. The old thing where it always was, back again' (*W*, 42-3). What can be said of the change is that it is an experience of pervasive nothingness that generates feelings of disorientation, sickness, and alienation: it is 'the presence of *what did not exist*, that presence without, that presence within, that presence between' (*W*, 43; my emphasis).

A similar experience of the disorienting strangeness of things and the self – also described as 'the change' (un changement) – is the central theme of Sartre's novel. So it is fitting that Roquentin begins his diary in an attempt to find some answers to Arsene's question – 'The change. In what did it consist?' – just as the drama of Sartre's story is the unfolding of Arsene's loaded statement that 'It is hard to say' (*W*, 41). Both men first try to understand the nature of the change but can only describe it as a 'sensuous' perception that they are facing the unknown (*W*, 42).

The best thing would be to write down everything.... To keep a diary in order to understand.... I must fix the exact extent and nature of this change.... If I only knew what I was frightened of, I should already have made considerable progress.[19]

Like Roquentin, Arsene initially suspects that the change is merely a sickness, or perhaps a product of creeping senility or madness. But once the 'slip' has occurred it begins to infect all aspects of experience. In the following passage, note especially how the change is described by Beckett's and Sartre's narrators; for both heroes it is gradually and subtly revealed through the accumulation of tiny adjustments that then give way to a monumental, unspeakable disclosure.

For the day comes when he says, Am I not a little out of sorts, today? ... and he asks himself if he is not perhaps a little seedy. The fool! ... Something slipped ... some tiny little thing [,] a little slip of one or two lines maybe, and then stop, altogether, not one missing, and that is all ... millions of little things moving all together out of their old place ... and furtively, as though it were forbidden. And I have little doubt that I was the only person living to discover them.... I perceived it with a perception so sensuous that in comparison the impressions of a man buried alive in Lisbon ... seem a frigid and artificial construction of the understanding (*W*, 41–2).

Something has happened to me.... It came as an illness does, not like an ordinary certainty, not like anything obvious. *It installed itself cunningly, little by little; I felt a little strange, a little awkward, and that was all.* Once it was established, it did not move any more, it lay low.... And now it has started blossoming.... The thing is that I very rarely think; consequently *a host of little metamorphoses accumulate in me without my noticing it, and then, one fine day, a positive revolution takes place* (*N*, 13–14; my emphasis).

Arsene and Roquentin arrive at similar conjectures about the nature of this change (for both it is reality denuded of its 'purpose') and the servant's experience parallels the scholar's in the way that neither can decide if the change has taken place inside or outside of himself: 'To conclude that the incident was internal', Arsene warns, 'would, I think, be rash' (*W*, 41); 'So a change *has* taken place', Roquentin avers, 'But where? It's an abstract change which settles on nothing. Is it I who has changed?

If it isn't I then it's this room.... ' (*N*, 14). Beckett's novel also rehearses Sartre's ideas about the disorienting impact 'the change' has on language. Using the Sartrean metaphor of a 'dark', 'reverse side' of normal experience (think of Roquentin's stroll down the Boulevard Noir), the ur-*Watt*'s original narrator 'we' registers a traumatic experience which renders words abstract and near meaningless. 'We's' plunge into another dark passage – Quin's hallway – anticipates this aspect of 'the change' for Watt ('the same things happen to us all', Arsene hints (*W*, 44)), and eventually Knott's entire home represents the 'reverse side' of reality. In this Sartrean realm, objects become separated from their identity and purpose as objects drift from their signifiers. A new anxiety arises for Watt and Roquentin as commonplace things demand an explanation that can never be granted: 'To explain had always been *to exorcise*, for Watt' but 'it was in vain that Watt said, Pot, pot.... For it was not a pot, the more he looked, the more he reflected' (*W*, 75; 78; my emphasis).

This thing I'm sitting on, leaning my hand on, is called a seat.... I murmur: 'It's a seat', *rather like an exorcism*. But the word remains on my lips, it refuses to settle on the thing.... Things have broken free from their names. They are there, grotesque, stubborn, gigantic, and it seems ridiculous to call them seats or say anything at all about them: I am in the midst of Things, which cannot be given names (*N*, 180; my emphasis).

The strangeness of things in this surreal world is complemented by the hero's sense of estrangement from the human body, whose different components now seem to take on unsettlingly independent and alien identities. Consider Roquentin's description of his encounter with the Autodidact:

This morning, at the library, when the Autodidact came to say good-morning to me, it took me ten seconds to recognise him. I saw an unknown face which was barely a face. And then there was his hand, like a fat maggot in my hand. I let go of it straightaway and the arm fell back limply (*N*, 14).

Beckett seems to have recalled this passage as he was struggling to develop his own speaker's experience of a disorienting obscurity in the ur-*Watt*. On page 209 of the typescript, 'we' encounters Arsene in Quin's darkened hallway. Like Roquentin, Beckett's protagonist struggles to make out his companion's familiar, but now obscured head, even as he encounters an alien hand. But in Beckett's version, the Sartrean effect has been strengthened: this is the speaker's *own* hand that suddenly looms up before him, grey and flaccid at the end of a limp arm. Holding the hand at a distance, 'we' then repeats Roquentin's gesture, gingerly grasping this inhuman flesh (in Beckett's text the hand is not described as a maggot but as a drooping fish) before allowing it to descend gently toward his side (WTS, 209).

If Sartre provided Beckett with an important model for the kind of monologue he would make his own in the Novellas, this influence had become untraceable by the mid-forties. As Pilling points out, though the narrators of these short pieces can hope to reach the end of their tales (to quote 'The Calmative's' speaker) 'with nothing changed', this is only because Arsene's traumatic revelation of the change has been absorbed in a distant past that has altered the speaker's worlds forever (*BBG*, 225). There is no longer a 'ladder' to fall *from* in these stories into the realm of the strange dark that now governs them. The tales themselves become like the house of Knott where uncertainty is the only constant and 'nothing changed … because all was a coming and a going' (*W*, 130) – 'but with the difference', to borrow from Pilling, 'that the "nothing changed" has now been seen from within' (*BBG*, 225).

If the disorienting quality of the Novellas can be partially attributed to his interest in Sartre and his experiments with monologue in the ur-*Watt*, this aspect of Beckett's postwar fiction also owes debts to the changes in his compositional practice that we have seen at work in the *Watt* drafts of the early forties. In several instances, the Beckett of 'Suite' draws on his newfound practice of allowing uncertainties and inconsistencies to push the story closer to the 'obscure'.

Initially, Beckett worked steadily and slowly, completing a page or so per day. But as he went on, his handwriting became looser and more slanted, suggesting that occasionally he was able to write much faster, and there were sessions when he apparently completed four or more pages. Likely connected to this increase in speed, as early as page 11 (the close of a passage begun 22 February when his protagonist reaches the home of the Turkish woman), Beckett had sketched out the personality of his speaker and the motifs that would govern this figure's experience: sojourn, expulsion, wandering, and vision. The way in which these familiar elements were to be structured in the new piece (so far an episodic fiction), though, does not seem to have been completely clear.

On the recto of page 10 of the 'Suite' manuscript, for example, we find the origins of one of 'Suite's' more perplexing episodes: the sudden and unexplained disorientation of the speaker upon arriving at the Turkish woman's house and his 'vision' of his emergence from another house. Under a slash drawn to indicate a new beginning two days after the previous date of composition (20 February), Beckett was stuck. Doodles on the verso of page 9 indicate that he was trying to get the narrative going by stimulating himself visually. But it seems that eventually he could 'go on' only by deploying one of the tricks he had used in the ur-*Watt*: jump-starting the narrative by fictionalising his own struggle to continue. As he did in Notebook 3, Beckett immerses his speaker in the 'dark' and then allows his visual imagination to double as his narrator's, thereby conjuring up a 'vague picture':

> Now I didn't know where it I was. I had a vague picture of a big red house 4 or 5 storeys high. I have good reason to believe that it was part of a terrace. It was evening dark when I arrived and I did not pay the attention to my surroundings that I would have, if I had thought they were going to close around me (MS 91–1, 10v–11r).

If the narrator acknowledges that he has arrived at the Turkish woman's house, how does he not know where he is? Does the 'now' refer to the storyteller's time or the protagonist's? Either way, Beckett apparently valued his speaker's sense of disorientation and the 'picture's' menacing quality. He seems to have puzzled over the non-sequitur nature of the passage, and, unsure what to do with it, eventually decided that he would reinsert it at the beginning of the story as the protagonist's first expulsion/ 'birth'. In an unusually enthusiastic note to himself he writes, '*Prepare as 1st departure' on the facing page, double-underlining and marking the note with a large star. But on reflection, the spatial and temporal ambiguities that this passage weaves into the story in its original position pleased Beckett. Instead of 'preparing' it by repositioning the event or explaining it, he hearkened to the voice of Pilate rather than to the high priests of revision. In the French text and final English version the vague picture appears in its original place.

In subsequent revisions Beckett seeks to heighten the vague quality of the 'picture' and modifies the passage to take on the more portentous status of a 'vision' (it is 'une vague image' in the *Temps* version) – a move that also creates a discrepancy when the speaker claims that he has never had visions except in his sleep, or as a child. In the Minuit text and then in the English typescript, he further obscures this passage so that the speaker never actually 'sees' anything at all: 'J'avais une vague image, même pas, je ne voyais rien' becomes 'I had a vague vision, not even that <a real vision>, I didn't see anything ... ' (TS of 'The End', 9). Is the protagonist asleep or arrested by a memory from childhood at the time of this vision (which is not a vision)? What might it mean for a speaker who is already dead to have a 'vision' within the dream that is his story? Like 'Suite's' narrator, who is condemned to resurrect himself in each of his tales, the questions worked into the story by this passage cannot be laid to rest. For the speaker himself remains under the shadow of profound uncertainty where Beckett found him in February of 1946.

Beckett's shift into French in the manuscript also reveals a related move that joins the act of writing with the narrator's struggle to continue. On 13 March and by now on page 25 (about halfway through his notebook) Beckett begins the final passage of the first part of his tale. As he did when neither writer nor narrator knew 'where [he] was' in the ur-*Watt*, he begins a new episode with the theme of 'continuing' uppermost in his speaker's mind: 'Once on the road', he pens hopefully, 'the way was all downhill' (MS 91–1, 25r). But Beckett also clearly wanted his narrative to take a new direction and on page 28 draws a line about a third of the way down the page and begins again in French. (The last English sentence is the description of the narrator's tutor's death: 'dead of an infarct' in the manuscript.) He then translates and revises the preceding paragraph – the episode in which the narrator covers the lower part of his face with a black cloth and goes begging. (In this initial French translation/revision, Beckett made cuts but also added detail; he omitted the narrator's age at the time when the *Ethics* were given to him – originally '13 or 14' – but inserted a description of the dark glasses.) Beckett's first sentence in French – a translation of an English sentence that begins 'Rising now for the moment ...' – was actually excised from the 1946 Temps version. But once again it is likely that we hear Beckett's own writerly concerns behind this portentous new beginning – as he transfers his own refusal to 'rest' to his (then immobile) character 'for the moment': 'Je ne me restait donc ...' (MS 91–1, 28r).

Similar revisions in this story set an important pattern for Beckett's compositional practice in the other Novellas and in *Three Novels* which naturally follows from his experiments in the ur-*Watt*: a willingness to 'accept' major parts of the manuscript virtually 'as soon as [it was] written down' and the attempt to 'vaguen' the writing by allowing incongruities and strengthening connections between events and episodes. (For example, Beckett went back to insert the 'phial' that first appears in 'The Calmative' in 'The End.') As one might suspect, the 'Suite' drafts also reveal early instances of a related compositional praxis for which Beckett was to become well known: paring the text back and eliding details in a further attempt to push the text closer to the 'obscure'. Here, these excisions especially concern those details that fill out the speaker's 'external' reality and experience. For example, the girl who appears immediately after the speaker's thoughts originally appears in the story to provide a link between the speaker and the world above.

Sometimes it was a girl who brought me the things I sent out for. I didn't have the energy to thank her. Besides it could have meant giving her money for sweets. I have no idea who she was. She used to fidget around the room for a time and then go away without saying anything (MS 91–1, 13r–14r).

But as she appears in the Temps, Grove, and Minuit texts, the girl has no apparent purpose for coming downstairs and no longer helps the speaker. This is how she is described in the English typescript:

Sometimes it was a little girl ~~that~~ <who> came. She had long red hair which <u>hung down</u> <hanging> into braids. I didn't know who she was. She lingered awhile in the room, then went away without a word (TS of 'The End', 11).

The narrator's isolation is preserved, his ignorance concerning his world emphasized, and Beckett conjures an appropriate atmosphere around a figure who, in a phrase that appears in the Minuit and Grove editions, 'Fortunately,/ ... did not need affection' (*N*, 15). The major excision Beckett made in the 'Suite' manuscript was likely conducted for similar reasons. This cut took out the majority of the manuscript's page 19, in which the narrator examines his face in a mirror (he sees a patchy beard and a small, puckered mouth that reminds the speaker of an anus) (MS 91–1, 19r). Beckett drew on this description later when he described his speaker's failures to solicit alms on the country roads, but it seems the introspection and self-appreciation that such mirror-gazing suggests was at odds with the indifference and general incomprehension Beckett desired for his hero. The speaker's ugliness is finally only of interest to him because it hinders his begging.

'A NEW BEGINNING, BUT WITH NO LIFE IN IT': *MERCIER AND CAMIER*

The Novellas' use of first-person narration fed directly into the techniques at work in *Molloy*. But Beckett's next novel, *Mercier and Camier*, has often been considered a regressive fiction, a throwback to a mode of writing not unlike *Murphy*'s 'realism'. And, like that book, *Mercier* is not perceived to have had much of an impact on Beckett's subsequent writing. Yet this judgment has often been passed with little attention paid to either novel's narrative technique. At the level of its story proper, *Mercier* is indeed a limited work that adds little that is technically interesting to Beckett's oeuvre. But at the level of narration, it presents an important extension of Beckett's approach to fiction that he further developed in his postwar novels, especially *Malone Dies* and *The Unnamable*.

By the end of 'Suite et Fin', Beckett was clearly feeling toward a narrative position that originates from beyond 'the end' and the grave, and his attempts in this regard became more pronounced as he kept writing. The last story in the original three novellas, 'Le Calmant', tells us plainly that the speaker is deceased, so it is not surprising that Beckett also called it 'Death'. ('La Fin' tells of the narrator's state in 'Limbo' while in 'L'Expulsé', the speaker is in his moribund 'Prime'.) But in *Mercier and Camier*, Beckett joins this unsettling narrative position with a voice resurrected from what must have seemed his own distant past: the speech of the writer-intellectual who creates and hovers over a fictional world in the full knowledge of its artificiality. This *is* the 'professor' but – as Beckett allegedly put it when watching his television play *Quad* in the slow-motion speed he decided upon as its final pace – 'it's a hundred thousand years later'.[20] And the millennia have worn down Beckett's erudite trickster into a cantankerous melancholic. Flashes of the professor's old style reappear (contrast the simple garden of 'Suite' with the 'strangulating profusion' of *Mercier*'s park, which has 'something of the maze, irksome to perambulate, difficult of egress, for one not in its secrets') but they do so accompanied by his now virulent scorn at his tale's 'stink of artifice'.[21]

The novels most often cited as influences on Beckett's book are Diderot's Sternean *Jacques le fataliste* and Flaubert's farcical *Bouvard et Pecuchet*. But although these books may have contributed to Beckett's invention of an itinerant 'pseudocouple' at the level of 'the journey of Mercier and Camier', they do little to illuminate the most important dimension of this novel with relation to Beckett's fictional development: the origination of the bitter, vengeful 'I' who is this story's teller.

But beyond the eastering valleys the sky changes, it's the foul old sun yet again, punctual as a hangman. Take a firm hold on yourselves now, we are going to see the glories of the earth once more ... our brethren are there to dispel our hopes if any, our multitudinous brethren, and the rising gorge, and all the hoary old pangs. So there [Mercier and Camier] are in view again ... Whose turn now, Camier's, then turn worm and have a good look. (*MC*, 105).

What is perhaps most remarkable about this novel is its style: the way that its presiding animus ironically deploys images of death, decay and abjection against any narrative expectations of renewal, betterment, or resolution. Setting the scene for an atmospheric sunrise, the 'novelist' typically chooses the image of an execution rather than a new beginning; this day's 'punctuality', like the 'glories' of this world, our 'brethren', and our 'hopes' all induce nausea and long-familiar pain. It is unsurprising, then, that the narrator's own task conjoins the work of an entertainer (concerned with the pleasure of his audience) with that of the sadist (whose malice is directed against the reader and his puppets alike): 'turn worm and have a good look'. Could this speaker's undisguised hatred of his creatures and his revulsion for his tale make him any more unlike Sterne's and Diderot's affable yarn-spinners?

> While I've been telling you this story, which you'll assume I've made up ...
> What about the man in the livery who was scraping away on the bass viol?
> Reader, you shall have it, I promise. You have my word on it.[22]

Both *Mercier* and *Jacques* appear to make overtures to the reader. But in a manner very unlike that of the Sternean model, Beckett's novel is fundamentally monologic: *Mercier*'s personal pronouns are not meant to indicate a readerly audience as much as emphasise the profound isolation of voice splitting itself, painfully, into a writing and an observing self.

> It takes a little time to grasp more or less what happened. It's your sole excuse, the best in any case. Enough to tempt you joking apart to have another go, another go at getting up, dressing up (paramount), ingesting, excreting, undressing up, dossing down, and all the other things too tedious to enumerate, in the long run too tedious, requiring to be done and suffered .... But one black beast is harder to keep at bay, the waiting for the night that makes it all plain at last.... It's night, forenight, and there are no more sedatives (*MC*, 108–9).

The 'you' that monitors the writing self here does not consider that self's task as one of playful philosophical speculation, much less of pleasurable distraction. In writing, 'you' are 'hav[ing] another go' at confronting a situation which remains inscrutable: composing stories is 'your sole excuse' for talking on about the reality of having lived (trying to 'grasp more or less what happened'), and, now – in an even more baffling turn of events – living on after death. Passages like these, though largely overlooked by Beckett's readers, do much of the important work of *Mercier* by connecting the book's fascination with solitude and weariness with the act of storytelling in ways that anticipate important dimensions of *Three Novels* (especially *Malone Dies*). Significantly, they also suggest a context for the book's narrative technique distinct from that of the Sternean model. The emphasis on the 'tedium' of solitude here (which inflects the very rhythms of *Mercier*'s prose as it is both the dominant experience of the speaker's former life and the experience of re-inhabiting that existence to write a chronicle about life), like the book's interest in disgust, death, and decrepitude, as well as the relation of fictional composition to 'waiting for the [final] night' recall Céline – though if so, *Mercier* owes less to *Voyage au Bout de la Nuit* (1932) than to *Mort à Credit* (1936). The story of *Mercier and Camier* clearly has little or no connection with the one told in Céline's later novel (which Beckett read and enjoyed in the late 30s). But in those passages which link the writer behind *Mercier* with his tale, it is difficult not to hear echoes of Céline's aging narrator, inventing stories for himself out of a disgusted desire for 'the end'.

Here we are, alone again. It's all so slow, so heavy, so sad.... I'll be old soon. Then at last it will be over.... Whom will I write to? I've nobody left. No one to receive the friendly spirits of the dead.... I'll have to bear it all alone.... I know I could talk about my hatred. I'll do that later on if they don't come back. I'd rather tell stories. I'll tell stories that will make them come back, to kill me, from the ends of the world. Then it will be over and that will be all right with me.[23]

As if in answer to Céline, and with the irony typical of Beckett's narrative, *Mercier*'s narrator suggests that such storytelling goes on after the grave – a place where the hatred for life and the concomitant necessity to 'bear it' is decidedly not over.

Once we acknowledge the narrator of Beckett's novel, its formal qualities and narrative trajectory become clearer. For although this book has often been described as a type of picaresque or quest narrative, the questions it poses are not primarily those which we ask of such narratives. 'Will the protagonists successfully attain the object of their venture?' is less interesting and relevant with regard to *Mercier* than the question: 'Will this *story* and its *teller* disintegrate through exhaustion and aimlessness before getting to *its* destination?' This strange question leads to others: 'Just what are the stakes which have been set for this contest?' And: 'What bourne might be at the end of it all – what haven beyond life and death, attainable only through keeping the "fable" going?' In casting up these questions the book hints at a new twist to the drama of composition in Beckett's work which from now on will threaten to eclipse the 'story' proper. For the tales of the wandering heroes that reappear in the novels are now staged as a *by-product* of another, more serious story; they are a gambit for release from a dire game. This game is no longer (primarily) Beckett's version of the Joycean sport of exhaustive reference, the Gidean ploy of Naturalistic subversion, or the demolition of reason by its own methods. This new game is established at the level of the novel's narration; it is a task for the speaker guided by a set of obscure and inflexible rules that he never fully understands. These rules dictate that the act of composition takes on the double status of punishment and reprieve. And the 'novelist' must start playing from the exhaustion of his resources, fuelled only by his ignorance, his desperation and his resolve: 'The journey of Mercier and Camier is one I *can* tell, if I *will* . . . ' (*MC*, 7; my emphasis).

For this reason, in *Mercier and Camier* the breakdown of narrative illusion that we have come to expect from Beckett's fiction takes place in a manner fundamentally different from the way it does in the earlier novels, occurring largely through the speaker's lapses, omissions, and laconic expressions of overpowering weariness. The essential playfulness and vigour of the speakers of *Dream, Murphy* and (at times) *Watt* is replaced by a more completely felt 'fatigue and disgust' (*W*, 247). As the story 'Mercier and Camier' goes on, its *other* plot – the one involving the speaker's struggle to carry on telling the tale – progresses as well, with its narrator degenerating sporadically. By Chapter V he allows himself a two-page discourse on weariness ('There is no time left and yet how it drags' (*MC*, 76)) and by VII he is mixing up his creatures and muttering 'no matter', 'nothing is known for sure, henceforth' and admitting that 'The whole question of priority, so luminous hitherto, is from now on obscure' (*MC*, 103). Extinction – his own and his puppets' – is never far from his mind, and by this stage he often desires both: 'Here would be the place to make an end' (*MC*, 103). But he rallies to erupt at the opening of VIII with a final diatribe on what tedium it is to populate his little world:

It's wearing naturally, all-absorbing, no time left for putting a shine on the soul, but you can't have everything, the body in bits, the mind flayed alive and the archeus (in the stomach) as in the days of innocency, before the flop, yes, it's a fact, no time left for eternity (*MC*, 109).

The game of infusing the novel's characters with meaning ('putting a shine on the soul') like the game of realism ('all the other things too tedious to enumerate') is energetically rejected in VII as the highest form of tedium, and there is a structural reason for this. As the narrative nears its end, the narrator has to work ever harder in order to deflate the novel's formal gravitation toward a type of closure. Passages like these, where the 'novelist' seeks to deflate not only his own narrative but the life behind it and any grand narrative beyond it ('the days of innocency, before the flop'), work in tandem with the book's perfunctory summaries: both contribute to the illusion that the novel is a particular type of game for a self caught in another game which it does not understand. Despite *Mercier and Camier*'s limitations, then, it is here that the act of composition begins to take on the status it will assume in Beckett's postwar novels: as a façade for, even a waste product of another system, narrative, or world: 'The life of afterlife' (*MC*, 123). Because this world, it is implied, is largely unspeakable, we have the story of Mercier and Camier.

CHAPTER 5

Images of the Author

The account I have given of Beckett's novels so far will do little to defend him from the criticism, voiced early and often by his readers, that his fictions are solipsistic – an offense that many would combine with the related charge of 'nihilism'. And the reading of *Three Novels* I am going to offer will not recuperate Beckett as a writer of value for such readers, at least not within their own terms. This is because these books set out to subvert the novel's narratives of self-discovery (especially in the fictional diary and the *Bildungsroman*); equally, they work to disturb our faith in an aesthetic that might either posit the artwork as a consolation for suffering (as in the writings of Schopenhauer and Proust) or, alternatively, regard the novel as a socializing tutor of thought and feeling (a role valorised by the realist novel's defenders from George Eliot to Martha Nussbaum and Jenefer Robinson). As I will show, *Three Novels'* subversive relationship to such traditions cannot be understood without reference to their complex and interconnected form. It is to this form we now turn.

Few readers of *Three Novels* have failed to remark on one of the strangest and most perplexing aspects of these books: the suggestion, reinforced by the many echoes and repetitions that create interconnections between the stories, that Malone is the author of Beckett's fictions from *Murphy* onward, or that the Unnamable is the 'ventriloquist' behind Malone's tale and Beckett's previous stories.[1] Such connections, which are perhaps the most apparent and disturbing links between the *Three Novels* (and which draw Beckett's earlier fictions into their strangely multiple worlds), developed in part from Beckett's early fascination with complicating what he termed 'closure' and 'ending' in the novel. By positioning Molloy's or Malone's (multiple) ends – and Beckett's previous novels – as fictions 'within' other narrative worlds, the status and the potential meaning of these narratives are altered and complicated. As we shall see, such strategies are also at one with another of Beckett's related interests that intensified in the forties: his enduring fascination with the novel's potential to stage authorship as *self*-authorship, and to dramatize the reflexive relation between the voice and the story it tells.

The key source for Beckett's experiments with self-reflexivity in the novel has, to my knowledge, only been suspected once. Theodor Adorno, in his manuscript notes on *The Unnamable*, posited a connection between Beckett's disorienting strategies in that book and Gide's mirroring techniques in *Paludes*, and although Beckett himself may have pointed out this debt to Adorno during their discussions, his suspicion has never been followed up.[2] But it is now clear that Beckett had long been fascinated with Gide's use of multiple narrative 'planes' to reinforce the inconclusive power of his art and had experimented with similar techniques from *Dream* onward. Remember, for instance, how *Dream* rehearses Gide's preoccupation with the image of the author within the fiction, presenting a doubled reflection of Beckett in the text (Mr Beckett and Belacaqua) as Edouard and his 'novelist' reflect their author in Gide's *Les Faux-Monnayeurs*. Or consider the mirroring effects generated by 'Mr Beckett' and *Watt*'s Sam. These are narrators who, by appropriating the name on the title page, suggest an affinity with the reality inhabited by their author, and therefore a relationship to one another – a situation that generates links between discrete works in Beckett's oeuvre and begins to suggest an extra-textual author who is and is not Beckett.

As this last point suggests, by the mid-forties Beckett was exploring techniques that not only transgress the novel's various fictional 'estates' but that also suggest the books are part of a collective form made up of multiple, discrete fictions – a form that Beckett hinted at when he referred to his novels as 'the series'. The Novellas seem to have been a miniature laboratory in this respect. For while it may be partly true that the thematic and tonal continuity of these tales is a practical result of Beckett's process of working out of a new mode of narration, his cultivation of the cross-connections between the stories after they had been written clearly suggests an attempt to forge links between them that hint at an extra-textual narrator. (For example, Beckett's insertion of details that link one tale and the speaker of one story with another – such as the phial in 'The End' and 'The Calmative'.) For this narrator, each novella is a part of his 'myth' or one of his 'stories'. As the speaker of 'The Expelled' puts it, 'you will see how alike they are' (*N*, 46).

By the late forties, Beckett was deploying devices that strengthen the suggestion of an occult order uniting his separate novels. In *Mercier and Camier*, characters from Beckett's other fictions begin to appear, as if the creatures of these worlds may have an extra-textual life apart from the 'regions' they inhabit (*MC*, 7). Watt's reappearance in *Mercier and Camier* relates the 'novelist' of *Mercier* with the Beckett of the title page (and therefore the Beckett of the previous novels) but the illusion that these characters are *aware* of the fictional universes beyond their text is also cultivated in Watt's discussion about his previous life at Knott's, his knowledge of Mercier's and Camier's infancies, and the dim memories Beckett's new hobos retain of Murphy (whose looks they compare to Watt's). Watt's comments also suggest an understanding of his common lineage with Mercier, Camier, and Murphy when he claims that 'One shall be born ... one is born of us, who having nothing will wish for nothing' – a genealogy Mercier and Camier seem to understand when, in the bar, they pretend to be Watt's children (*MC*, 114, 115). Other details that connect *Mercier*'s world with the larger terrain of Beckett's previous fictions include Mercier's and Camier's feeling that they have seen the derelict from 'The End' and 'Old Madden' somewhere before (*MC*, 42; 117) (Arsene was the 'maddened prizeman' in the Watt manuscripts); the reappearance of *Watt*'s Mr Graves (as a 'pastoral patriarch') at the inn; the return of Mr Gall as the manager of a country pub (recalling Watt's piano tuners and Murphy's Lord Gall of Wormwood); Quin's reincarnation in the final bar scene.

These tricks are joined by others at the level of narration. For if the exhaustion and sardonic laughter of *Mercier and Camier*'s narrator invokes Céline, the posture adopted by this speaker reveals him, like *Murphy*'s 'novelist', as another Gidean puppeteer presiding over his recalcitrant creatures. And this technique is joined by a related move also borrowed from Beckett's early master: the characters' suspicion of their author's guiding hand.

Strange impression, said Mercier, strange impression sometimes that we are not alone.
I am not sure I understand, said Camier.
Now quick, now slow, that is Camier all over.
Like the presence of a third party, said Mercier. Enveloping us. I have felt it from the start. And I am anything but psychic.
Does it bother you? said Camier.
At first, no, said Mercier.
And now? said Camier.
It begins to bother me a little, said Mercier (*MC*, 100).

Like the 'novelist' of *Les Caves du Vatican*, the composer of *Mercier and Camier* leaves us in no doubt that this 'third party' 'enveloping' the landscape is he. He advertises his presence ('Now quick, now slow, that is

Camier all over') and hints at his control over the diegesis: 'The journey of Mercier and Camier is one I can tell, *if I will*, for I was with them all the time' (*MC*, 7; my emphasis).

Mercier's paranoia reappears in one of its more complex manifestations in Moran's narrative. As many have noticed, Youdi's godlike relation to Moran is deliberately elicited by Beckett.[3] But Youdi also seems to engineer Moran's downfall in ways that suggest he is a figure for the *writer* – as he is, insofar as we read *Molloy* as one of Malone's/the Unnamable's self-inscriptive fictions. This becomes evident in Youdi's comments on the outcome of the Molloy mission, which he ponders like an aesthetically pleasing object, invoking Keats's opening meditation on form in *Endymion*. But the medium here is not art but a 'life' – Moran's life – which has been shaped into 'a thing of beauty' by an 'author' who cannot help rubbing his hands in 'joy' as he contemplates his work (*T*, 165). Like Edouard, Mercier, and Victor, Moran is aware of his tormentor's gaze; at times, he even has the uncomfortable sense that that he is *within a work of art*. Observing the scene that has been set for his transformation, Moran senses such an order that appears beyond that of the workings of chance:

I soon stopped on the crest of a rise from where I could survey, without fatigue, the camp-site and the surrounding country. And I made this curious observation, that the land from where I was, and even the clouds in the sky, were so disposed as to lead the eyes gently to the camp, as in a painting by an old master (*T*, 153).

Moran's suspicion of a guiding hand behind his experiences resurfaces in his account of his miraculous crippling. As he finishes dragging his doppelgänger into the copse, he notes that this strange task was in some way one that he was *meant* to perform – by whatever powers have crippled him in the first place: 'Already my knee was stiffening again. It no longer *required* to be supple' (*T*, 152; my emphasis).

A few examples will suffice to demonstrate that Beckett found precedent for such techniques in Gide's writing – an oeuvre that repeatedly depicts characters overseen by an interfering consciousness to whose presence they are often blind but whose controlling hand or imposed order they may suspect. Anticipating the links between the Novellas or *Three Novels*, Gide cultivates intertextual references between fictions in ways that suggest such an 'arranger' behind their multiple worlds. When the 'novelist' of *Les Caves du Vatican* (who is positioned in that text as 'l'auteur de

Paludes') makes an unambiguous reference to *Promethée mal enchâiné* (by pointing out that the 'gl' in Baraglioul should be pronounced as in *migli-onnaire*, referring to a character in *Promethée mal enchâiné*), *Les Caves du Vatican* indicates an extra-textual 'novelist' who is distinct from Gide, yet who seems to preside over his various fictions. This figure generates a disorienting effect that reasserts the constructed and artificial nature of the text's world by 'appear[ing] to draw the reader out of the world of fictionality into the real, extratextual world of a flesh-and-blood author, but in fact reinsert[ing] him into an unreal textual universe' – an effect that Beckett of course cultivates in *Mercier, Malone Dies,* and *The Unnamable* (Babcock, 78). These refractions of the author's image are intensified when the relationship between the various narrators and Gide himself is deliberately elicited, as when (like the Beckett who writes as a 'Mr Beckett' in *Dream* and a 'Sam' in *Watt*) Gide names the narrator/listener of *Isabelle* 'Gide'.

Characters also recur in Gide's different fictions. *Les Nourritures terrestres'* Menalque reappears in *L'Immoraliste*, and as noted, in a far more complex fashion Edouard and the others who appear as fictional characters created by *Les Faux-Monnayeurs'* 'novelist' are also characters in Gide's notebook about that fiction, *Journal des Faux-Monnayeurs*. As we have already seen, Gide also hints at his characters' awareness of their status *as* characters in *Caves*, though he used this tactic again in *Les Faux-Monnayeurs*. Here an unsettling ambiguity is sometimes preserved between the time and space within the narrative (at the character's level of experience) and that of the narrative as a text (the reader's level) through an ambivalent use of 'here' and 'now'. Gide flaunts this trick at the novel's opening when Bernard states 'C'est le moment de croire que j'entends des pas dans le corridor'. As Arthur Babcock explains, the line may be may be read in at least two ways, 'one tending to naturalise the text, the other opening onto the world of self-consciousness' (Babcock, 84). Benard's expression might be translated into English as, 'This is a fine time to think that I hear steps in the corridor'. But a more literal reading of the French suggests a self-awareness he as a character is not supposed to have: 'The time has come for me to think that I hear steps in the corridor'. '"Time" in what sequence,' Babcock asks, 'if not that of the melodramatic novel? Is Bernard aware, as Lafcadio sometimes seems to be, that he is a fictional entity?' (Babcock, 84). This strange effect is heightened when, in a fashion that anticipates Mercier's (far more resentful) acknowledgment of *his* 'author', Bernard also seems to recognise the presence of his 'novelist' when he speaks of '*à nous deux*'.

GIDE'S MIRRORS

Such experiments have a key origin in Gide's idea of the novel as the most lawless of genres, a form that could reject the naïve artifice of realism *and* the Symbolist urge to jettison contingence by engaging directly with the artworks' contradictions – for instance, through playing up the pretence at the '*Free will of [the novel's] creator & free will of [his] creature*' (MIC60, 41; Burrows's emphasis). But though we have so far considered such techniques mainly with reference to the creature and his 'novelist', Gide was also interested in using similar devices to explore a related concern: staging the act of composition as one of self-inscription.

It is worth remembering that Gide sometimes composed in front of a double mirror – a practice that he fictionalized in *Les Cahiers d'André Walter* (1891), and that hints at the complex relationship his works stage between their many authors, and the way those authors behold themselves in the act of writing their own narratives.[4] Like another of his writer-avatars, Edouard, Gide often felt that he only existed to himself as a series of 'others' – with whom his (continually changing) observing self sought to identify through an act of imagination:

I am never anything but what I think myself – and this varies so incessantly, that often, if I were not there to make them acquainted, my morning's self would not recognise my evening's. Nothing could be more different from me than myself.... I live only through others – by procuration, so to speak, and by espousals; and I never feel myself living so intensely as when I escape from myself to become no matter who (*C*, 68).

As this passage suggests, for Gide writing is central to the author's self-comprehension, which is paradoxically diffused and refracted in that act of writing. But if this experience of self-otherness and existence by proxy undergirds Gide's view of the self in general, it is most keenly apparent to the author engaged in an autobiographical project – the writer who is in some way involved (like Edouard) in keeping a journal. The diaristic practices Gide imposes on his characters thus reflect the autographic nature of Gide's practice and fictional theory: as Justin O'Brien hints, 'the journal is Gide's form *par excellence* and ... his imaginary works might almost be considered to be extracted from his own *Journals*.'[5]

To adequately represent his view of writing and the self (the self that exists *within* a fiction or between interconnected fictions, as in the *Journal des Faux-Monnayeurs* and *Les Faux-Monnayeurs*), Gide created characters involved in the same activity as their narrator, 'doubling' or mirroring the writer as his own interlocutor, and framing one act of composition within another. He first theorised this structure and other forms of the mise en abyme device in one of his journal entries in 1893. Here Gide describes his fascination with a formal arrangement by which 'the subject of the work itself' is 'transposed at the level of the characters', a structure he illustrates with reference to the convex mirrors in the paintings of Memling, the play within the play in Hamlet, 'the device from heraldry that involves putting a second representation of the original shield "en abyme" within it' and other forms of internal duplication (*J*, 30–1). In the following I appropriate one of Justin O'Brien's coinages for the sake of distinguishing the specific subset of this device that I am concerned with here as 'composition en abyme', a form of internal duplication that can be defined in terms of a doubled relationship: 'as a coupling or a twinning of activities related to a similar object' (Dällenbach, 18).

This kind of doubling – which paradigmatically figures an author composing a story that contains a version of himself composing a story, and so on – lies at the heart of Gide's project, for this technique most fully allows him to explore the struggle with the gulf between reality and literature that is the true subject of his fiction. Through dramatizing his own authorship and creating characters involved in the same activity as their narrator, the writer doubles or mirrors himself as his own interlocutor. In this way, the composition en abyme works to expose 'the way in which the writer constructs the writing and vice versa' by dramatizing the fluid and contingent nature of both (Dällenbach, 18). The writing self only exists through its reflections/fictions and the fictions through their authoring self; both are continually in flux and in correspondence with each other. Gide calls this dynamic 'retroaction':

As the book issues from us, it changes us, modifying the course of our life, just as in physics those free-hanging vases, full of liquid, are seen, as they empty, to receive an impulse in the opposite direction from that of the liquid's flow. Our acts exercise a retroaction upon us. 'Our deeds act upon us as much as we act upon them', said George Eliot (*J*, 30).

Retroaction dramatises 'the influence of the book upon the one who is writing it, and during that very writing'; it is the process by which the author is created *by* his work as he creates that work (in a composition en abyme this situation is potentially doubled at the level of the diegesis where the 'fictional' author tells his tale, and so on) (*J*, 29). Such a reflexive relation between the writer and the text, as H. Porter Abbott has pointed out, may well be the universal condition of first-person writing, but its homeland, as it were, is the diary or journal – the form that exposes writing *as* action and 'exposes a drama of interpretation, blended ... with a drama of creation'.[6] Within the many real and fictional journals that make up Gide's work, retroaction is staged on multiple levels through the composition en abyme: a 'relationship of relationships, the relation of the narrator N to his/her story S being the same as that of the narrator/ character n to his/her story s' (Dällenbach, 18). This structure is a most Gidean form of internal duplication, for in fictions that take as their subject the fictions of the subject, the composition en abyme mirrors the writer's composition of his own fictions. As in the mirrors of *Le Traité du Narcisse* (1891), for example, in which Narcisse dreams of an Adam who in turn longs to contemplate his own visage, the composition en abyme reproduces an image of the subject perceiving the image (of himself) that he has made.

As Adorno indicated, such mirroring effects are most evident in Gide's *Paludes*, a diary fiction that Beckett knew well, lectured on, and alluded to in his fiction. In this work a high level of ambiguity is generated in the text through at least two interrelated strategies. The first is that the title *Paludes* is shared by the embedding work (Gide's *Paludes*) and the embedded work/journal (the narrator's fiction), and it is also the title of the work/journal written by the character (Tityre) whose personality the narrator assumes *within* the embedded work. Within these '*Paludes*', Gide exploits the self-referentiality of the first-person pronoun to create an echo effect by which the various 'je's' are rendered ambiguous and can at once refer to the 'je' of Tityre, the 'je' of the narrator and, at times, the hidden 'je' of the author. The ambiguous 'je' of *Paludes* most frequently suggests both the narrator and author, as in the leitmotif phrase 'I am writing *Paludes*'.[7] One effect of this simultaneity is that the narrator annexes the name on the book's cover, rivalling the 'real' Gide (and the world in which he writes) even as the opposite occurs in a dramatised reflection of Gide's own process of composition. We follow the Gide of the title page 'down' into the fictions nested within his *Paludes*, hearing his 'je' become the narrator's, and then the narrator's 'je' Tityre's. The effect of these shifting 'planes' (to use Beckett's term for the various levels of *Les Faux-Monnayeurs*) on which are transposed the 'I' of the novel, is disorientation. Is this Tityre's voice or his maker's? Are we in Gide's *Paludes* or the narrator's fiction of the same name? The borders between the fiction and reality are blurred.

In *Les Faux-Monnayeurs* Gide returns to and amplifies the kinds of regression and ambiguity in *Paludes*: the figure of the writer reappears within the novel's 'double mirror' as Edouard composes his own *Les Faux-Monnayeurs*, although this fiction will logically contain *another* novelist composing a fiction (Edouard realises that this is the only way to present the 'struggle' between the artist and reality that will be the subject of his novel), and so on. *Les Faux-Monnayeurs* therefore presents a new form of reduplication: a literary gesture at infinite regression. Like *Paludes*, the 'je' of Gide, the 'novelist', and Edouard oscillate within this structure by virtue of the text's cultivated ambiguities. For example, consider the following passage from Edouard's journal in which the protagonist's voice, the 'novelist's', and that of the Gide of the *Journal des Faux-Monnayeurs*, all blur together: 'This episode must be very much shortened. Precision in the reader's imagination could be obtained not by accumulating details but by two or three touches put in exactly the right places' (*C*, 83). At other times, Gide's *Les Faux-Monnayeurs* refers to Edouard's novel by name to generate an even more disorienting kind of transposition. As Dällenbach points out, in the following passage the use of the deictic 'here' (rather than 'there') joins with the perfect tense ('has been able' instead of 'will be able') to strengthen the 'superimposition': 'It will be difficult in *Les Faux-Monnayeurs* for it to be credible that the character who will play me here has been able, while remaining on good terms with his sister, not to know her children' (Dällenbach's translation, 32; *C*, 84).

Anticipating the way in which Beckett connected multiple, discrete fictions through author-figures who preside 'over' one another, *Les Faux-Monnayeurs* is *itself* a narrative frame that is somehow related to *Les Caves du Vatican* via the *Journal des Faux-Monnayeurs* – which contains fragments of Lafcadio's Journal. Lafcadio's Journal, along with the *Journal des Faux-Monnayeurs* that contains *it*, reappears in *Les Faux-Monnayeurs* as passages of Edouard's journal. Given these dizzying perspectives, it comes as no surprise that by this point in his career, Gide conceived of the fiction within the fiction as a 'mirror'. (Edouard refers to his journal as his 'pocket mirror' (*C*, 142).) For the kinds of self-reflexivity displayed in *La Tentative amoureuse* and to an extent *Paludes* do not proceed in one 'direction', but seem to refract one another in a number of paradoxical ways. For example, if Lafcadio's Journal in *Les Caves du Vatican* corresponds to that Lafcadio's Journal from the *Journal des Faux-Monnayeurs* – a relation that Gide invites – the *Journal des Faux-Monnayeurs* (which 'frames' *Les Faux-Monnayeurs* itself, which contains Edouard's Journal and *his*

'novelist', etc.) is paradoxically *contained by that which is 'within' itself.*
Reductively, and in a way unfaithful to these complexities, one can sketch
a series of *Les Faux-Monnayeurs*'s 'nesting' fictions as follows:

Gide's *Journal des Faux-Monnayeurs* (which contains Lafcadio's Journal/
Edouard's Journal): Gide's *Les Faux-Monnayeurs*: the 'novelist' of *Les Faux-
Monnayeurs*: Edouard's Journal: Edouard's (virtual) *Les Faux-Monnayeurs* and
Journal des Faux-Monnayeurs, and so on.

A correspondence between these fictions assumes a roughly 'circular'
pattern when limited in this manner, moving from journal to journal,
each journal containing an image of a novelist and a novel that contains –
and so on. But of course this scheme is incomplete. The web extends to at
least two other texts, *Les Caves du Vatican* and Gide's own *Journals*, which
further the network of reflections and commentaries upon Gide's many
staged acts of composition.

THE CELL WITHIN THE CELL

Related strategies appear in Beckett's fiction after the war, but here they
take on a different and more troubling significance than in Gide's writing. In *Three Novels*, and especially in *Malone Dies* and *The Unnamable*,
the games Beckett's authors play with the novel are left behind for an
exploration of the way such authors are constructed by and entrapped
within their own fictions. To achieve this, Beckett began to deploy composition en abyme across a range of discrete self-inscriptive fictions.

The general structural dynamic behind *Three Novels* is hinted at in an
essay Beckett wrote sometime in March of 1947, only a month or two
before he began *Molloy* on 2 May that year. In 'Peintres de l'Empêchement'
(composed under the provisional title 'le nouvel objet') Beckett hints at
his interest in a form of internal duplication as a central motif and governing formal characteristic of the artwork. Recalling the terminology he
had first used in his discussion of the structure of *Paludes* and *Les Faux-
Monnayeurs* ('planes') (MIC60, 33; 37), Beckett argues that the modernity
of the van Velde's paintings is inseparable from their use of a self-reflexive
form that depicts the process of unveiling that brought it into being:

Un dévoilement sans fin, voile derrière voile, plan sur plan de transparencies impar-
faites, un dévoilement vers l'indévoilable, le rien, la chose à nouveau (*Dis*, 136).

Such planes may be 'the void', the 'nothing', or 'the colours of the spec-
trum of black', but Beckett discovers a final image 'buried' beneath these

levels: an image that reveals the incarceration of the artist within his work.

Et l'ensevelissement dans l'unique, dans un lieu d'impénétrables proximities, cellule peinte sur la pierre de la cellule, art d'incarcération (*Dis*, 136).

This perplexing image within an image suggests that Beckett could replace the original title centring on the artist's evasive 'new object' with a subsequent focus on the artist's 'impasse' because the two are inextricable; the first can finally be stated only in terms of the second. At the heart of the modern work Beckett perceives a mise en abyme of potentially infinite regression: the artist's cell (which contains him) depicted within itself – an image that must contain *another* artist caught in the same act of composition as his creator, and so on. In the depths of this mirror, Beckett's vision of incarceration recurs as both the ontological condition of the artist (the stone of the cell that imprisons him) and the governing condition of the artwork that holds his doubled reality (the cell painted upon this stone).

In *Malone Dies* and *The Unnamable*, this structure is imposed across an array of discrete fictions, granting the *author*-figures of these books an extra-textual memory that extends to Beckett's previous works – an illusion bolstered by the many echoes and extra-textual references Beckett cultivated in *Three Novels*.[8] The closest formal relative of Beckett's original composite meta-fictional structure (which seems to have initially included only *Molloy* and the fiction that would become *Malone Dies*) is *Les Faux-Monnayeurs* and Gide's *Journal des Faux-Monnayeurs*: Beckett's version also comprises a 'fiction' ('*Molloy*', that is also composed of two 'journals') generated by a 'real' 'diary' referencing '*Molloy*'s' creation and containing a record of fictional composition alongside a record of the vicissitudes of its author (Malone's diaristic narrative). But unlike Gide's more straightforward and playful construct, Beckett's 'author's' 'journal' in *Malone Dies* does not comment directly on his 'fiction' ('*Molloy*') in the way that *Journal des Faux-Monnayeurs* stages its novel's (*Les Faux-Monnayeurs*) construction. Nor does Beckett's project reveal the 'real' 'author' of Beckett's project as 'Beckett'. Instead, Beckett reincorporates his fictional world within another fiction, and, drawing on techniques explored in the Novellas, he cultivates repetitions of theme, phrase, and event between *Molloy* and *Malone Dies* to suggest that '*Molloy*' is a fiction that bears the mark of another fictional author's (Malone's) abiding consciousness.

Beckett prepared the ground for this 'ventriloquist's' 'diary' even as he wrote *Molloy*. As Bair pointed out (Bair, 374), even though the first French edition was published after Beckett had written *The Unnamable*, it was only in the English edition of 1955 that the sentence 'This time, then once more I think, then I think it will be over' was altered to read 'This time, then once more I think, *then perhaps a last time*, I think it'll be over' (*T*, 8; my emphasis) – an anticipation of Malone's 'journal' behind this fiction that is repeated in Molloy's description of his tales as 'cries': 'Yes, let me cry out, this time, then another time perhaps, then perhaps last time' (*T*, 26). Such passages indicate an awareness of the larger pattern that sounds the voice of Malone behind Molloy, as the latter revisions sound that of the Unnamable behind Malone. This echo is especially audible at those points where Molloy reveals himself as a composer of a record/ work of imagination by which he inscribes himself in the text – the role, of course, that Malone is also engaged in 'behind' Molloy, and Beckett 'behind' Malone – or when Molloy's position as a bedridden diarist is repeated at the level of his 'author':

My knees are enormous. I have just caught a glimpse of them, when I got up for a second. . . . But from time to time I shall recall my present existence compared to which this is a nursery tale. But only from time to time, so that it may be said, if necessary . . . Oh it's only a diary, it'll soon be over (*T*, 62).

The echo effect of this extended composition en abyme means that, as Malone guides Molloy to divide himself into a narrator and protagonist, his 'I' generates and multiplies perspectives analogous to those of Gide's author-protagonist-diarist in *Paludes* or Edouard's narrator in *Les Faux-Monnayeurs* as his creature begins *his* diary (which will also, potentially, contain another diary – that of Edouard's fictional diarist).

In *The Unnamable*, this multiple first-person pronoun also generates a framing dynamic *within* the novel when, for instance, the Unnamable not only sees Malone in his void and remembers telling his stories, but channels him: 'The answer to all that is this, I quote Malone, that I was entirely absorbed in the business on hand . . . ' (*T*, 322). Or consider the passages where Mahood (who is also, perhaps, working at the behest of the mysterious 'they' who told the 'stories' that are also Beckett's other novels *to* the Unnamable) ventriloquizes the Unnamable to tell the story of the crippled wanderer. At such moments, as the voice of the text shifts into storytelling mode, there are at least three 'I's sounding, each 'within' the next: the crippled wanderer's, the Unnamable's, and Mahood's:

In the meantime it's Mahood, this caricature is he. What if we were one and the same after all, as he affirms, and I deny? ... I've been he an instant, hobbling through a nature which, it is only fair to say, was on the barren side and, what is more, it is only just to add, tolerably deserted to begin with. After each thrust of my crutches I stopped ... (*T*, 317–18).

I had no wish to arrive, but I had to do my utmost, in order to arrive.... Still Mahood speaking (*T*, 323).

The reader's disorientation in these situations is only enhanced by the Unnamable's own confusion about this 'I' – an anxiety that is not alleviated by the eventual addition of a 'fourth' subject, Worm:

That brings us up to four, gathered together. I knew it, there might be a hundred of us and still we'd lack the hundred and first, we'll always be short of me. Worm, I nearly said Watt, Worm, what can I say of Worm.... Perhaps it's by trying to be Worm that I'll finally succeed in being Mahood, I hadn't thought of that. Then all I'll have to do is be Worm (*T*, 341).

CHAPTER 6

'Oh It's Only a Diary': Molloy

Within its multiple fictional frames, *Molloy* gestures toward several novelistic types: notably, the picaresque, the *Bildungsroman*, and the fictional autobiography and diary. Yet Beckett's novel is involved with these genres most profoundly at a subterranean level. That is, it is less concerned with subverting such forms of the novel than with engaging the biographical master-narrative that underpins them. To borrow from Michael Holquist, this is the story the novel traditionally tells about a 'historical self': 'the subject of a biography whose events are arranged as a function of the author's attempts to explain those events'.[1] The emergence of this self, as John Morris has argued, is most apparent in the autobiography (and its fictional manifestations), the genre in which 'formal continuity is a principle of philosophic, not merely narrative, coherence'; coherence in the autobiography 'is [therefore] in some sense the real subject of the work, the gradual evolution of an always-identifiable self'.[2] Events within this story acquire a symbolic value as they build toward the self's recognition of purpose – which is, tautologically, self-recognition. At the same time, the self grows toward an understanding of its story's position within larger spiritual, economic, social, or familial narratives. The historical self moves, in other words, toward what we might call *wisdom*: a sensual knowledge that is both a form of integration with one's world and self-integration.

We have seen that Beckett's work begins with the attempt to undermine both Romantic and Naturalistic models of such coherent selves and their stories in the novel, an ambition that led him into conflict with a number of fictional paradigms. But, as his extension of Gide's composition en abyme strategies suggest, by the time of *Molloy* Beckett's focus had shifted toward forms of autographic writing, such as the real and fictional autobiography and (most apparently in the case of *Malone Dies*) the diary and the diary novel. *Three Novels* work, ultimately, to subvert the underpinnings of these forms in the novel's biographical master-narratives of education, self-recognition, and wisdom. Further, through a 'blurring of [their] outline[s]' (*LC*, 49), Beckett's novels trouble the boundaries between autographic writing – which is traditionally inspired by a drive toward sincerity – and its ostensible opposite: fiction, and specifically, the modern novel. By means of their multiple frames, *Three Novels* stage acts of self-writing as acts of fictional composition and vice versa, confounding the diaristic drive toward self-recognition through joining this trajectory with the modern novel's resistance to closure and its exposure of form as always a form of *composition*. At a more basic level still, Beckett's fictions of this period work to uncouple the novel's moorings in a faith in the expressive, ordering and recuperative powers of language.

Molloy's troubling of the novel's roots in such a biographical master-narrative begins to come into focus when we consider it with relation to one of the specific forms of the novel toward which it gestures: the fictional diary. As his readers have recognized, Beckett had a profound interest in diaries, both fictional and real; and this fascination had an impact on his writing, most apparently in *Malone Dies*.³ But we should also consider that the interconnected form of the original two *Novels* requires us to consider the (fictional) diary as a context for *Molloy* as well; within the frame of the 'diary' of Beckett's original master-narrator (Malone), *Molloy* takes on the status of two prolonged fictional/autographic 'entries' within the 'big child's exercise-book' which Malone claims is '[his] life' (*T*, 276) (as noted, Molloy also imagines describing his narrative as 'only a diary' (*T*, 62)). In formal terms, *Molloy* itself deploys a diaristic fascination with the retroactive current between the narrating voice and its tale by foregrounding the text's role (both as a narrative and as a material artefact) within its writer's story. Unsurprisingly, then, the journal has had a significant if not always acknowledged impact on the way that *Molloy* has been understood.

In considering what it might mean to read *Molloy* with relation to the diary we could do worse than to look to Gide as a point of departure. For Beckett's early master was also one of the foremost theorists and practitioners of the diary in the twentieth century. Like generations of diarists, Gide's interest in the journal revolves around the form's intimate relationship to the biographical master-narrative noted earlier and, specifically, the diary's traditional use as a strategy to uncover an authentic, integral self obscured by habit, self-evasion, and custom.⁴ In the several traditions that uphold this notion, the diarist allows his pen to follow the spontaneous (and therefore, in this view, sincere) impulses of the inner self – whose contours emerge, as in a mirror, in his journal's pages.

But although Gide drew on this function of the diary in *Les Cahiers d'André Walter*, his work was almost immediately animated by an opposing impulse that reemerges with greater (and stranger) force at the heart of *Molloy* and *Malone Dies*: to use forms of autographic writing to critique the truth-telling and expressive capabilities of language. He did so through repeatedly attacking a Puritan model of the diary that values the form's relation to sincerity as an aid in the recovery of psychic and spiritual wholeness (a model whose most influential fictional exemplar is Defoe's *Robinson Crusoe*). In *La Symphonie pastorale* and *La Porte étroite*, for instance, Gide inverts the narrative trajectory of the Puritan diary by staging the Christian journal of self-discovery and salvation as a practised form of 'self-abnegation' whose key moments revolve around acts of misprision and self-deception.

As we shall see, Gide's inversion of the Christian model of the journal of self-discovery was important to Beckett. But by the forties, the use of the diary as a tool for the integration of the inner self had been given new life by psychotherapy – which sought to harness the form's excavatory powers to decode the private symbolism of the patient's unconscious. The most significant contributor to this reinvention of the journal is Jung, whose concept of Active Imagination has had a major influence on the practice of diary-keeping in the twentieth century, especially in the United States (where the impact of the Puritan tradition of journaling is still felt). As Jung argued in the Tavistock Lectures (the third of which was heard by Beckett in October of 1935 (*DF*, 218)), the patient exercising Active Imagination comes to recognise his private symbolism through working to objectify the contents of his unconscious in writing, painting, or other deliberate, repetitive, quasi-creative activities. In this way, the patient participates in what Gide would call a retroactive relationship with his medium even as he discovers the values of his archetypal material, generating a collaboration of his conscious and unconscious data. In the psychotherapeutic diary, for example, the writing itself 'has a definite effect upon [the writer]. Whatever he has put into it works back on him and produces a change of attitude'.[5] Like his Christian predecessors, the Jungian diarist uncovers and integrates his person in the act of writing, ideally achieving 'a living birth that leads to a new level of being, a new situation'.[6]

This model has had an important impact on the way that *Molloy* especially has been understood – which is not surprising given the fact that the most convincing and widespread readings of this novel concern its relationship to the mythology of psychoanalysis. J. D. O'Hara, for example, has suggested that Molloy's tale has at its centre an encounter with the Jungian archetype of wisdom or *Sophia*,[7] a reading that builds on Vivian Mercier's early account of the novel as 'an allegory of the Ego and the Id', anticipates aspects of Phil Baker's important *Beckett and the Mythology of Psychoanalysis* and affirms the reading recently offered in *The Grove Companion to Samuel Beckett*:

While Molloy enacts a Jungian quest for an integrated self, and encounters his Anima and Shadow, Moran enacts a Freudian drama of repression, a patriarchal drama that complements Molloy's maternal needs (*GC*, 381).

Such accounts have often remained silent on questions of genre and form, but the implicit suggestion is that *Molloy* (and Malone's '*Molloy*') is not simply a fiction that deploys the mythology of psychoanalysis, but a work that charts a character's private world of unconscious symbol through an act of self-exploration: this is a 'Jungian quest for an integrated self' conducted through an act of writing staged at the level of Malone's narrative (as it is in one of Molloy's own asides) as a 'diary'.

Yet if *Molloy*'s/'*Molloy*'s' closest analogue in such readings is the psychotherapeutic journal (whose ambition, in Jungian terms, is wisdom), once again it is less concerned with this specific model than the biographical master-narrative that underpins it. Molloy's/Malone's 'diary' stalls the diary's drive toward self-perception through hindering the process of recognition that would decode the symbolic nature of its 'events' – effectively blocking the retroactive 'work[ing] back' of the diarist's 'material' (Jung, 'Tavistock', 173). In doing so, this book explores not *sophia* – that integrative knowledge of oneself and one's world – but what Beckett, for his part, calls *moria*: folly.

All I am is feeling. Molloy and the others came to me the day I became aware of my own folly. Only then did I begin to write the things I feel (SB qtd. in d'Aubarède, 217).

Folly here signifies Beckett's mature response to the concern that drove his early experiments with the novel: the inadequacy of language to express reality, and the radical resistance of experience to reification within form.[8] Inseparable from this notion is the emphasis on feeling over cognition that we have seen became increasingly important for Beckett during the late thirties and the wartime years, and reemerges in his 1945 essay 'La peinture des van Velde ou le Monde et le Pantalon'. Here Beckett describes his fascination with an art that could not be 'moins intellectuelle' and posits a response to the artwork based upon remaining in a sense of unknowing rather than the resolution of this sense through the exercise of analysis (*Dis*, 131). While the critic – whose task in this regard mirrors the psychoanalyst's – seeks to get the 'nonsense' of the writing 'back together' (rabibocher) into a coherent narrative, Beckett gestures at an art that complicates the conditions under which any reintegration of the work might occur (*Dis*, 119). Folly here signifies *feeling* bafflement and *existing in* a state of radical ignorance, a serious experience that (as Beckett's final poem and his essay suggest) is also always sliding into an encounter with the ridiculous and the meaningless.

Beckett's *Three Novels* deploy this experience of folly against the structural drive toward self-integration and self-understanding which dominates those forms of the novel from which it borrows: the picaresque, the *Bildungsroman*, the fictional autobiography, and the fictional diary. And it is largely this tension that produces the strange energies in Beckett's books. Each of the *Three Novels*, as Leslie Hill puts it of *Comment c'est*, 'invites an allegorical reading' even as it tends to 'disqualify ... the possibility of doing so' – to the extent that a reader sensitive to the fiction's powers of negation and deferral may conclude that *Molloy*, for example, 'remains radically and disturbingly empty of apparent symbolic purpose' (Hill, 138). And yet it would be more faithful to this text to say that it keeps *shifting between* meaning and its opposite – folly – in a way that is hard to describe. This is because the text's power to suggest an always-emerging, potentially profound meaning, and also to complicate and hinder this meaning from fully taking hold, involves matching its drive toward the symbolic and the serious with a counter-pull toward the baffling, the insignificant, and the ridiculous. Rather than cancel each other out, these currents are mutually reinforcing; together, they generate a rich tonal ambivalence that confuses and overdetermines the sense – that is, the meaning and the emotional charge – of the *Molloy* text. The result of this complication of the novel's means and ends is not simply 'undoing', but an experience of *intensification*.

Despite the claims of Beckett's critics, the primary result of this intensification – of feeling, of potential meaning – is not the demolishing of ideas, or the dismantling of emotions (which are, according to his detractors in this regard, underpinned by ideas). As Beckett stated, *Molloy* is not concerned with ideas or concepts per se.[9] Rather, through folly, the novel works to resist the form's traditional and enduring ambitions to translate feeling into knowledge, and sense into symbol. *Molloy* draws us toward, and reels us back from, the threshold of recognition. Feeling here does not pass from the gut (or the heart), as it were, toward the mind; like the hero's identity in this narrative, it remains unresolved – strangely portentous and meaningless, and charged with the power to unsettle and surprise.

One of the strangest episodes in *Molloy* is its hero's encounter with the person he often refers to as Lousse or Sophie, O'Hara's 'feminine wisdom' who eventually initiates Molloy 'into the physical world', thereby allowing him to become, in Jung's terms, *'a filius sapientiae'* – a wise son (O'Hara, 'Jung', 137). Despite this important role within the story of Molloy's life, however, at the outset Lousse (here only 'the lady') is presented as a comic figure whose dog he inadvertently kills and who then saves him from the 'bloodthirsty mob' by means of a speech.

He has killed Teddy, I grant you that, Teddy whom I loved like my own child, but it is not so serious as it seems.... For Teddy was old, blind, deaf, crippled with rheumatism and perpetually incontinent, night and day, indoors and out of doors. Thanks then to this poor old man I had been spared a painful task, not to mention the expense which I am ill able to afford.... You may say, she said, that he did wrong to run away, that he should have explained, asked to be forgiven. Granted. But it is clear he has not all his wits about him, that he is beside himself, for reasons of which we know nothing and which might put us all to shame, if we did know them. I even wonder if he knows what he has done (*T*, 33).

Presented as if to a jury in a court room, the speech has a technical decorum, a thoroughness, and an attempted grandiosity familiar to the reader of *Watt* (note Lousse's use of hypophora and asyndeton). Yet these potentially 'serious' qualities of the speech serve only to heighten its ridiculous effect, which is largely achieved by the grandstanding sentimentality of Lousse's appeals ('Teddy whom I loved like my own child') and her shameless indulgence in the details of her own, her husband's, Molloy's, and her pet's rather embarrassing sufferings (one especially imagines what it might mean for a dog to be 'perpetually incontinent, night and day'). As Molloy indicates, if the speech is undertaken out of an interest to preserve him, it is quickly taken over by Lousse's urge to stay 'in her stride' (*T*, 33).

　　Is this the voice of Wisdom, Jung's archetype Sophia-Sapientia? The Molloy text suggests otherwise: recall that Jung's figure speaks 'with the magic authority of the female' and initiates the male into the 'wisdom and spiritual exaltation that transcend reason'.[10] And if Lousse's symbolic importance in this regard begins to seem doubtful in the light of Jung's description, Molloy's own comments don't encourage us: 'There emanated such tedium from this droning voice that I was making ready to move on', he admits (*T*, 33). Rather than manifesting wisdom or those attributes of the archetype's 'negative side' (death, the abyss, the devourer, etc.), Lousse more often seems a ridiculous and eccentric person, an identity that is only strengthened as the episode progresses. Nevertheless, and in a manner that is difficult to grasp, the encounter does at times *also* seem to suggest to Molloy and the reader a powerfully symbolic (and terrifying) significance, ruling out any reading of Lousse as *simply* a ridiculous or meaningless figure. Yet even as Molloy insists on the strangeness of the episode and its effects on him, multiple comic deflations in the narrative keep hinting that the encounter is 'not so serious as it seems' (*T*, 33). The text's fluctuation between nonmeaning and seriousness thus keeps any mythic or archetypal reading of Lousse from assuming its status within a narrative of psychic reintegration or self-discovery even as it grants the *Molloy* text its weird and compelling gravity.

The first major event in this episode is the burial of Teddy. Molloy describes the 'dispersion' of the crowd, the 'fatuous colloquy' with the policeman, and the tiresome journey to Lousse's ('I had my bellyful by the time I got there') in a manner that keeps this part of the story in the domain of farce (*T*, 35). Teddy is here an inert, comic object – poked with a cane, continually slipping off the bicycle seat – who invites Molloy's sympathy as little as the reader's.

Someone was poking the dog, with a malacca. The dog was uniformly yellow. ... His death must have hurt him less than my fall me. And he at least was dead. We slung him across the saddle and set off, like an army in retreat, helping each other I suppose, to keep the corpse from falling, to keep the bicycle moving, to keep ourselves moving, through the jeering crowd (*T*, 35).

'Like an army in retreat'; 'through the jeering crowd' – Molloy depicts this unlikely trio as a group of clowns who set off the 'bloodthirsty mob'. The interment of this ridiculous pet by its owner (who allegedly intended to put him down anyway) and his accidental killer is then interrupted by Molloy's explanation that his leg prevented him from digging, a point that leads him to this startling reflection: 'I was virtually one-legged, and I would have been happier, livelier, amputated at the groin. And if they had removed a few testicles into the bargain I wouldn't have objected' (*T*, 35). From this statement, Molloy takes off on one of his extended digressions – in which he proceeds to describe his long-lived antagonism with his testicles.

For from such testicles like mine, dangling at mid-thigh at the end of the meagre cord, there was nothing more to be squeezed, not a drop. So that non che speme il desiderio, and I longed to see them gone, from the old stand where they bore false witness, for and against, in the lifelong charge against me. For if they accused me of having made a balls of it, of me, of them, they thanked me for it too, from the depths of their rotten bag, the right lower than the left, or inversely, I forget, decaying circus clowns. And, worse still, they got in my way when I tried to walk, when I tried to sit down, as if my sick leg was not enough, and when I rode my bicycle they bounced up and down (*T*, 36).

As elsewhere in this book, the text's power to arrest our attention is partly generated through its apparent discontinuity. The considerable warmth of feeling that Molloy then directs against his 'balls' occasions laughter (this is, after all, a passage initiated by a revenge fantasy – against his own body), and the comic tone is further bolstered by the passage's striking imagery: the personification of Molloy's testicles as rebellious 'circus clowns' who make a fool of their owner. To mention only the obvious, this move also invites several clever puns as these insurrectionists 'testify' against Molloy and, true to their comic profession, hinder his every move, bouncing up and down ridiculously 'at mid-thigh' when he rides his bicycle.

But, to appropriate a phrase Molloy uses later of his tale, 'making a balls of it' is not all that is happening here (*T*, 77). If, to borrow from Thomas Pynchon, 'When we speak of "seriousness" in fiction ultimately we are talking about an attitude toward death',[11] *Molloy*'s power to move us consists largely in its startling pairing of an unruly comic energy with a profound longing for an ultimacy that is often figured *as* death – in a manner that uses the comic to reinforce the intensity of the serious, and vice versa. Note that, although Molloy concludes, with another pun, that he 'must be attached to [his balls] after all', the passage also invokes the darker currents of the Romantic tradition in its putrefied images, its fascination with mutilation (recall Beckett's penchant for Keats's 'awful sweetness and thick soft damp green richness' in works like 'The Pot of Basil' (SB to TM, 27/4/30 to 11/5/30, *LSB 1*, 21)), and its quotation from Leopardi's sombre 'To Himself'. Molloy's digression inflects the gravity of Leopardi's text with laughter ('I feel/ Not hope alone, desire/ For dear deceits in us has come to fail')[12] by situating this meditation on the *death* of desire within his discussion of the fate of his 'balls'. But this passage also requires us to hear behind its laughter the cry for oblivion which powers Molloy's narrative as a whole, lurks behind his fantasy of self-castration and closes Leopardi's poem:

Lie quietly. Despair
This final time. Fate granted to our kind
Nothing but dying. Now despise yourself,
Nature (the brutal force
That furtively ordains the general harm),
And this infinity of nothingness (Leopardi, 118).

This complex ground bass of (deathly) seriousness lingers as the narrative shifts back into Molloy's account of Teddy's burial, where this event now begins to take on an air of quiet, even respectful ceremony.

It was Lousse who dug the hole while I held the dog in my arms. He was heavy already and cold, but he had not yet begun to stink. He smelt bad, if you like, but bad like an old dog, not like a dead dog. He too had dug holes, perhaps at this very spot. We buried him as he was, no box or wrapping of any kind, like a Carthusian monk, but with his collar and lead (*T*, 36).

Holding Teddy's corpse like the infant-substitute the dog has been, Molloy is put in a reflective mood which, if tinged with irony, is not without sympathy in its consideration of the dog's past life of digging holes, possibly where he will now be interred. And when Teddy is placed in the earth with his humble effects and without shroud or coffin, Molloy compares this silly animal's commital to the entombment of a monk from the highly ascetic order that inspired Matthew Arnold in his *Stanzas from the Grande Chartreuse*. The strange, almost solemn tone that now begins to play around this laughable scene becomes unignorable in Molloy's startling and cryptic statement that:

On the whole I was a mere spectator, I contributed my presence. As if it had been my own burial. And it was (*T*, 37).

The intimation that begins to flicker into view here – that this ridiculous burial is in some way a significant, even inscrutably symbolic episode for Molloy – is subtly sustained in the sentences that describe the setting of this now weirdly ambivalent event.

It was a larch tree. It is the only tree I can identify, with certainty. Funny she should have chosen, to bury her dog beneath, the only tree I can identify, with certainty (*T*, 37).

'Funny' the choice is, in several senses. As other readers have noticed, with the image of the larch tree Beckett locates Teddy's burial under a sign that in his oeuvre veers between the obsessional, the nostalgic, and the fearful, and that presides over birth before it signifies death.[13] This image is in keeping with Beckett's intention at this time to create a network of links between his texts that would complicate and overdetermine their individual narratives within a collective form composed of all of his novels since *Murphy*. But the burial also persists in appearing as if it betokens an order that is unclear to the reader and the protagonist alike within the *Molloy* text. But what order?

The intimation of an occult significance behind Teddy's burial is reinforced through a series of images that suggest a larger structure of meaning behind the individual events of the Lousse encounter. These images are linked through their association with burial; appropriately, they are also involved with issues of perception and the difficulty of apprehending meaning. To ask a question that is as ridiculous as it is perhaps important: What is the connection, if any, between the red specks (so carefully described) on the leaves of this heavily encoded larch tree and the red specks that are the ticks (buried alive) in Teddy's ears?

The sea-green needles are like silk and speckled, it always seemed to me, with little red, how shall I say, with little red specks. The dog had ticks in his ears, I have an eye for such things, they were buried with him (*T*, 37).

This image reminds us that, immediately preceding the burial, Molloy claims he can only speak of his life as though it were a type of *serious joke* – a point he illustrates through another image/story about storytelling, the interpretation of order, death and buried animation.

My life, my life, now I speak of it as something over, now as a joke which still goes on, and it is neither, for at the same time it is over and it goes on, and is there any tense for that? Watch wound and buried by the watchmaker, before he died, whose ruined works will one day speak of God, to the worms (*T*, 36).

Sardonic in its recollection of the watchmaker analogy from the teleological argument (an argument that indicates a symbolic order in the structure of the world), this passage also rises to a meditation on the relative proximity of human knowledge to that of an animal's – an association that reemerges in the final image of burial that trails the Teddy episode. Like her dog and his human replacement, Lousse's parrot is another of her pets and an object of laughter (and a long-standing Beckettian symbol for words detached from meaning). But his death also figures an entrapment that will continue beyond the grave, a state that is somehow connected with Molloy's present condition: 'Him too one day she would bury. In his cage probably. Me too, if I had stayed, she would have buried. If I had her address I'd write to her, to come and bury me' (*T*, 38).

The final sentiment in this sentence – a desire to be buried alive by Lousse *now* – recalls, in its strange associations (a mother figure burying her husband/pet/son), an inversion of Molloy's deathbed musings on his real mother: a woman that he has, in a sense, put in the ground, perhaps while still 'alive', or who perhaps still remains unburied:

The truth is I don't know much. For example my mother's death. Was she already dead when I came? Or did she die later? I mean enough to bury. I don't know. Perhaps they haven't buried her yet. In any case I have her room. I sleep in her bed. I piss and shit in her pot. I have taken her place (*T*, 7–8).

The fear that stirs like an unquiet corpse beneath the comic surface of this novel – that Molloy's mother is not dead, or is dead and is still alive – thus resurfaces from its shallow grave to 'harrow' the Teddy episode through the uncanny logic that grants this narrative its weird continuity:

And there are days, like this evening, when my memory confuses [Lousse and Ruth/Edith] and I am tempted to think of them as one and the same old hag, flattened and crazed by life. And God forgive me to tell you the horrible truth, my mother's image sometimes mingles with theirs, which is literally unendurable, like being crucified, I don't know why and I don't want to (*T*, 59).

Needless to say, such connections trouble the relationship between the text's emotional charge and any 'meaning' extractable from its strange pattern. It is true that a symbolic structure always seems about to emerge (with the implacability of the repressed) from *Molloy*'s complex tonal and relational matrix. Yet this matrix also works continually to prevent such a structure from fully realizing itself. Even as the recurrent laughter of this novel suggests that all is 'not so serious as it seems', from even such ludic circumstances as Teddy's burial we begin to glimpse a scene compounded of echoes that proceeds with all the gravity of a forbidden ritual. In this scene Molloy replaces Teddy just as the dog acted as a surrogate for Lousse's son and her son a replacement for her husband. At the same time, Molloy the son is 'taken for' two absent fathers – his own and, through Teddy, the partner of Lousse – as his mother's 'image' is mingled with those of Lousse and his lover Ruth/Edith. And so a son/father is interred by his lover/mother (whom he has anal sex with and who likewise gives him an anal birth) even as, to use Molloy's phrase, he 'take[s] her place' – burying her (alive) while acting as a 'spectator' at his own entombment. So it is fitting that, from this impossible perspective, and with a thought that now reveals both its wild hilarity and horror, Molloy thinks: 'All I need now is a son' (*T*, 8).

What is this weird laughter that interrupts the critical urge to make sense of the novel? And if Molloy never grows into a wise son, what lesson can the reader hope to learn from his text? The mythology of psycho-analysis cannot offer a way out of the labyrinthine interpenetration of identities and emotions that is *Molloy* because the novel keeps destabiliz-ing the very symbolic configurations it summons even as they flicker into view. Even in leaving Lousse behind, the text only deepens the unsettling ambivalence of her role. Molloy recalls that, as he departs, Lousse 'did not try and hold me back but ... went and sat down on her dog's grave, perhaps, which was mine too in a way' (*T*, 59). Does Molloy imagine that Lousse (whoever or whatever she is) sits on this (whose?) grave in sadness at losing him, perhaps remembering her husband and her dog? Or does she sit on this grave in order to keep those whom she has buried – Molloy among them – *from climbing out again*? Does this image of a woman (who is, Molloy points out, perhaps a man) perched upon a grave con-vey acceptance or grief or indifference or – somehow – all of these emo-tions? Or is it charged with another sense altogether, a meaning that is far darker, unyielding?

In *Molloy*, the role of the emerging text within the story of its writer's life, his diary/fiction, not only proves ineffectual for the means the diary has consistently sought in the course of its history – self-betterment, self-revelation, or a new birth – but it operates in such a way as to deepen the writer's original situation of uncertainty: the diary's retroactive principle here works to undermine Molloy's sense of himself rather than resolve it. If the writer's 'sense of identity [remains] wrapped in a meaningless-ness often hard to penetrate' (*T*, 31), this is not simply because his 'arche-typal material' never reveals its 'inherent ideas' – a process that would allow his writing to work upon him even as he 'works out all [its] values' (Jung, 'Tavistock', 173). Molloy's 'diary' remains in a state of perpetual beginning because his writing (that is, his reaction to his extant narrative) proceeds from his reading of a self and a text that is both a work of mem-ory and imagination, and that confuses an ancient past with the moment of writing. If his 'history' is anything to go by, Molloy will set down his pencil only to pick it up again to write, 'Here's my beginning' (*T*, 8). The voice that speaks in Molloy's diary thus confounds the form's quest for a language uncontaminated by artifice or illusion because it knows that it speaks only lies. To speak in this universe *is* to lie.[14] But these are lies of a strange and compelling sort – lies that break down the barriers between truth and untruth, the allegorical and the literal, and the meaningful and the meaningless. It is through his ongoing reaction to these lies that Molloy writes on, recognizing that he 'would do better, at least no worse, to obliterate texts than to blacken margins' (*T*, 13) – that his situation is 'senseless, speechless, issueless' – *and* that his diary 'must mean something' (*T*, 8).

NARRATIVES OF ABNEGATION: *MOLLOY* II, *LA SYMPHONIE PASTORALE*, AND *LA NAUSÉE*

Molloy's resistance to the diary's master-narrative of self-discovery and salvation suggests its importance within the context of a wider division between twentieth-century fictions that stage themselves as or include diaries. On one hand, the diary has continued to attract those who hold to the view that art can be united with life – that the inner self can be named and that the diary's recuperative powers might allow the writer to achieve psychic wholeness and discover a meaningful narrative in his experience. As H. Porter Abbott has argued, those who hold to such notions, whether religious or not, share in the heritage of Tennyson, whose great verse journal *In Memoriam* (1849) provides a powerful example for those striving to 'see in part/ That all, as in some piece of art,/ Is toil cöoperant to an end'.[15] This ambition has generated a significant number of real and fictional diaries in the latter half of the twentieth century, notably by Anaïs Nin, Marion Milner, Tristine Rainer, and their followers (writers with close ties to psychotherapy who promote the journal as an 'antidote' to the 'unrelatedness, incoherence, and disintegration of the modern man')[16] as well as by a line of religious writers (in French literature: François Mauriac, Georges Bernanos, and Julien Green, among others). Against such defenders of the diary's integrative and salvific powers, others have deployed the form to critique and unravel its attendant myths: notably, Gide, Sartre, and Beauvoir.

Beckett's novel belongs in the company of the critics because *Molloy's* second narrative borrows from and critiques the strongest (that is, the religious) formation of the journal of self-discovery and salvation. In this endeavour he is preceded by the examples of Gide and Sartre. In *La Symphonie pastorale* and *La Nausée*, these writers respectively subvert models of the Puritan and the Catholic diary novel to chart the erosion of the world-picture of their protagonists, and to co-opt and pervert the Christian terminology of sin and salvation. Working against the tendencies of their respective religious models, Gide and Sartre resist granting their heroes final or redemptive insights even as they trace a narrative movement (borrowed from the Christian model) that proceeds toward the surrender of a life of illusion. Deeply sceptical of language, Gide's and Sartre's ironic fictions represent powerful counters to the religious journal's faith in a sincere or pure language of the heart, and the integral self this language might reveal.

I mentioned that Gide's experiments in the diary quickly assumed the form of an attack on the diary's claims for sincerity and specifically the way the Puritan diary harnesses this view of writing in the interests of a salvific narrative. But a closer examination of what is perhaps Gide's most remarkable Puritan diary fiction – *La Symphonie pastorale* – reveals that this book was more than a purely critical model for Beckett; it represents an example of a particular type of fiction that, following Gide, he termed the novel of 'abnegation' or 'renouncement' [*sic*] (MIC60, 23). This narrative type is a key fictional response to important choices that Beckett outlined for the modern novelist.

As with many of the insights Gide provided Beckett, the paradigm for the novel of abnegation derives from Dostoevsky, whose rejection of the European tradition's interest in the individual in society led him to focus on the self's relationship to himself or to God (D, 15; MIC60, 23). The novel of abnegation is therefore preoccupied with a different set of questions from those posed by the realist novel; with 'no social motive' driving the characters, it explores deeply individualized states and what Moran calls 'questions of a theological nature' (MIC60, 23; *T*, 167). Yet this type of novel also borrows from and inverts the Christian 'paradox of renunciation' ('[that to] save [one's] life [one must] lose it' (MIC60, 27)) by charting the loss of the individual's sense of self in a manner that requires the novelist to choose between two paths open to him in the modern age. For Gide, these paths are represented in the writings of Dostoevsky and those of his antagonist, Friedrich Nietzsche.

According to Gide, Nietzsche and Dostoevsky struggle with the same modern problem, the notion that 'God [is] a myth'. For Nietzsche, this situation leads to a terrible freedom – man now realises that he can replace God's will with his own. This recognition that 'all is lawful' entails a new imperative: man must become a superman, 'ruthless' in his act of self-willing and 'outstripping' his humanity (D, 150). But Dostoevsky follows an opposing path, seeking not to 'exalt' the hero above his fellows but to *abase* him through a process of self-dispossession. Referring to Stavrogin, the anti-hero of *The Possessed*, Gide writes:

[T]o one and the same problem Nietzsche and Dostoevsky propose different, radically opposed solutions. Nietzsche advocates the affirmation of the personality – for him it is the one possible aim in life: Dostoevsky postulates its surrender. Nietzsche presupposes the heights of achievement where Dostoevsky prophesies utter ruin (*D*, 150).

The novel of abnegation follows a Dostoevskian stripping away of its protagonist's personality and those stays that have supported the false self – the ties of family, convention, and society – to the point that its hero has 'nowhere to turn' (*D*, 145). A major theme of this type of narrative, and which follows from its attention to the erosion of illusions, is the opening of blind eyes: the reader's eyes and the protagonist's.

We exist on given premises, and readily acquire the habit of seeing the world, not so much as it actually is, but as we have been told and persuaded it is.... Yes, I firmly believe [Dostoevsky] opens our eyes to certain phenomena ... to which we have been so far blind (*D*, 107).

Beckett emphasized the links between these writers – Nietzsche, Dostoevsky, Gide – in his lectures, and as he prepared himself for what was at least his third attempt at a monograph on Gide in the summer of 1934, he read Nietzsche again, focusing on the most complete exposition of the 'superman' doctrine in *Thus Spake Zarathustra* (*BC*, 47).[17] Yet Beckett's treatment of the novel of abnegation emerges only after the war in *Molloy* II. This response comes into relief as we compare it with Gide's own attempt within a fictional diary: *La Symphonie pastorale*, a *récit* whose original title – *L'Aveugle* – highlights its connection with the trajectory for the novel sketched in *Dostoïevsky*.[18] In Gide's diary novel the theme of self-perception is exchanged for a narrative focusing on blindness, just as the form's quest for a transparent language of the heart is displaced by a governing irony. Targeting the Puritan notion of the journal as a guide to a more authentic, fuller religious life, Gide casts his fictive diary within a drama of self-betrayal that leads toward the 'surrender' and disintegration of its hero's 'personality' (*D*, 90).

A summary will suffice to sketch the outline of Gide's text. In two notebooks written by Gide's protagonist – a Protestant minister who takes a blind girl into his home – we follow the diarist's loss of himself and his world 'as [he had] been told and persuaded it is' (*D*, 107). The vision that Gide's character loses is that of a Christian universe ruled by a benevolent patriarchy, a pastoral world figured through Gide's pun on the title of Beethoven's sixth symphony. Emphasising the links between the

Shepherd who watches over the world and the Pastor who watches over his flock, the diarist insists that the universe is ruled by a beneficent God whose kindness is figured in an ordered nature: 'God's creation is harmonious, directed to the fulfilment of man's happiness, through love'; 'Only men's blindness to this Will of God leads to their unhappiness' (Brée, *Gide*, 204). Predictably, this moral harmony gives way to dissonance as the story charts the Pastor's fall from the innocence of self-delusion into a fuller, more troubling sense of self and world. Even as Gide transposes the sixth symphony's most idyllic movement – the 'scene by the bank of a stream' – as the setting for Gertrude's literal 'fall' to her death (the pun is Gide's), the Pastor is forced to confront the truth that he has hidden from himself: that '[The sixth symphony's] ineffable harmonies painted the world as it might have been, as it would be without evil and without sin'.[19] The destruction of this world-picture is figured in the fragmentation of the Pastor's family. By the end, he has exchanged a position of paternal and spiritual headship for one of weakness – notably, he is abandoned by his son. The Pastor's 'utter ruin' is ironically expressed in his final supplication: an 'Our Father' riddled with silences.

As we shall see, the contours of Gide's narrative of blindness and negative self-revelation indicate its importance as a precursor to Beckett's text. But it also seems that Gide's journal of abnegation had a direct impact on Beckett's novel, specifically with regard to the character of Moran. For the most prominent psychological need that recurs throughout Gide's *récits* reappears writ large in Moran's character, a trait Walker has described concisely as 'the insidious attraction of restraint, discipline and austerity' which for certain individuals 'are roundabout forms of self-indulgence' (Walker, *Gide*, 44). In ways that create uneasy disjunctions between their comments on their actions and their submerged motivations, both Gide's and Beckett's heroes invoke the language of religious and filial piety to mask their desire for control and dominance. And these narrators have a common aim in doing so: manipulating their adolescent sons, both of whom are named Jacques.

In Gide's text, the Pastor's rivalry with his son emerges beneath the disapproval and condescension that pervades his narrative as a whole. Despite Jacques's age (both Jacques characters are, as Moran puts it, 'on the threshold of life' (*T*, 92)), the Pastor's son must always remain bound to his father as an obedient child. The Pastor thinks of Jacques as 'My big boy', adding, in a spasm of distrust so comically exaggerated in Beckett's own narrator, 'One thinks them tender-hearted, when really they are only coaxing and wheedling one' (*PS*, 18). Like Moran, Gide's Pastor expresses his pleasure at his continued patronisation of his son into adolescence under cover of praising Jacques and maintaining higher principles: 'Jacques has one excellent point – that the simple words I often used to him as a child: "I appeal to your conscience," have always been sufficient to check him' (*PS*, 41). This particular mode is so markedly discordant with the Pastor's ostensible message (his virtue, his charity) that at times it arouses our laughter. Consider, for instance, the Pastor's account of outraged virtue at his wife's surprised reference to the blind girl as 'that'.

I shivered in my soul at this use of the word 'that', and had some difficulty in restraining a movement of indignation. As, however, I was still under the spell of *my long and peaceful meditation, I controlled myself.* Turning towards the whole party, who were standing round in a circle, I placed my hand on the blind girl's head and said *as solemnly as I could*:
   'I have brought back the lost sheep' (*PS*, 14; my emphasis).

Even if Gide's Pastor can pass himself off as the Good Shepherd to his pharisaical flock (he can't), he is not as successful with the reader. Beneath his veneer of affronted piety, we sense a self-consciously staged scene ('the whole party [was] standing round in a circle') where the Pastor can play Christ ('I … said as solemnly as I could') (*PS*, 14). This homecoming scene sets the stage for all that follows. Depicting himself as a selfless shepherd acting out higher principles, the Pastor reveals himself as a self-serving, deluded individual whose relation to himself and his family is best described through book's dominant metaphor of blindness. It is this blindness and the Pastor's continued abuse of his authority that eventually forces Jacques to flee his father and abjure his faith.

   Typically, Beckett pushes this particular ironic mode much further – until it becomes fundamentally comic. For instance, note Moran's acknowledgment that he 'sometimes' goes 'too far' when he 'checks' his Jacques:

For I was sometimes inclined to go too far when I reprimanded my son, who was consequently a little afraid of me. I myself had never been sufficiently chastened. Though I had not been spoiled either, merely neglected. Whence bad habits ingrained beyond remedy and of which even the most meticulous piety has never been able to break me. I hoped to spare my son this misfortune, by giving him a good clout from time to time, together with my reasons for doing so (*T*, 96).

In passages like these, Moran, too, claims to act out of a desire for his son's benefit – here saving him from 'bad habits'. Yet the language of appropriate and measured discipline ('when I reprimanded my son'; 'sufficiently chastened') is comically upset by the cruder idiom Moran uses to describe how the exercise of such benevolent authority actually works: the 'good' in 'giving him a good clout' does not refer to the virtue of the act but to the satisfying nature of its violence. As it turns out, Moran's defence here turns out to be an opportunity for a spot of self-pity and self-congratulation, too: unlike his lucky son, Moran has been 'neglected' (but not 'spoiled'); never fear, though, for despite this handicap Moran has dutifully striven to reform himself by 'the most meticulous piety'.

As with the Pastor, Moran's relationship to his son thus reveals a deep-seated sense of self-importance that is inextricable from a disingenuous piety.[20] Take, for example, Moran's 'libertarian view' that a certain inner attitude should prevail on the Sabbath over outward observances:

It must have been about eleven o'clock, still too early to go to church. I was savouring the day of rest, while deploring the importance attached to it, *in certain parishes*. To work, even to play on Sunday, was not of necessity reprehensible, *in my opinion*. It all depended on the state of mind of him who worked or played and on the nature of his work, of his play, *in my opinion*. I was reflecting *with satisfaction* on this, that this slightly libertarian view was gaining ground (*T*, 92–3; my emphasis).

Like the Pastor, Moran likes to think of himself as both theologically liberal and inherently orthodox in his commitment to deeper truths. But of course we are not deceived by Moran's reading of himself; here the true subject of his meditations emerges awkwardly every time he reminds us that we are hearing '[his] opinion': Moran's theology here is lower on his list of interests than his own intelligence, virtue and broad-mindedness. What he really 'savours' about the Sabbath is the way it enables him to 'deplore' the actions of others ('in certain parishes'), and of course his 'satisfaction' arises less from his contemplation of the spread of a theological perspective than from his pleasurable self-regard: 'Seeing something done which I could have done better myself, if I wished, and which I did do better whenever I put my mind to it,' he admits, 'I had the impression of discharging a function to which no form of activity could have exalted me' (*T*, 92–3). In a final ludic twist to this episode, Moran immediately violates his rather exalted view that one's state of mind is more important than going through the motions in his deceptive manoeuvrings with Ambrose ('Would I be granted the body of Christ after a pint of Wallenstein?' (*T*, 97)). In short, Gide's and Beckett's fathers are characterised by the vice they continually suspect in their sons – that of hypocrisy.

Beckett's treatment of character and narration borrows from Gide's book, but in its inversion of the Christian terminology of sin and redemption, and its positioning of the diary as form of confession in which the diarist travels toward of a form of self-recognition, it also recalls another tradition whose context is Catholic and whose most notable critic in the twentieth-century novel is Sartre. Sartre's own Catholic roots are well known, and while the diary never achieved the status among Catholics that it did among Protestants, it did have an influential following which by the thirties had generated an impressive fictional model. This model was likely suggested to Sartre by two diary novels that appeared in the 1930s: Mauriac's *Le Noeud de Vipères* (1932) and Bernanos's *Journal d'un Curé de Campagne* (1936).[21] Both novels follow the writing protagonist's journey toward the moment of death, an instant that grants a profound self-awareness to the diarist as well as the revelation of grace. These books also deploy an array of conventional diaristic motifs – the importance of the writer's room, his sensitivity, loneliness, and introversion, and the theme of the mirror – to stage the act of writing as a tool for the uncovering and salvation of the hidden man. It is therefore appropriate that writing in these books is figured as an act of confession. The penitent in this drama is initially hindered by his poor self-insight, but as he keeps writing the journal begins to take on the qualities of a silent companion – a confessor – who draws out the truth about the writer and guides him toward wisdom. It is for these reasons that the diarist begins to sense an obscure prompting which, when he recognises it, begins to whisper to him of grace:

As I sit here scribbling in the lamplight, pages no one will ever read, I get the feeling of an invisible presence which surely could not be God – rather a friend made in my image, although distinct from me, a separate entity.[22]

[The voice in this diary is] like a voice always speaking to me, never silent day or night. I suppose this voice will cease when I do? Or else – (Bernanos, 119).

What power is leading me on? Is it blind – or is it love? Perhaps it may be love ... [23]

With this whispering voice comes the eventual emergence of a new self in the diary's pages – a moment of culmination in texts that are filled with mirror imagery. The dramatic emergence of this new yet somehow familiar visage figures what Mauriac in his own diary terms 'le miracle de la pureté du coeur unie à celle du langage ... ; la double perfection de l'âme et de la parole', or more precisely, the double perfection of the soul *through* the word: the writer's revelation of his true self through a discovery of a pure language of the heart.[24] When the confession is complete, the writer realises that he has known only a distorted image of himself and of God. He now encounters himself for the first time in the light of grace:

All my life long I have been the prisoner of a passion which never really possessed me. Like a dog barking at the moon, I was held in thrall by a reflection. Fancy waking up at sixty-eight! Fancy being reborn at the very moment of my death! (Mauriac, *The Knot*, 177).

For the first time in years – perhaps for the first time ever – I seem to stand before my youth and look upon it without mistrust; I have rediscovered a forgotten face. And my youth looks back at me, forgives me (Bernanos, 309).

Beckett would have been attracted to Sartre's critique of this model for several reasons, not least because *La Nausée*'s raid on the Catholic diary novel originates in Sartre's attempt to engage the dilemma that we have seen drives both Beckett's and Gide's experiments with the novel: the irreconcilability of form with a formless reality. Perhaps the most elegant reading of Sartre's novel in English was provided by Frank Kermode, who described the 'dissonance between paradigmatic form and contingent reality' in *La Nausée*.[25] But it is H. Porter Abbott who has connected this problem with Sartre's response to Bernanos and Mauriac and the broader continuum of modern diary fiction. As Abbott points out, in Sartre's 1939 broadside 'François Mauriac and Freedom', he attacks Mauriac for the same reasons that Gide and Beckett targeted Balzac: Mauriac's 'omniscient and omnipotent' relationship to characters and plot in the novel. Robbing his characters of their freedom and subjecting them to a preordained plot, Mauriac becomes the opposite of an artist:

Like most of our writers, he has tried to ignore the fact that the theory of relativity applies in full to the universe of fiction.... M. Mauriac has put himself first. He has chosen divine omniscience and omnipotence. But novels are written *by* men and *for* men. In the eyes of God, who cuts through appearances and goes beyond them, there is no novel, no art, for art thrives on appearances. God is not an artist. Neither is M. Mauriac.[26]

Given this scrupulous attention to form, Sartre's choice of the diary reveals his willingness to highlight the problem the novel often conceals. In giving structure to his beliefs about a formless reality, he at once represents and belies them – a problem that, like Sartre's response to it, should now be familiar: Sartre stages his struggle with the novel within the fiction. Literature in *La Nausée* is the type of fraud Roquentin seeks to avoid in his own diary: 'You seem to start at the beginning.... And in fact you have begun at the end'; 'Beware of literature', he cautions himself, 'I must follow the pen, without looking for words' (*N*, 62). But if the structure of beginning, middle, and ending is always waiting to capture even the most lawless of forms ('Something begins in order to end ... it achieves significance only through its death' (*N*, 59)), the novel's use of the diary further highlights the form's underpinnings in a master-narrative that tends toward specific ends: the hero's attainment of self-insight, his achievement of a 'new birth', his discovery of a language of the heart.

It is for this reason that Sartre attacks the diary's faith in sincerity. Like his religious antecedents, Roquentin is a hero of insight, yet his discovery that existence is absurd and that there is no order to experience forces Sartre to undercut his diary's movement toward revelation. No truth about this contingent world must be allowed to attain the status of a final truth, just as Roquentin's realization of who he really is must never attain the status of a spiritual awakening: 'I want no secrets, no spiritual condition, nothing ineffable; I am neither a virgin or a priest, to play at having an inner life' (*N*, 41). Sartre capriciously kicks against the goads by borrowing the hallmarks and stages of the Christian diary novel only to invert them. Like Mauriac's and Bernanos's protagonists, Roquentin is 'fallen' and 'cast out' – but into a contingent world. On Easter, when he finishes his first diary, Roquentin sets out to be 'saved' and 'washed ... from the sin of existing'. Most poignantly, Sartre inverts the redemptive mirror imagery of the diary by allowing his hero to discover a new self which is inhuman, formless, irretrievably alien:

My gaze travels slowly and wearily down over this forehead, these cheeks: it meets nothing firm, and sinks into the sand.... What I can see is ... on the edge of the vegetable world, at the polyp level.... The eyes, nose, mouth disappear: nothing human is left (*N*, 30–1).

In sum, Sartre seeks to confound the narrative trajectory of the Catholic diary of self-discovery and salvation even as he uses it for his own ends: to explore a vision of a godless universe and a nonessential self.

Sartre's parody of the Catholic paradigm provides an important context for *Molloy*'s significance as a work of novelistic critique even as it helps to make sense of the viciously ironic energies circulating in Beckett's novel. Like Gide and Sartre, Beckett co-opts the terminology of Christian sin and redemption to plot an alternate trajectory to the one charted by the religious paradigm: the hero's descent into uncertainty and self-renunciation. So it is appropriate that with the opening of Moran's account, we find ourselves in an Eden before the fall. And although the concords of the Pastor's world-symphony are here transposed into the tones of petit-bourgeois self-content so despised by Roquentin, Moran's garden is unmistakably a place that figures a divine, patriarchal order at work in the world. Like the Pastor in his descriptions of Beethoven's scene by the bank of a stream, Moran enjoys this garden in all 'innocence and simplicity': 'Personally I just liked plants', he states, 'I even saw in them at times a superfetatory proof of the existence of God' (*T*, 100).

I offered my face to the black mass of fragrant vegetation that was mine and with which I could do as I pleased and never be gainsaid. It was full of songbirds, their heads under their wings, fearing nothing, for they knew me. My trees, my bushes, my flower-beds, my tiny lawns, I used to think I loved them. If I sometimes cut a branch, a flower, it was solely for their own good, that they might increase in strength and happiness. And I never did it without a pang. Indeed if the truth were known, I did not do it at all. I got Christy to do it (*T*, 128).

Moran as gardener once again illustrates those qualities we have seen in his interaction with his son: a self-congratulatory obsession with power ('I could do as I pleased and never be gainsaid') ostensibly wielded for the good of others ('it was solely for their own good'). As in the Pastor's creed, suffering and pain in this world are simply a part of God's loving will working for the happiness of mankind, with Christ as agent.

The terminology Beckett used for describing Moran's ensuing transformation is unambiguous: to Jr's amazement on beholding his father's altered state, Moran angrily repeats that he has had 'a fall' (*T*, 156). Moran's authority is then gradually lost, his son flees the father he now fears and distrusts, and this blind Adam, cast out of his garden, undergoes a process of negative self-revelation. In depicting his hero's journey toward the loss of his old self, Beckett drew chiefly on Sartre's parody of the Catholic diary's salvific mirror imagery, but he combined this move with a new rewriting of *Les Caves du Vatican*'s central 'mutation'. Playfully, Beckett inverts Gide's version: Anthime's transformation from a crippled, hostile atheist to a healthy and devout Catholic reappears in Beckett's text as Moran's transformation from a devout Catholic to a cripple in open defiance of his God (and the novel's chief representative of patriarchal authority in Moran's world, Youdi). In all senses, this reversal transforms Beckett's character into a fallen derelict who, like his quarry, now embodies his maker's postwar vision of 'humanity in ruins'.[27] Notably, Beckett completes this mutation through burlesquing Gide's Nietzsche:

It is natural that every important moral change, or as Nietzsche would say, transmutation of values, should be due to some physiological disturbance. With physical well-being, mental activity is in abeyance, and as long as conditions continue to be satisfactory, no change can possibly be contemplated (*D*, 153).

As with Anthime's mutation, the permanent crippling is literally an overnight affair, but Moran receives a 'taster' of what is to come as soon as the Molloy mission's disintegrative 'poison' begins to work on him ('as long as conditions continue to be satisfactory, no change can possibly be contemplated' (*D*, 153)). This anticipatory pain occurs while Moran is treating his son's upset stomach and is positioned immediately after the novel's first mirror scene. In his bathroom, Moran claims that 'the mirror, the chromium' instil 'a great peace' in him;[28] his own clearly defined identity is a consoling contrast to the vagueness that begins creeping round him after receiving his orders. Like Mauriac's diarist at the beginning of *his* project, Moran here initially perceives an illusory self. But, ironically, it is the *integrity and solidity* of Moran's reflected self that is deceiving. Moran even wonders about the cut of his moustache (a recurrent symbol, as Baker has shown, of paternal authority in Beckett)[29] until the sudden pain that shoots through his knee puts a stop to this comforting interlude and knocks him off his stool. This is Moran's first fall and as such it incites the first incident of open rebellion against patriarchal authority: Jacques Jr's mockery of his stricken father. This rebellion will of course be rehearsed by Moran himself with relation to God and Youdi, first in the Molloy country and then in the composition of his narrative.

Moran's future defiance is assured when his counterconversion/crucifixion begins in earnest: the pain strikes him repeatedly on his journey, waking him from sleep just as the Madonna's kindly violence disturbs Anthime. (Both incidents involve a sudden, stabbing pain that afflicts the characters at night and heralds a physical and spiritual transformation.) Beckett's version preserves a perfect symmetry in this regard: like Anthime, his crippling inhibits him from humbling himself before God, and specifically from bending the knee *to take communion* – 'It would have been impossible for me to kneel, for example', Moran points out (*T*, 140). Never mind, since taking communion is an experience he has already failed to enjoy in a spiritual sense after hearing of the Molloy affair. Like Gide's atheist/Catholic, Moran's 'body and soul [keep] pace' with one another (*L*, 41): 'as I made my way home [after communion]', Moran recalls, 'I felt like one who, having swallowed a pain-killer, is first astonished, then indignant, on obtaining no relief' (*T*, 102).

The physical transformation of Beckett's hero during this phase is important at the level of plot, too, since it complements his inner transformation – figured through novel's use of mirror imagery – to invert the Christian diary's trajectory toward a moment of spiritual rebirth and self-recognition. Appropriately, the crippling therefore necessitates the departure of Moran's son (anticipating the fracturing of the pastoral chain in which Moran is one link) and sets up Beckett's hero for a three-day stint in the wilds that recalls Christ's death and resurrection. (Christ, of course, emerges from his death with his divine identity vindicated; Moran undergoes the culmination of a process that will result in the disintegration of his old self.) In the novel's second and third mirror scenes, Beckett reinforces the uncertainty and anxiety that he introduced in the bathroom scene: Moran drags himself down to the stream near his camp and, after washing his face and hands, waits for his image to swim back into view: 'I watched it as it trembled towards an ever increasing likeness. Now and then a drop, falling from my face, shattered it again' (*T*, 146). This 'shattering' scene fittingly revisits the static image Moran beheld in the mirror of his ordered home just as it anticipates the even stranger visage he then encounters in his mind's eye:

And then I saw a little globe swaying up slowly from the depths, through the quiet water, smooth at first, and scarcely paler than its supporting ripples, and little by little a face, with holes for the eyes and mouth and other wounds, and nothing to show it was a man's face or a woman's face, a young face or an old face, or if its calm too was not an effect of the water trembling between it and the light (*T*, 149).

Here the conjoining of radical self-estrangement with a hovering sense of revelation invokes Sartre: as in Roquentin's vision ('The eyes, nose, mouth disappear: nothing human is left' (*N*, 30–1)), the force of this passage consists in its depiction of an individual face emerging from and returning to the indifferent, the unstable and the inorganic ('the water trembling'). And as with Roquentin, whose re-writing of the Catholic diary's conversion narrative leads him toward a vision of the unrecognisable, Moran paradoxically perceives what Bernanos calls the 'forgotten, rediscovered face' as an experience of erasure and erosion (Bernanos, 16):

And what I saw was more like a crumbling, a frenzied collapsing of all that had always protected me from all I was condemned to be. Or it was like a kind of clawing towards a light and countenance I could not name, that I had once known and long denied (*T*, 149).

The language of damnation (being 'condemned') here complements the way that Beckett deploys the Christian diary's language of illumination and recognition ('a light and countenance I could not name') against itself: this is neither the face of a man who has found salvation, nor the face of his saviour.

Following these experiences, Moran begins to inhabit his new self, a process which is staged over the requisite three days, at the end of which he has killed and buried his double and emerged defiant of his masters. Instead of enjoying the lights of the city (as in the scene with the shepherd (*T*, 160)), the new Moran feels only scorn for the 'foul little flickering lights of terrified men', and goes from dreading the punishments of Youdi to laughing at them (*T*, 162). Moran's new identity is confirmed when he uses false piety to deceive a credulous farmer on the return journey.

Moran's defiance is then reenacted at the level of the text's composition. As in the Catholic journal, writing and confession are fused in Moran's report. But the reflexive properties of the Christian model, like those of its pyschotherapeutic descendant, once again work here in reverse: through writing Moran only deepens his guilt and his sense of ignorance about what has happened. His subject (Molloy and his dealings with him) can never truly be confessed since in telling the story, he enters again into the journey where 'all is dark': 'For in describing this day I am once more he who suffered it.... And as then my thoughts would have none of Molloy, so tonight my pen. This confession has been preying on my mind for some time past. To have made it gives me no relief' (*T*, 116). 'And yet', he admits, 'I had changed and was still changing [in the act of writing]' (*T*, 154). Like Sartre's novel, Beckett's also co-opts the Catholic paradigm's treatment of the journal as a companion voice that confesses and advises the penitent. But, predictably, Moran's 'paltry scrivening', like the voice he hears, leads him only deeper into the sense that even the meagre understanding he has is 'all wrong':

> I have spoken of a voice telling me things. I was getting to know it better now, to understand what it wanted. It did not use the words that Moran had been taught when he was little.... So that at first I did not know what it wanted. But in the end I understood this language. I understood it, I understand it, all wrong perhaps. That is not what matters (*T*, 176).

What matters is that the act of writing is at one with the acts of counterconversion and defiance it relates, for to modify Molloy's saying, to *confess* in this text is to lie. This is a truth that Moran-writer embraces in the novel's most troubling and striking inversion of the Christian diary's movement toward a language of sincere self-expression: his confession that the confession itself has been false – and that delivering it has only deepened its writer's resolve to reject the masters he once feared: '[The

voice] told me to write the report.... Then I went back into the house and
wrote, It is midnight. The rain is beating on the windows. It was not midnight. It was not raining' (*T*, 176).

Molloy represents a rejection of the diaristic tradition's master-narrative
even as it figures the culmination of the 'Dostoevskian' trajectory in
Beckett's writing by parodically undermining any solution to the problem of an unknowable reality through an experience of individual
overcoming. *Molloy* II is the most complete of Beckett's narratives of
abnegation in that it presents the process by which a man (bearing several talismans of human and divine patriarchy) becomes an *under*-man
through a journey that charts the stripping away of his 'personality',
rather than his triumph. 'I was a contrivance', Moran claims before his
'fall', a slave to 'the inerrable contraption I called my life', and a devotee
of the human race's 'slow ascension towards the light' (*T*, 114, 115, 131).[30]
This journey, like those charted in Dostoevsky's stories, 'draws us away
from Rome ... far, too, from worldly codes of honour' (*D*, 132), toward
a resignation of the false self and a state of 'utter ruin'. But if Moran's
'growing resignation of being dispossessed of self' (*T*, 149) invokes Gide,
Sartre, and Dostoevsky, it also exceeds these exemplars. Beckett takes
Gide's suggestion (that this modern hero must lose his 'personality')
further than either of his antecedents: 'I have been a man long enough',
Moran acknowledges in the final page of his report, 'I shall not put up
with it any more, I shall not try any more' (*T*, 176). Unlike Dostoevsky,
who makes a 'religion of suffering' out of his characters' ordeals, or
Sartre, who founded a philosophical system based upon the absurdity
of existence, Moran's *via negativa* provides little hope of a meaningful
return to religion or philosophy (*D*, 144). Moran may, in some sense, be
'free' of the world of order and convention, but this 'freedom' remains
profoundly uncertain in its qualities. His fallen state is not a ground for
choice or autonomy. Instead, Beckett's tale generates a complex series
of parodic echoes that hinder attempts to assign value to Moran's statements. Consider his closing prayer:

And I recited the pretty quietist Pater Our Father who art no more in heaven
than on earth or in hell, I neither want nor desire that thy name be hallowed,
thou knowest best what suits thee. Etc. The middle and the end are very pretty
(*T*, 168).

Like the Pastor's final 'Our Father', Moran's prayer ironically echoes
the *Hirtengesang* (shepherd's song of thanks) in the final movement of

Beethoven's sixth symphony, even as it parodies Dostoevsky's 'quietist' answer to the problem of suffering as outlined by Gide. Moran's state, then, has none of Raskolnikov's penitence, though it does remind us of Gide's Pastor's abjection. But we must also acknowledge a defiance in Moran's sneering prayer that is fiercer and stranger than anything found in Gide's universe. In depicting Moran 'vanquishing' his way through the snow, uttering curses against God, men, animals and things, Beckett seems to comically rework the cold rage of a character from another fallen world: Dostoevsky's Stavrogin (*T*, 166).

Unlike Stavrogin or the Pastor, however, Beckett's hero has not understood his position by the close of his tale and the story fails, in an important sense, to end. Moran is still caught in an ongoing process of 'conceiving' his 'ruin' even as he composes his report (in writing, as in his homeward journey, he notes that he is proceeding 'towards what I would have called my ruin if I could have conceived what I had left to be ruined. Perhaps ... I have not done conceiving it, it takes time ... (*T*, 166)). Moran is therefore unable to achieve that '*utter* ruin' Gide praised as the point of Dostoevsky's stories, and on which their movement toward redemption turns.

His rage, his fear of the disorienting world into which he has fallen (the birdsong of Moran's garden has given way to the 'terrible battlecry' of the eagle owl that now haunts his sleepless nights (*T*, 92)), and his lingering terror of his masters' reprisals all indicate that Moran represents a negation of the options Beckett understood as answers to the problems of his historical and philosophical moment. Gide's Dostoevsky, like his Nietzsche, cannot provide a way out of a world that also precludes the preordained endings of Mauriac's and Bernanos's salvation narratives. At the end, Moran asks: 'Does this mean I am freer now than I was?' (*T*, 176). He can only answer 'I do not know' as he composes to the dictation of a voice whose origin and meaning he may never understand (*T*, 176).

CHAPTER 7

'The Art of Incarceration': Malone Dies

The situation is familiar to any reader of diary fiction – the isolated writer, his descriptions of his room, his repeated observations about the act of writing, his reflections upon his narrative – yet Malone's condition heightens the introversion and isolation we expect in the diary novel to an absurd degree even as it wildly extends and parodically hijacks the Catholic journal's final stage-setting: that of the isolated penitent's deathbed. To be sure, it is possible to hear a number of exemplars behind Beckett's 'final' dying diarist: the failing Jules Renard and the tormented Johnson of *Prayers and Meditations* come to mind. But the similarities between *Malone Dies* and *Le Noeud de Vipères* especially suggest an influence that possibly fuelled the vicious and driven qualities of Beckett's book, as well as its halting rhythms. Both diarists are 'disgusting' old men, victims of 'incurable disease', 'sunk in the [bed or chair]' where they write and where they suspect they will die (Mauriac, 18). Both write to plot vengeance upon the world and upon their descendants (in Louis's case his wife and children; in Malone's his fictional creatures), 'revelling, for the last time, in a last outpouring of misery, impotence and hate' (*T*, 198). Both ironically note their progress toward death with reference to the holy calendar. (Recall that Malone's creature, Molloy, also describes the passage of time through reflecting on the Angelus, just as Moran notes the tolling of his beloved church bells.) Both are strangers to a world that has changed almost beyond recognition (a passing airplane reminds both diarists of this fact). Both are strangers to love. For both, time is pressing; their decaying bodies force them to make haste with their revenge.

These similarities create a common tone between these books – a rhythm of submerged and spiteful violence, of sporadic desperation, and the consciousness of being dead while yet alive. And this commonality reinforces the ironies of Beckett's inversion of the Christian journey toward rebirth, prayer, eternal companionship, and illumination in Malone's striking image of being 'born into death' and his anticipation of a *void* at the end of his project never to be filled with supplication: 'Then [I will] be alone a long time, unhappy, not knowing what my prayer should be nor to whom' (*T*, 226). The voice Malone hears in his diary recalls the voice of the spirit heard by the Catholic diarist, but this companion is no comforter; his 'paraclete' is 'psittaceous' – a parrot (*T*, 250). And within the frame of Malone's diary, this parrot has the effect of ventriloquizing the voice Molloy hears at the end of his 'diary' ('Don't fret, Molloy' (*T*, 91)) and the strange tongue Moran begins to understand. Like Jackson's caged bird ('nihil in intellectu' (*T*, 218)), Malone's companion only 'stammers out' its pensum, and as with Lousse's parrot and Malone himself, it will likely be buried in its prison (*T*, 32). Similarly, Malone may, like Bernanos's priest, realize that his 'big child's exercise-book' is his 'life' (*T*, 276), but this truth will never lead him toward a meaningful self-encounter; Beckett's fictional diary holds up a world in which fraudulence, hatred, and impotence are indistinguishable from virtue, and the self reappears in the text's mirrors only to be fled or destroyed by its maker. The closest within the *Three Novels* to a paradigm of diary fiction, *Malone Dies* works most ambitiously to subvert the twin claims of the Catholic model it hijacks: that suffering has a meaningful end, and that absolution exists all around us, even in the very medium of language: 'All is grace' (Bernanos, 317). Even as his hand trails off the page – replicating the conceit Mauriac deploys in the salvific moment that closes Louis's journal – Malone indicates that the only revelation available to him is a fuller knowledge of his end *as* the end of 'it all': 'never anything there any more' (*T*, 289).

But there is of course much more to Malone's narrative than its subversion of a paradigm of the Catholic diary novel. Beckett's book joins this trajectory with an assault on at least two other 'faiths': first and most apparently, the trust in the novel's powers for cultivating and socially integrating the individual implied in realist narratives of *Bildung*; and second, a romantic faith in the potential of the imagination to transcend suffering. As I will show, Beckett's novel undermines these notions through staging Malone's failed attempt – through the act of writing – at a jailbreak from the self and its prisons.

As the Unnamable will do, Malone deprecates 'his' previous efforts and admits that they were 'failures': 'For my stories are all in vain', he admits as his dying body calls him back to himself; 'deep down I never doubted, even the days abounding in proof to the contrary, that I was still alive and breathing in and out the air of the earth' (*T*, 234). Murphy, Watt, Molloy – his stories were all too serious, too 'earnest'. Now, at the threshold of his death he tries a different tack: he will 'play'. Whatever else this 'playing' signifies, it is an attempt to momentarily evade Malone's ontological solitude through 'forgetting himself': leaving his bedridden suffering to create, observe, and finally torment and kill another. To do this, Malone needs to construct a 'convincing' narrative with enough detail to resemble a 'real life',[1] while avoiding the mistake he has always fallen into: committing himself too 'seriously' to the fiction and thereby *investing it with his own image*. He must distance this fictional being from himself or the notebook will become another mirror. Then Malone will once again fail to escape his solitude, and the story will reflect back to him another image of himself in his prison.

What tedium. And I call that playing. I wonder if I am not talking yet again about myself. Shall I be incapable, to the end, of lying on any other subject? I feel the old dark gathering, the solitude preparing, by which I know myself.... That is not how to play. Soon I shall not know where Sapo comes from, nor what he hopes.... I must simply be on my guard, reflecting on what I have said before I go on and stopping, each time disaster threatens, to look at myself as I am. That is just what I wanted to avoid. But there seems to be no other solution. After that mud-bath I shall be better able to endure a world unsullied by my presence (*T*, 189).

Yet Malone's urges here are more complex and more confused than the simple need to escape. He also intends to return to himself – to 'earnestness' – in the moments before his death to fulfil a different desire. Previous attempts to escape from himself have not succeeded, but neither have they provided him with what he thinks of as an 'authentic statement', an autographic image to counterpoint the fictional avatars that hold up to Malone their distorting mirrors. This return will also enable Malone to achieve an additional aim: to enjoy his death in a double perspective. Having positioned himself 'outside' himself (by 'show[ing] [him]self' in the same notebook he composes his fictions) Malone will be able to observe his own death and the consequent death of his surrogate 'inside' him.

My concern is not with me, but with another, far beneath me and whom I try to envy, of whose crass adventures I can now tell at last, I do not know how. Of myself I could never tell, any more than live or tell of others.... To show myself now, on the point of vanishing, at the same time as the stranger, and by the same grace, that would be no ordinary last straw. Then live, long enough to feel, behind my closed eyes, other eyes close (*T*, 196).

In spite of his best efforts, however, Malone's story becomes yet another image of the author, and in doing so thwarts the effort at 'play' and absence from the self. The story becomes another mirror and cell as Beckett carefully develops the relationship between Malone and his characters, first with Mr Saposcat, then between Malone, Mr Saposcat, and his son. For example, Mr Saposcat's dominant trait is a Malone-like 'earnestness' and, just like his maker, 'Mr Saposcat applied his mind, with the earnestness he brought to everything he did' (*T*, 188); Malone claims his 'body is what is called, unadvisedly perhaps, impotent' (*T*, 186), and the Saposcats 'drew the strength to live from the prospect of their impotence' (*T*, 187); Malone 'was born grave as others syphilitic' (*T*, 195), so Sapo's face 'was as always grave' (*T*, 206); like his maker, Sapo has never learned the 'art of thinking' and can 'make no meaning of the babel raging in his head' (*T*, 193), and so on. The irony is unmissable. Attempting to escape from dying in an act of 'play' 'unsullied by [his] presence', Malone's failure becomes plain when Sapo's father suggests that '[his son] ought to play more games' (*T*, 193).

Worst of all, even Malone's fear of creating a character in his own image is replicated at the level of the diegesis in the person of Mr Saposcat, who cannot bear to look into his son's eyes because they resemble his own. As Knowlson notes, these pale blue eyes also resemble Beckett's, and *his* father's. The scene thus assumes the doubled image of the author we have encountered in some of Gide's mirrors: Beckett inscribes his own origins in the text at the diegetic level (the relation between the Saposcats, father and son), and reflects on that act of inscription at the extradiegetic level (Malone's anxiety at the relation between his characters), a reflection that of course also mirrors Beckett's authorial relation to Malone. Malone's act of beholding the image of Mr Saposcat looking anxiously into a mirror thus becomes a doubled image of the author beholding *himself experiencing* the inevitable beholding of himself (in the mirror of his fictions): 'All hangs together', Malone admits; 'I am in chains' (*T*, 219).[2] This apparently unbreakable authorial chain of 'the long dead and the yet unborn' is also mirrored in Malone's technique of naming the father after the son, a strategy that Beckett has of course deployed with his own creatures: 'The man's name is Saposcat. Like his father's' (*T*, 187). As Beckett's own fictive characters adopt his name, so his 'final' author-figure 'en abyme', Lemuel, joins Malone, *his* creator and the arch-narrator of Beckett's own fictions circa 1947, with the Samuel on the title page.

This disturbing mirroring within the text is inextricably linked to the novel's critique of a view of literature's power to edify us, a point implicitly acknowledged by those who have considered the status of *Malone Dies* as an anti-realist fiction.[3] Such readings highlight the way Beckett's fictions reject those aims that the realist tradition has often sought for its protagonists: the eventual rewarding of virtue, the triumph of the spirit and the genius over circumstance and social integration and self-knowledge. In *Malone Dies*, this rejection is most overt in Beckett's parodic allusions to Balzac and his tradition. As Ruby Cohn was the first to point out, in the tale of Saposcat, Beckett flaunts a debt to *Louis Lambert* by assigning the peasant family the surname 'Louis' in the original French and 'Lambert' in his English translation. Her suspicion is borne out by a series of ironic allusions to and inversions of Balzac's story of troubled genius. Malone echoes Balzac's account of Louis's 'précoce intelligence' when he describes Sapo as a 'precocious boy', but while Louis is a voracious reader (by five he has read the Bible and by ten over 2,000 books) and neglects his lessons because he is formulating a complex mystic system (based on Balzac's Swedenborgian theories), Sapo is a 'dolt' who hides his books under a stone, attends his lessons with a 'blank' mind, sneers at his teachers, and smashes a classroom window (*T*, 190). Like Lambert, Sapo takes solitary walks in the countryside, but rather than the stirrings of genius that Madame de Staël recognizes in Balzac's hero, Sapo exhibits only incomprehension before nature – a stupidity confirmed by the 'murmur' in his head: 'You are a simpleton' (*T*, 191). There is a physical resemblance between the two: both heroes have abnormally large heads, but whereas Lambert's swells with transcendent theories, Sapo's teachers are 'all the more irked' by their failure to get anything into his remarkable skull (*T*, 191).

Beckett's treatment of Balzac might seem to be unsurprising on one level, yet there are problems with readings of *Malone Dies* that describe it as chiefly parodic of realism. First, it should be squarely acknowledged that if *Lambert* is Beckett's target, this book is not a good example of the kind of Naturalism Beckett took issue with in his remarks on the novel. Second, the parodic verve of Beckett's book cannot be separated from the way that it deliberately stages the *writing* of fiction in ways that Balzac's does not. Third, in parodying Balzac, Beckett targets *Lambert*'s deep investment in the broad romantic and mystic tradition that Balzac's novel draws on for its effects – a tradition holding that the inward being and the imagination can transcend the suffering of the material world, and whose trajectory is ultimately toward a reconciliation with the divine. As Beckett's counterblast to this tradition comes into closer focus, the unsettling strangeness of *Malone Dies*, and *Three Novels* more generally, gains definition – even as these books become more troubling and more resistant to our criteria for valuing the novel.

THE SADEAN IMAGINATION

Balzac's early novel draws heavily on Swedenborg's mysticism for its effects, but it is also deeply invested in formations of Romanticism that, by Balzac's time, had absorbed the figure of the mystic within a greater cult of inwardness and genius. *Louis Lambert*'s debts to this cult need little emphasis. But it is worth pointing out that when Balzac's hero describes his transcendent imagination as his greatest gift *and* curse –

The poet's sensitive nerves are perpetually shocked, and what ought to be his glory becomes his torment; his imagination is his cruellest enemy[4]

– he speaks less as a Christian mystic than as a descendant of the inward-looking and sorrowful youth who first appears in Goethe's early novel, and who numbers among his inheritors the speakers of Keats's and Leopardi's great odes as well and the poet of Baudelaire's 'L'Albatros'. Yet as Lambert acknowledges, the imagination in this tradition is not merely the cause of the subject's torment, but of his transcendent power. And if, like the writers he admires, Balzac's genius early 'acquired that acuteness which must surely characterize the intellectual perceptiveness of great poets and often bring them to the verge of madness' (Balzac, 30), for Lambert, as for Coleridge, the imagination is ultimately the wish to 'lose and find all self in God'.[5] Closely allied to this view (which unites writers as diverse as Wordsworth, Shelley, Keats, and Blake) is the belief that the imagination enriches the life of the writer in the act of creation. As Jonathan Wordsworth puts it, 'We create because, in the intensity of creation, we lead a fuller life, losing ourselves in that which we are making', a view set forth concisely by Byron in the famous lines initiating Childe Harold's third pilgrimage:[6]

> 'Tis to create, and in creating live
> A being more intense, that we endow
> With form our fancy, gaining as we give
> The life we imagine[7]

It hardly needs to be said that Beckett's novel sets itself against this formation of the romantic imagination as transcendent of suffering, allied to the wish to encounter the divine, and as a form of experiencing a more intense and fuller life through the act of creation. But to understand how exactly Beckett counters this myth, it is necessary to turn to the relation between violence and writing in Beckett's text. For while it is likely that Beckett draws on Zola's story of incest and domestic brutality in *La Terre* for some of his themes (an influence posited by James Acheson), in a manner wholly alien to Zola the sadism in Malone's stories goes beyond the book's actual and implied killings, rapes, incarcerations, and beatings to inextricably link violence with the act of *fictional composition*.[8] At the level of the writer writing, then, *Malone Dies* does not reject that most enduring of romantic legacies – that of the imagination – so much as draw on a different model or precursor of it, a model in which the act of writing is understood as a form of *perpetual negation*.

Beckett found this model in the work of the Marquis de Sade, a writer with whom he had long been acquainted. Censorship prohibited Beckett from reading Sade in the early thirties, but he was acquainted with him through other sources at this time; for example, he drew on Mario Praz's account of 'The Divine Marquis' in *The Romantic Agony* to make glancing allusions to *Justine* and *Juliette* in *Dream* and to *Les 120 Journées de Sodome* in 'A Wet Night'.[9] But by 1934 Beckett had read enough of the real thing to take issue with it; in a letter to McGreevy in September he criticizes Sade's fury at the 'impossibilité d'outrager la nature' as 'mièvre' and at one with the anthropomorphizing tendencies of an earlier age (SB to TM, 9/8/34, *LSB 1*, 221). By 1938, Beckett's enthusiasm for Sade is evident when he mentions to George Reavey that he 'should like very much to do [a translation of *Les 120 Journées de Sodome* for Jack Kahane]', a book he calls 'one of the capital works of the 18th century' (SB to TM, 20/2/38, *LSB 1*, 604). In any event, Beckett backed out of the translation, worried about 'what effect it [would have] on [his] lit[erary] situation in England or how it might prejudice future publications of [his] own there' (SB to TM, 20/2/38, *LSB 1*, 604), but by this time he had read at least volumes 1 and 3 of Maurice Heine's three-volume edition of *Sodome*. In a letter to McGreevy he enthusiastically speaks of the work's demanding form: 'You would loathe it', he acknowledges to his Catholic friend, but baits him with the following: 'It fills me with a kind of metaphysical ecstasy'; 'The composition is extraordinary, as rigorous as Dante's' (SB to TM, 21/2/38, *LSB 1*, 607).

Letters to Georges Duthuit indicate Beckett was rereading Sade intensively and making translations from Maurice Blanchot's essay *Lautréamont et Sade* (1949) in late 1950 and early 1951. 'There are some very good things in [Blanchot's essay]', he wrote, 'A few tremendous quotations that I did not know, in the style of the one I knocked up for you from the 120 Days'; 'Hard to single out one passage to translate, but I managed to and started on it'. He went on to discuss his further reading around the subject, suggesting that he 'could spice things up by putting in a few extracts from Klossowski (*Sade mon Prochain*) and Maurice Heine (forward to the *Dialogue entre un Prêtre et un Moribund*)'.[10] In January of 1951, he again wrote to Duthuit, mentioning that he had translated four letters by Sade ('one of them extremely beautiful'), and referring to *La Philosophie dans le Boudoir* (SB to GD, ?8/1/51, *LSB 2*, 222). A few days later he discussed his reading of Maurice Heine's *Le Marquis de Sade* (1950), a text that posits Sade as a key founder of the *roman noir* or Gothic novel (SB to GD, ?10/1/51, *LSB 2*, 224). It was also around this time that Beckett 'finished the Blanchot [translation]', pointing out that 'Blanchot is by far the most intelligent' of Sade's interpreters (SB to GD, 12/1/51, *LSB 2*, 224–25). In early January of 1952, he was still thinking about Sade, referring to 'the sun passage' in *Les 120 Journées* (likely a reference to a passage at the end of the sixth day or at the end of the twenty-fourth day) (SB to GD, 3/1/52, *LSB 2*, 311).[11]

It is not difficult to surmise why Sade's work was of interest to Beckett at this time. Most apparently, Sade is a writer for whom the act of composition is inextricable from a state of solitary incarceration. And in an important way, the circumstances that Sade suffered in the Bastille, Conciergerie, the Charenton asylum, and his other prisons were only the most obvious dimension of this condition. As Blanchot argues in his 1949 essay, Sade's system should be understood as the 'primary effect of absolute solitude' which exists from birth:

Nature wills that we be born alone, there is no real contact or relationship possible between one person and another. The only rule of conduct for me to follow, therefore, is to prefer whatever affects me pleasurably and, conversely, to hold as naught anything which, as a result of my preferences, may cause harm to others. The greatest pain inflicted on others is of less account than my own pleasure.[12]

The foundations of this system would have resonated with a Beckett who had long been a disciple of Leopardi and Leibniz. But as Blanchot indicates, solipsism in Sade's thinking does not translate into romantic despair or philosophical theory but into *power* – the right of the Sadean hero 'to be himself and to enjoy himself … is the primary meaning of his solitude' (Blanchot, 52). And this power, which allows the Sadean hero to destroy his victims with impunity, is most fully realised not in life but in the world of imagination, and specifically in the act of *writing*. This is why, when Clairwill laments the limitations of her powers for destruction ('What I should like to find is a crime the effects of which would be perpetual, even when I myself do not act

[,] a disturbance so formal that even after my death its effects would still be felt'), Juliette counsels, 'Try your hand at moral crime, the kind one commits in writing.'[13] Likewise Belmore to Sade's most infamous heroine:

> Oh, Juliette, how delicious are the pleasures of the imagination.... All the earth is ours in these enchanted moments; not a single creature resists us ... we devastate the planet ... and repeople it with new objects, and immolate these in their turn; the means to every crime is ours, we commit them all; we multiply the horror an hundredfold (Sade, *Juliette*, 522).

In the Sadean imagination Beckett found the necessary counter to the romantic myth of genius described in Lambert's ascent toward the 'purer forms' and the 'angels'. For it is through a similarly radical, ascetic solitude that Sadean man revels in those imaginative powers through which he seeks to more fully realise his ends: vengeance upon mankind and his greatest delusion, God. This vengeance marks the Marquis as the transmitter of a particular legacy which obtains an important inheritor in the Beckett of *Three Novels*:

> the idea that God smites equally the just and the unjust, and perhaps the former rather than the latter; ... that pain and death are everywhere in Nature, that crime is Nature's law; and the conception of God as a Being of supreme wickedness ('the supreme evil, God'), and the revolt of men against the divinity he disowns (Praz, 234).

Both the figure of the writer alone in his room and the notion of a consciousness composing a world and threatening it with dissolution had preoccupied Beckett for some time. But while his previous fictions had hinted at an antagonistic and even sadistic impulse at work in the 'novelist', in *Malone Dies* the disturbing relation between such urges and the creative enterprise reach their fullest expression yet. For although Malone's aims are multiple and contradictory (to know himself better, to console himself in the face of death, to escape himself, to return to himself in a moment of earnestness), the negative force of his writing becomes increasingly important until his project could be summed up as: Retribution. 'Let me say before I go any further', Malone writes at the outset, 'that I forgive no one'; 'Now it is the present I must establish, before I am avenged' (*T*, 180; 184). In the manner of Clairwill's fantasy of a legacy of death beyond death, this strange vengeance is wreaked on Malone's imaginative world and specifically Saposcat/Macmann. 'All I ask', Malone admits, interrupting the Sapo tale, is to know, before I abandon him whose life has so well begun, that my death and mine alone prevents him from moving on, from winning, losing, joying, suffering, rotting and dying, and even had I lived he would have waited, before he died, for his body to be dead. That is what you might call taking a reef in your sails (*T*, 198).

The thought here is complex: Malone transports himself to the moment of his death (the moment 'before I abandon [Sapo]') and then imagines projecting his power beyond that moment through inhabiting the imagination of his creature. In this fantasy, Sapo's dawning knowledge that he is utterly subject to Malone leads him to the realization that either Malone's death will signal his abortion ('prevent[ing] him from moving on', even to his own death), or Malone's life will mean that Sapo will eventually long for death (waiting 'for his body to be dead'). In either scenario, Sapo will serve his master's need for a subtle and, in its own terms total, experience of power and reprisal.

But of course Sapo will not have been the first victim. This 'man alone' has already butchered a series of individuals before him:

But let us get on with ... my demise.... Then it will be all over with the Murphys, Merciers, Molloys, and Malones.... How many have I killed, hitting them on the head or setting fire to them? ... A sudden wish, I have a sudden wish to see, as sometimes in the old days, something, anything, no matter what, something I could not have imagined. There was the old butler too, in London I think, there's London again, I cut his throat with his razor, that makes five. It seems to me he had a name. Yes, what I need now is a touch of the unimaginable ... (*T*, 237).

Here Malone does not recount the variously tortured ends of Beckett's old heroes for the sake of reassuring himself about the approaching end of a job well done ('Then it will be all over'); he recalls these entertaining spectacles to work himself into a state of almost breathless excitement as he turns to ponder new thrills ('A sudden wish, I have a sudden wish to see ...'). Recapturing his previous fictions this way, Beckett also alters their meaning: the motivation behind the strange deaths of Murphy and the old gentleman, which already suggested a sadistic role for the 'novelist' of that book (chance has no part in Malone's fictional worlds, either), is now nakedly revealed to be an exhausted version of the Sadean lust for new stimulation: a quality which Malone, in this most unromantic of novels, fittingly describes as the 'unimaginable'.

'The end of a life', Malone points out, 'is always vivifying', but it is not only the killing that excites him (*T*, 212). In several portions of the book that indicate its connections to the Gothic novel's origins in Sadean fantasy, Malone reveals that he also enjoys humiliating and torturing the figures conjured by his imagination. For instance, when he speaks of 'playing' with 'a hunchback' who 'came running, proud as punch of his fine hunch', Malone gloats that 'It did not occur to him that I might have to ask him to undress' (*T*, 180). And in one remarkable instance which has been virtually ignored by Beckett's readers, Malone fantasizes about strangling, imprisoning, and molesting a little girl from the crowd of 'All the people [he has] ever caught a glimpse of':

> I might be able to catch one, a little girl for example, and half strangle her, three quarters, until she promises to give me my stick, give me my soup, empty my pots, kiss me, fondle me, smile to me, give me my hat, stay with me, follow the hearse weeping into her handkerchief, that would be nice. I'm such a good man, at bottom, such a good man, how is it nobody ever noticed that? A little girl would be into my barrow, she would undress before me, sleep beside me, have nobody but me, I would jam the bed against the door to prevent her running away, but then she would throw herself out of the window … (*T*, 274).

Malone's pleasure in his imagined power over another ('half strangle her, three quarters'; 'I would jam the bed against the door') is integral to this fantasy, as is the notion that he would add a final, suitably perverse excitement to his descent into the grave ('A little girl would be into my barrow'). The image of the moribund Malone being 'fondled' by the girl is particularly disturbing, but it is nevertheless impossible to read this passage without recognizing the outrageous comic energy that informs even its darkest impulses. The notion of eliciting a 'promise' from the girl to 'follow the hearse weeping into her handkerchief' as if she were a Dickensian innocent mourning a beloved relative is particularly ludic, as is Malone's pretence that he is blissfully unaware of the absurdity of his daydream and his role within it: 'I'm such a good man, at bottom, such a good man …'. As so often in *Watt*, there is a pleasure here in observing a character getting carried away with his own private reasoning (which becomes ever more removed from reality) even as we are brought up short by the image of the girl jumping out of the window. As this image suggests, though, *Malone*'s comedy only adds to the disquieting power of the text, for it draws us into an uneasy collusion with the writer through what Blanchot, writing of Sade, terms 'a strange humour' wrung by a 'style [which] reveals an icy joviality and, in its extravagance, a kind of cold innocence' (Blanchot, 70). 'But', we may well ask with Molloy, 'what business has innocence here? What relation to the … spirits of darkness?' (*T*, 10). As with Molloy's 'diary' ('It's not clear' (*T*, 10)), we are not enlightened through Malone's self-inscriptions, only confounded by his text's capacity to edge us toward uncomfortable and incommensurate ways of feeling. The rhapsode ends appropriately, with a parody of enduring love. The girl grows to adore Malone and after his death dutifully 'put[s] a plug in [his] arse-hole'. In indulging himself with this final vision, Beckett's overheated hero at last feels he has gone too far: 'Easy, Malone, take it easy, you old whore' (*T,* 275).

If, like Sade's, Malone's writing is inseparable from his desire for vengeance, this drive is itself Sadean in its targets, centring on mankind and his illusions, chief among which is 'the consolations of religion' (*T,* 240). The figure who stands in as Malone's 'old debtor' in this regard is of course his hero, whose torments begin in earnest in the second part of the story where he appears as the aged derelict named Macmann who is still 'addicted' to the 'chimera' of divine punishment (*T,* 240). Lying cruciform in the rain, this 'son of man's' identity assumes its double meaning as Macmann's author wreaks his vengeance on everyman *and* his greatest folly, thereby inscribing Sade's signature at the heart of Beckett's text: An animus that cannot find its target in life assumes – within the imagination – the demiurgic powers of the creator it denies.

The living. They were always more than I could bear, all, no, I don't mean that, but groaning with tedium I watched them come and go, then I killed them.... I stop everything and wait. Sapo stands on one leg, motionless, his strange eyes closed. The turmoil of the day freezes in a thousand absurd postures. The little cloud drifting before their glorious sun will darken the earth as long as I please (*T,* 194).

Here Beckett's narrator revisits the fascination with tedium, solitude, and sadistic, absolute power that began to emerge in *Mercier and Camier,* joining these elements with the (virtually) dead writer's renewed antagonism against 'the living': *Mercier*'s hated sun, like the 'novelist's' 'multitudinous brethren' on earth, need no longer be tolerated since Malone can blot them out as easily as he stills the globe or freezes his characters in mid-stride. This passage suggests that *Malone Dies* is an anti-novel in rather specific sense: it is a book that subjects its protagonist to serial cruelty at the hands of an 'all-unfuckable' power (*MC,* 26). In doing so, Beckett's book joins forces with Sade's attack on what Richardson termed 'virtue rewarded' in the novel (Sapo/Macmann's idiocy is innocuous if not innocent) and the form's origins in narratives of *Bildung* as well as narratives of confession – both of which call for a meaningful progression in the life of an individual toward an awakening under the hand of chance or providence. As in Sade's texts, this parodic rejection of virtue and its allies is most fully realized in *Malone Dies* through a grotesque and farcical eroticism that provokes both horror and laughter. This aspect of Beckett's novel needs little emphasis, but it is worth pointing out that the lover/'keeper' Malone chooses for his incarcerated hero could have been drawn directly from *Les 120 Journées de Sodome*. Consider, for example, Sade's description of Thérèse, one of the castle's aged 'ladies in waiting'.

Thérèse was sixty-two; she was tall, thin, looked like a skeleton, not a hair was left on her head, not a tooth in her mouth, and from this opening in her body she exhaled an odour capable of flooring any bystander. Her ass was peppered with wounds, and her buttocks were so prodigiously slack one could have rolled the skin around a walking stick; the hole in this splendid ass resembled the crater of a volcano what for width, and for aroma the pit of a privy.... She had one twisted arm and limped in one leg.[14]

In *Sodome*, the prisoners of the castle are forbidden to relieve themselves anywhere but in the chapel. Malone's story goes one better in its mingling of the sacred and the profane: the novel's only crucifixes are ornaments on and *in* the body of his fearsome Moll:

The thin yellow arms contorted by some kind of bone deformation, the lips so broad and thick that they seemed to devour half the face, were at first sight her most revolting features. She wore by way of earrings two long ivory crucifixes which swayed wildly at the least movement of her head (*T,* 265).

This description, which joins the body of an antic corpse with that of a sufferer of advanced Paget's disease, has few rivals in the literature of the grotesque. Moll as nurse/lover presents a wild physical parody of the nurturing image of the Madonna: these lips, rather than soothing or praying 'devour'; the arms are not fit to cradle or to sustain but terrify; the crucifixes speak only of death and in their crazed movement, madness. The figure of Christ which completes the crucifixion scene that is Moll's face is of course in her mouth, 'between' the two thieve-earrings, 'a long yellow canine bared to the roots and carved, with the drill probably, to represent the celebrated sacrifice' (*T,* 265). Macmann enjoys letting his tongue rove over this 'rotten' fang in their love play, and this weird eroticism provides one final opportunity for Beckett to target *Louis Lambert* and its metaphysical underpinnings. Recall that Lambert sends his beloved, Mlle de Villenoix, several letters in which he describes his affections in terms drawn from his readings in the mystics: 'This rapture', he writes 'has made me apprehend the eternal contemplation in which … spirits abide in the presence of God' (Balzac, *Louis*, 83). Lambert also speaks of his beloved's face as 'the image of [her] soul' (Balzac, *Louis*, 83). Such visions of 'l'amour pur' reappear distorted in Malone's mirror when Macmann writes a series of poems to his mistress in which 'Love' guides 'Sucky'/ 'Hairy' 'To the lifelong promised land/Of the nearest cemetery' (*T*, 264). When it is already 'too late' to do him any good, Macmann still 'had time to compose ten or twelve more or less in this vein, all remarkable for their exaltation of love regarded as a kind of legal glue, a conception frequently to be met with in mystic texts' (*T*, 264).

The ending of *Malone Dies* has been troublesome for Beckett's readers in its combination of violence and detachment, but here too it follows in Sade's tradition. Malone initiates the final phase of his tale with Moll's murder ('Moll. I'm going to kill her' (*T*, 265)) and in a vicious parody of morning sickness, Moll loses her hair and crucifix-tooth and quickly perishes amid convulsions. The immediate introduction of Lemuel, a (possibly) 'Aryan' sadist, then considerably darkens the atmosphere of the book. How far one is meant to identify Malone with this final hero is an issue the novel does not resolve, but as with Sapo, a series of parallels are cultivated between the 'author' and his creature. Most notably, Lemuel is the guardian of a cast of characters who now reappear from Beckett's past fictions for a curtain call: Murphy, Watt, Moran, Molloy, and Macmann. And Lemuel's bloodstained hatchet of course blurs into the 'stick' or 'pencil' that Malone wields as *his* murder weapon. These and other connections make the book's final scenes more difficult to understand without acknowledging Sade as an influence, for it is here that Malone most openly takes revenge on 'the consolations of religion' and 'the society of nice people' in a way that does not, I think, permit the type of ethical recuperation Beckett's readers have often sought for it. Some may feel that Lady Pedal's stupidity and callous piety warrant a broken hip and her abandonment on the island. But the killing of Maurice and Ernest is more difficult to rationalize, especially because it is conducted in a manner imitative of the strangely detached and serial nature of Sadean violence – a violence that makes no discriminations as it has no ultimate end but *more violence*.

When [Lady Pedal] had disappeared Lemuel released Macmann, went up behind Maurice who was sitting on a stone filling his pipe and killed him with the hatchet. We're getting on, getting on. The youth and the giant took no notice.... A little later Ernest came back to fetch them. Going to meet him Lemuel killed him in his turn, in the same way as the other (*T*, 288).

Malone's matter-of-fact, even bored tone here ('We're getting on'), like his description of these 'decent, quiet, harmless men, brothers-in-law into the bargain' not only emphasises the innocuous normalcy of his victims and the shocking nature of the brutality enacted upon them, but it positions them as mere numbers – abstractions – within an endless series: just as one man follows the other to death 'in his turn, in the same way', 'there are billions of such brutes' still living (*T*, 288). 'So long as it is what is called a living being you can't go wrong, you have the guilty one' (*T*, 260), Malone points out – a truth which hints that although his story may end with an echo of Goethe's deathbed plea for 'light', any recollection of Enlightenment-man in this novel is countered by an even more powerful impulse toward a realm in which the 'dark triumph[s]' (*T*, 203). In this mirror world, the ideals of the age of Enlightenment (like those of the age of Romanticism) appear only to be inverted: as Blanchot puts it in his summary of Sade's philosophy, 'To declare that all men are equal is [for Sade] equivalent to saying that no one is worth more than any other, all are interchangeable, each is only a unit, a cipher in an infinite progression' (Blanchot, 41). In such a world the premise of equality means that members of the herd, like Big Lambert's pigs, are all fundamentally alike *in their suitability for destruction*.

'Lemuel is in charge', we read as we near the end: 'he raises his hatchet on which the blood will never dry but not', Malone interjects – the violent tenor of the text shifting suddenly – 'to hit anyone' (*T*, 289). Like *Molloy*, this novel cannot resolve itself, not least because, as Beckett claimed of Gide's modern 'psychological' works, it sets out to explore a mind that cannot 'become unified' (Daiken). We are reminded that this world – its dark laughter, strange violence, and vengeance – is 'only' such stuff as dreams are made on. But still we are left wondering: if Lemuel does not raise this hatchet (or pencil or stick or light) in aggression, how should we interpret this final gesture? Is it one of defiance or triumph or valediction? And what comfort in the thought that the cost of an end to violence in this world is this world's end?

Conclusion: Beckett and the Modern Novel

The question of Beckett's stature in twentieth-century literature is no longer in question. But as David Pattie recently pointed out,

the nature of his contribution is a matter of debate. He is variously the last of the humanists, portraying the individual soul surviving in the utmost extremity; the last of the modernists, in whose work the experimental urges of the inter-war years reach their endpoint; one of the first post-modernists, pulling apart the underlying mechanisms of a literary and dramatic text; a philosopher, in whose work the history of Western thought can be discerned; an anti-rationalist, perhaps even a mystic; and so on, and so on.... And yet there is no consensus (Pattie, 226–7).

In this sense, for academics at least, Beckett is perhaps 'a uniquely frustrating figure' (Pattie, 227). This difficulty with categorising Beckett may be one of the more salient reminders that the terms that we often deploy to segment literature in the twentieth-century have a limited utility. But it is also highlights the fact that Beckett placed a principle of uncertainty at the very heart of his artistic theory and practice. In this study, I have argued that this principle of uncertainty itself has a genealogy within the novel.

Behind Beckett's novels of the thirties and forties there is an insistent question concerning the limits of the form: How, Beckett asks, can one explore an ultimately unknowable reality, and especially the disunified reality of the inner self, by means of a literary construct that is 'linear' and 'teleological', and was assigned (by its masters in the nineteenth century and by the complacent novelists and critics of Beckett's own age) the task of transcribing the vicissitudes of an external, social world?

I have argued that, for Beckett, this question is inseparable from a European tradition of the novel that obtains a major contributor in the work of Gide – whose fictions cannot be reconciled with any theory of art that overcomes the dilemma of representation. Gide's works do not present themselves as an aesthetic rendering of a sociohistorical reality

(*La comédie humaine*), or reveal new unities in individual experience via the revelatory power of art (*À la recherche du temps perdu*), or assume that a principle of identification is possible between word and world (*Finnegans Wake*). They complicate these formulations of the novel's means and ends because of his conviction that art and reality are fundamentally *irreconcilable* – that reality is unknowable in itself, and art is always artifice. In Gide's hands, the novel's function becomes to disturb and critique received forms, even as the novel exposes its own author and interrogates the imposed order of his means: 'The received notion of artistic perfection gives way to the search for the aesthetic structure which encompasses – indeed cultivates – uncertainty, and reveals holes in the fabric of conventional constructions' (Walker, *Gide*, 180).

Beckett's novels and theory from 1930 to 1950 extend this conceptualisation of the writer's task. This continuity becomes immediately apparent when we examine Beckett's argument in his 1930 lectures on Gide and the novel ('Artistic statement – extractive of essential real. Reality – unavailable' (MIC60, 105)), or his 1934 recognition of a 'rupture of the lines of communication' between subject and object (*Dis*, 70). And instead of fading away, this preoccupation with an incommunicable reality reappears at the heart of *Three Dialogues* in 'B.'s' 1949 call for an art that recognises the 'increasing anxiety of the relation' between the artist's 'means' and his 'aliment' – an art that, rather than exploring 'expressive possibilities', or 'enlarging its repertory' submits 'wholly to the incoercible absence of relation, in the absence of terms, or ... in the presence of unavailable terms' (*PTD*, 121, 120, 124).

Unlike many of Gide's other heirs (for example, Claude Simon), Beckett's dilemma is never primarily the philosopher's question: 'comment savoir?' It is always the writer's question: 'comment dire?' And whether or not he adhered to any of the faiths or nihilisms his readers have often claimed for him, Beckett's writing surely explores the ramifications of a loss of confidence (deeper and more searching than Gide's own) in *literature* as it had been conceived – a crisis that begins as his refusal to affirm his faith, as it were, in the novel.

It is therefore unsurprising that Beckett's writing challenges those notions of art he inherited from Proust and Schopenhauer, writers who value the literary as a potent if transitory consolation for suffering. The rediscovery of the self in Beckett's novels is not, as he stated of Proust's writing, a 'solution'; it is the rediscovery of the walls that make up the prison house of language. Equally, Beckett rejects the Romantic notion that the artwork refines and illuminates the inner self of the 'pure Ideal man, whose unchanging oneness it is the great task of [the self's] being, in all its changes, to correspond' (Schiller, 17). These are not narratives of self-cultivation in any immediately recognisable manner. Nor does a book like *Malone Dies*, in its intense focus on the writer and his story, aim to portray a morally expansive or ideologically instructive social and economic world. For all these reasons, but mainly for the last, Beckett has often been brought before the court of Realism on the charge of 'solipsistic nihilism'.

One of the most prevalent and long-standing models for valuing the novel in English has chosen to target Beckett in this way because of the challenge his work poses to what Martha Nussbaum has called 'the project'. 'The project' seeks to uncover how literature assists us (through a composed and sensible reflection upon the emotional 'lessons' of the text) in arriving at 'essential truths about human life' and answers to the question 'How should one live?'[1] By this standard, Beckett's novels would seem to fail. For as we reflect upon their emotional movement (and the 'ideas' that Nussbaum argues undergird such feelings in fictions) they do not provide a suitably plural or necessarily ethical image of the world. Unlike say, George Eliot's novels, Beckett's texts exhibit 'an absence of human diversity' and 'an absence of human *activity* that seems foreign to our experience of emotional development, even at the cultural and social level' (Nussbaum, 250). This is why such readers cannot, above all, accept the strange way that the Beckettian voice echoes *within* its stories:

One thing that becomes very clear, as we read these novels, is that we are hearing, in the end, but a single human voice [and] Beckett emphasises this fact, by identifying Moran with the author of his other novels. And the solipsism of this voice's sense of life is so total that we get no sense of the distinctive shape of any other lives in this world (Nussbaum, 250).

It should now be clear that Beckett's own project originates as a critique of such narratives of 'emotional development ... at the cultural and social level' (Nussbaum, 250) by (comically) undermining the claims of 'the project's' ally, social realism. Chiefly, Beckett interrogates Realism's claim to represent the world, and therefore its insistence, finally, on the priority of a world 'common to all' (Nussbaum, 252). It is not surprising that Beckett's critics have often allied themselves with those philosophical traditions concerned with universality, since they often require the novel to function as a pedagogic tool through which we consider the individual's actions with relation to the acts of all others. But as Philip Fisher has recently reminded us, the literary will always elude those who seek to read it through such criteria because it will always resist the implicit claims of such imperatives: that is, the voice that speaks in the novel always *speaks out* against the notion that it is not exceptional; it always resists the dictates of systems that require it to will for the whole and for all time: 'in literature universality and reciprocity are structurally excluded'.[2] Lest we forget, even those novels championed by readers who call for the depiction of a 'common world' are themselves founded upon a collocation of what are always *individual* wills:

Novels … are accounts of my world or of someone's world, and not of the world per se. When Tolstoy and George Eliot multiply the positions by using several centres, and when they alternate between them, they only underline the narrative fact that any larger narrative world is made up of Lydgate's world plus Fred Vincy's plus Casaubon's, plus Dorothea Brooke's, *but only one at a time* (Fisher, 251; my emphasis).

Beckett's novels require us to take this point further. They work to remind us that, no matter how politically committed or acceptably diverse the novel's worlds may appear, its realms and voices always proceed from and are always mimed by but a single voice. This voice, in the very act of utterance, sets itself apart and asserts its radical singularity even as it 'devis[es] it all for company'.[3]

There is another, related reason that readers like Nussbaum object to Beckett's novels. The startling laughter, rage, terror, vulgarity, sadism – and perhaps most damningly, the 'deeply religious sensibility' – that pervade Beckett's fictions offend those who cherish the novel for its guidance into a universe whose crowning virtues are the cultivation of moral reflection, an enlarged sense of 'the group and its history' and the development of sympathy (Nussbaum, 251–2). Yet the unsettling comic power of *Three Novels* brings considerable pressure to bear on criteria for valuing the novel chiefly as a sentimental education or as a representation of a world in general. What types of novels are *Three Novels*? The project and its followers cannot say. *Molloy* does not fit into the categories those like Nussbaum's critic and ally, Jenefer Robinson, have set in their accounts of a moral realism as the only 'serious' fiction:

Not all novels invite the kind of serious, sustained emotional attention I am about to discuss. There are bad novels that try to teach us something and fail, there are genre novels that merely aim to entertain, and there are novels that are more like intellectual puzzles or games.[4]

If we are not to dismiss them, *Three Novels* necessitate a more prob-lematic set of criteria for valuing the novel. Such criteria would need to be based in literature's capacity for (at times deeply disturbing) pas-sages of complex and intense feeling, and the way in which such feelings may not be recuperable into a form of (common) knowledge. Through such a model we might come to see the novel as what Fisher has called '[a system] for the articulation of a personal world, along with that world's claim to be prior to, and, finally, more essential than any shared, com-mon world or "mere world"' (Fisher, 252). For the states that Beckett's fictions explore require 'an absence of diversity' by definition. And that is why they are rarely encountered, or appear in a significantly diminished form, in those works considered serious by readers who desire a vision of socializing plurality from the novel. An unremitting state of profound isolation, a sense of fear passing swiftly into terror, radical uncertainty – these intense states in Beckett's universe unfold with breathtaking rapid-ity into a laughter that is at once defiant, vengeful, exhilarated, and even tinged with a strange joy. Such books, in their fierce ambivalence, explore an emotional terrain where words like 'ironic' and 'inconclusive' simply fail when held up to the charged density of the Beckettian text – its cap-acity to harness the potentially stalling power of doubt in the interests of an on-wardness without name.

Beckett ostensibly claimed to J. D. O'Hara that those who find 'positive values' in his work discover something that he does not.[5] And this study, for its part, has not found such values endorsed or embodied in his fic-tion as they often have been in the novel's history. It also appears that, as Coetzee has argued, fiction for Beckett 'is the only subject of fiction' and 'therefore, fictions are closed systems, prisons' (Coetzee, 'The Comedy', 38). But if this account of Beckett's writing affirms that his novels resist the 'daydream gratification of fiction' with their increasing attention to 'the annihilation of illusion', it also means that these fictions – in a way that signals their particular importance – continually interrogate how and why we value the literary itself (Coetzee, 'Samuel Beckett', 49). Beckett's novels pose a thorny problem for those who require an endorsement of (or education in) values in literature as a prerequisite for valuing the literary. But this does not mean that the surprising and difficult experience of reading his novels is *itself* without value. This is not least because, as I have hinted above, these books work to test the codes and systems we bring to the act of reading. In doing so, *Three Novels* realise Beckett's ambitions for an artwork that remains foreign and irretrievably other (étranger) to those who would recuperate its 'nonsense' within any terms common to all (*Dis*, 118).

The discomforting, sceptical power of Beckett's fiction is brought to one culmination in *The Unnamable*. Continually highlighting its status as a work of fiction, this novel is remorselessly involved with the strange capacity of highly individualized feeling in the literary text to work against systems that might impose their problems and solutions on that text. This is a minimal work – Beckett's speaker is a disembodied voice imprisoned within a grey void – but it is capable of sounding the reaches of horror as well as delight. Consider one passage in which the Unnamable imagines a circle of unseen tormentors who observe him at the bottom of a furnace, forcing him to scream:

for them it's the end, for me the beginning, my end begins, they stop to listen to my screams, they'll never stop again, yes, they'll stop, my screams will stop, from time to time, I'll stop screaming, to listen and hear if anyone is answering, to look and see if anyone is coming, then go, close my eyes and go, screaming, to scream elsewhere (*T*, 387).

At first, this passage appears to give voice to the terror of potentially endless terror. But notice the way that the self-consciousness in the Unnamable's act of telling this story also inflects the text's emotional current in curious ways that do not mitigate that feeling but ramify it into others. The imagery here starts off as infernal, but then, as the the Unnamable changes his mind about never stopping his screams ('yes, they'll stop') and the strangely quotidian 'from time to time' enters ('What tenderness in these little words', Molloy says of this phrase, 'what savagery' (*T*, 83)), his imaginary screaming begins to suggest something like a *performance* – like the crying of a naughty child who runs about looking for an audience for his tantrum. With the next sentence, the current of Beckett's text has reversed from that of terror to laughter: the Unnamable admits that he has no mouth to scream *with*. A situation loaded with as much anguish (for is it not terrible to be denied the ability to scream because one has no mouth?) as comic potential then gives rise to a wholly unexpected feeling: the Unnamable's embarrassment. Defensively acknowledging his strange deficiency with the irascibility of Dostoevsky's Underground Man (but there it is.... I have no mouth, and what about it' (*T*, 388)) the Unnamable *defiantly* enters into a wildly satiric fantasy that refigures his screaming as 'howling' – a word that now expresses both the dark laughter and the (potentially unceasing) cries of torment that make up his text.

Yes, my mouth, but there it is, I won't open it, I have no mouth, and what about it, I'll grow one, a little hole at first, then wider and wider, deeper and deeper, the air will gush into me, and out a second later, howling.... That would start things off, the whole fabric would be infected, the ball would start a-rolling, the disturbance would spread to every part, locomotion itself would soon appear, trips properly so called, business trips, pleasure trips, research expeditions, sabbatical leaves, jaunts and rambles, honeymoons at home and abroad and long sad solitary tramps in the rain, I indicate the main trends, athletics, tossing in bed, physical jerks, locomotor ataxy, death throes, rigor and rigor mortis, emergal of the bony structure, that should suffice (*T*, 388).

As in *Molloy*, these unsettling rhythms disrupt attempts to discover an extractable 'meaning' in the text even as they assert the Unnamable's resistance to the oppressive 'they' who (possibly) force him to speak. But this work's metafictional properties – the way that it continually reflects upon the act of storytelling that constitutes the Unnamable himself – further hinder the attempt to read the book through given systems or archetypes. For instance, Beckett's readers from Kenner to Badiou have consistently understood this book as an exploration of unbridled Cartesian doubt; the uncertainty the Unnamable experiences, they argue, is at heart the uncertainty of a philosophical problem. Such interpretations often include a reading of the Unnamable's closing statements, where he imagines a door that may release him:

perhaps they have carried me to the threshold of my story, before the door that opens on my story, that would surprise me, if it opens, it will be I, it will be the silence, where I am, I don't know, I'll never know, in the silence you don't know, you must go on, I can't go on, I'll go on (*T*, 418).

Is this the moment of a revelation that spells the end to philosophical scepticism? Such a reading can only be partly true for it must neglect a strange fact: the door of which the Unnamable speaks first appears in another story he fabulates a few pages earlier. In the only sense that it can, Beckett's text gives us the answer as to what lies on the other side of its 'final' door. But the answer is: another fiction about fiction.

They love each other, marry, in order to love each other better, more conveniently, he goes to the wars, he dies at the wars, she weeps, with emotion, at having loved him, at having lost him, yep, marries again, in order to love again, more conveniently again, they love each other, you love as many times as necessary, as necessary in order to be happy, he comes back, the other comes back, from the wars, he didn't die at the wars after all, she goes to the station, to meet him, he dies in the train, of emotion, at the thought of seeing her again, having her again, she weeps, weeps again, with emotion again, at having lost him again, yep, goes back to the house, he's dead, the other is dead, the mother-in-law takes him down, he hanged himself, with emotion, at the thought of losing her, she weeps, weeps louder, at having loved him, at having lost him, there's a story for you, that was to teach me the nature of emotion, that's called emotion, what emotion can do, given favourable conditions, what love can do, well well, so that's emotion, that's love, and trains ... and the door, the house door is bolted, who bolted it, he the better to hang himself, or the mother-in-law the better to take him down, ... the door, the door interests me, a wooden door, who bolted the door, and for what purpose, I'll never know (*T*, 410–411).

Drawing Balzac's *Le Colonel Chabert* (1832) from his ragbag of memories, the Unnamable regales us with a wildly accelerated, ludic revision of this painful tale of a soldier, left for dead in the Napoleonic wars, who returns home only to find his wife remarried. Yet even if Beckett's target is familiar, his parody is now more troubling and difficult to understand. For if the Unnamable's version is one that neither he nor we can take 'seriously', it is also in some curious way connected, through 'emotion', to the question of freedom – the most serious subject in Beckett's universe. In passages like this one, this book complicates the systems we have for valuing the novel by effectively reinserting the problems of philosophy back into the problems of reading a literary narrative – even as it baits those who would require fiction to teach us a 'meaningful' moral lesson. If there is a lesson here, the Unnamable cannot tell us what it is because he does not know; 'emotion' in this story does not develop into wisdom but remains unresolved, baffling, foolish. More troubling still, Beckett's text reminds us that to answer the question – to force open the door – we surrender the particular power of whatever constitutes our encounter with *The Unnamable* for something else entirely. We turn our experience of reading the novel into what Molloy calls 'an incident of no interest *in itself*, like all that has a moral' (*T*, 85; my emphasis).

It is impossible to live according to the 'philosophy' of works like this one, and not only because their worlds, as Beckett's critics have argued, arise from a single, closeted voice. As Georges Bataille acknowledged, no one can follow in Molloy's footsteps.[6] But Beckett's project was never intended to speak for society or to transcend suffering, nor did he aim at taking up the role of moral tutor to the emotions. His novels will not act as repositories of or guides to the forms of knowledge that the novel has often claimed since these works arise from and return to states of profound isolation and unknowing. Instead, as Gide claimed of his own fiction, these books work 'to disturb' (*inquiéter*): to surprise and so unsettle the very foundations of our assumptions about value and meaning. In doing so, as Blanchot writes – controversially – of Sade's project, they work 'to modify the bases of all comprehension' (Blanchot, 72).

Notes

INTRODUCTION

1. SB qtd. in Gabriel D'Aubarède, 'Interview with Beckett', *Samuel Beckett: The Critical Heritage*, ed. Lawrence Graver and Raymond Federman (London: Routledge and Kegan Paul, 1979), 215–17, 217.
2. Samuel Beckett, *Disjecta* (London: John Calder, 2001), 78.
3. Frederik Smith, *Beckett's Eighteenth Century* (Basingstoke: Palgrave, 2002), 3.
4. See James H. Reid, *Proust, Beckett and Narration* (Cambridge: Cambridge University Press, 2003); Daniela Caselli, *Beckett's Dantes: Intertexuality in the Fiction and Criticism* (Manchester: Manchester University Press, 2006); Barbara Reich Gluck, *Beckett and Joyce: Friendship and Fiction* (Lewisburg, PA: Bucknell University Press, 1959); Phyllis Carey and Ed Jewinski, *Joyce 'n Beckett* (New York: Fordham University Press, 1992).
5. Shane Weller, *Beckett, Literature and the Ethics of Alterity* (New York: Palgrave Macmillan, 2006), viii. For notable contributions to this debate see H. Porter Abbott's 'Narrative', *Palgrave Advances in Samuel Beckett Studies*, ed. Lois Oppenheim (New York: Palgrave Macmillan, 2004), 7–29. See also David Hesla, *The Shape of Chaos: An Interpretation of the Art of Samuel Beckett* (Minneapolis: University of Minnesota Press, 1971); Lance St. John Butler, *Samuel Beckett and the Meaning of Being: A Study of Ontological Parable* (New York: Palgrave Macmillan, 1984); Thomas Trezise, *Into the Breach: Samuel Beckett and the Ends of Literature* (Princeton: Princeton University Press, 1990); Anthony Uhlmann, *Beckett and Poststructuralism* (Cambridge: Cambridge University Press, 1999).
6. David Pattie, 'Beckett and Bibliography', *Palgrave Advances in Samuel Beckett Studies*, ed. Lois Oppenheim, 226–46, 227–8.
7. On Beckett and philosophy I direct the reader to P. J. Murphy's 'Beckett and the Philosophers' in *The Cambridge Companion to Beckett*, ed. John Pilling (Cambridge: Cambridge University Press, 1994), 222–40. For a useful summary of the way that literary theory has deployed philosophy in the interests of a positive estimation of Beckett's writing, see David Pattie's 'Beckett and Bibliography' in *Palgrave Advances in Samuel Beckett Studies*, ed. Lois Oppenheim (New York: Palgrave Macmillan, 2004), 226–46. See also Shane Weller's account of the debate between the philosophers and their literary-critical allies in *A Taste for the Negative: Beckett and Nihilism* (London:

Legenda, 2005), and *Beckett, Literature and the Ethics of Alterity* (New York: Palgrave Macmillan, 2006).

8. See Beckett's comment to Gabriel d'Aubarède, cited earlier. He also noted (misleadingly) that 'I never read philosophers' and 'I never understand anything they write' (SB qtd. in d'Aubarède, 217). To Tom Driver, Beckett allegedly commented that 'When Heidegger and Sartre speak of a contrast between being and existence, they may be right, I don't know, their language is too philosophical for me. I am not a philosopher.' Tom Driver, 'Interview with Beckett' *Samuel Beckett: The Critical Heritage*, ed. Lawrence Graver and Raymond Federman (London: Routledge and Kegan Paul, 1979), 217–23, 219.

9. John Fletcher's *The Novels of Samuel Beckett*, 2nd edition (London: Chatto and Windus, 1970), is one of the few books to try to address Beckett's novels as novels, but is unlikely to be of much help to the contemporary researcher. Fletcher's book is a general survey (first published in 1964) and, in the event, does not discuss Beckett's novels in their relation to the genre in much detail. It brackets the novels according to Fletcher's idea of a teleological development in Beckett's fiction toward 'The Hero as Voice' (Fletcher, 179). Frederik Smith has conducted the most recent, and perhaps the most insightful, study of Beckett's relationship to literary traditions (including the eighteenth-century novel) in his *Beckett's Eighteenth Century*.

10. Jonathan Boulter, *Interpreting Narrative in the Novels of Samuel Beckett* (Gainesville, Florida: University Press of Florida, 2001), 2.

11. James H. Reid, *Proust, Beckett and Narration* (Cambridge: Cambridge University Press, 2003), 1.

12. SB to TM, 13/3/1948, qtd. in Deirdre Bair, *Samuel Beckett: A Biography* (New York: Harcourt Brace Jovanovich, 1978), 374.

13. Rachel Burrows, 'Notes on Samuel Beckett's Lectures', Beckett Manuscript Collection, Trinity College Dublin Library, MIC60, 27 (hereafter cited by manuscript number).

14. Samuel Beckett, *Dream of Fair to Middling Women* (London: John Calder, 1993), 179.

15. Leslie Hill, *Beckett's Fiction: In Different Words* (Cambridge: Cambridge University Press, 1990), 74–5.

16. Sarah Lawell, *Critics of Consciousness: The Existential Structures of Literature* (Cambridge: Harvard University Press, 1968), 267.

17. Samuel Beckett, *The Letters of Samuel Beckett: 1929–1940*, ed. Martha Dow Fehsenfeld and Lois More Overbeck (Cambridge: Cambridge University Press, 2009), vol. I, SB to TM, 15/8/1931, 81.

18. Shane Weller, *A Taste for the Negative: Beckett and Nihilism* (London: Legenda, Modern Humanities Research Association and Maney Publishing, 2005), 31–4.

19. Samuel Beckett, *Proust and Three Dialogues with Georges Duthuit* (London: John Calder, 1999), 49.

20. Christie McDonald, 'The Proustian Revolution', in *The Cambridge Companion to The French Novel: From 1800 to the Present*, ed. Timothy Unwin (Cambridge: Cambridge University Press, 1997), 111–25, 111.

21. This journal was a well-regarded Parisian monthly, started in 1909 by Gide. It published part of Joyce's 'Anna Livie [*sic*] Plurabelle' in no. 212, May 1931, 633–46. Joyce sent Beckett an autographed copy of the edition containing the translation in 1931. James Knowlson, *Damned to Fame: The Life of Samuel Beckett* (London: Bloomsbury, 1996), 128. The journal was temporarily revived after the war in 1953 as *La Nouvelle nouvelle revue française*, but then reverted to its old title. It published 'Mahood' (no. 2, Feb. 1953, 213–34) and 'Samuel Beckett et la peinture' (no. 54, June 1957, 1125–6). 'Souffle' (a translation of 'Breath') was included in *Cahiers du Chemin* (15 April 1971), 21–2. See C. J. Ackerley and S. E. Gontarski, *The Grove Companion to Samuel Beckett* (New York: Grove Press, 2004), 413.

22. James Knowlson and Brigitte Le Juez have both acknowledged that Beckett lectured on Gide in 1930, but neither has demonstrated Gide's importance to Beckett's novels.

23. Ackerley and Gontarski, *The Grove Companion to Samuel Beckett*, 227. Beckett's comment in *Proust* is as follows: 'The periods of transition that separate consecutive adaptations [to the real] represent the perilous zones in the life of the individual … when for a moment the boredom of living is replaced by the suffering of being. (At this point, and with a heavy heart and for the satisfaction or disgruntlement of Gideans, semi and integral, I am inspired to concede a brief parenthesis to all the analogivorous, who are capable of interpreting the "Live dangerously", that victorious hiccough in vacuo, as the national anthem of the true ego exiled in habit. The Gideans advocate a habit of living – and look for an epithet. A nonsensical bastard phrase. They imply a hierarchy of habits, as though it were valid to speak of good habits and bad habits. An automatic adjustment of the human organism to the conditions of its existence has as little moral significance as the casting of a clout when May is or is not out; and the exhortation to cultivate a habit as little sense as an exhortation to cultivate a coryza') (*PTD*, 19–20).

24. John Pilling, *A Companion to* Dream of Fair to Middling Women (Tallahassee, FL: Journal of Beckett Studies Books, 2004), 90–1; my emphasis.

25. Consider Knowlson's point that Rudmose-Brown rejected any 'system' or orthodoxy, and especially the interference of such systems in the practice of personal freedom – a stance that Knowlson claims Beckett's tutor then passed on to his young pupil. Gide's early dictum that 'We must all play our parts' also seems to have been important to Rudmose-Brown. (Gide elaborated this saying as 'everyone … had a part to play in the world which was his very own and unlike any other; so that every effort to submit to a common rule became in my eyes treachery'. André Gide, *If It Die*, trans. Dorothy Bussy (London: Random House, 2002), 214.) Rudmose-Brown rehearsed this notion tirelessly to the young Beckett as 'Every one of us must strive, unflinchingly, to be himself'. Knowlson argues this dictum could be understood as a guideline for Beckett's entire career (*DF*, 51).

26. Rachel Burrows, 'Interview with Rachel Burrows', Interview by S. E. Gontarski, Dougald McMillan, and Martha Fehsenfeld, *Journal of Beckett Studies*, 11/12 (1982): 1–15, 9.

27. André Gide, *The Counterfeiters*, trans. Dorothy Bussy (London: Penguin Books, 1966), 167.

28. The original source for this dictum is John 12:25: 'He that loveth his life shall lose it; and he that hateth his life in this world shall keep it unto life eternal.' *Holy Bible, Authorised King James Version* (London: Collins' Clear-Type Press, 1957), 21.

29. Beckett noted that Gide's first book, *Les Cahiers d'André Walter*, was a 'piece of dogmatism'; Gide, he suggested was at this stage 'Like a Christian Laforgue' (MIC60, 10). As Alan Sheridan points out, the late 1880s 'was a time when, for the young Gide, everything that mattered most to him was imbued with a religious spirit'. Alan Sheridan, *André Gide: A Life in the Present* (London: Penguin, 1998), 46. Gide himself acknowledged as much: 'art and religion were devoutly wedded in my heart and I tasted my most perfect ecstasy there where they most melted into one'. André Gide, *If It Die*, trans. Dorothy Bussy (London: Random House, 2002), 167.

30. Gide, *If It Die*, 206.

31. André Gide, unpublished journal entry, October 1894, trans. and qtd. in Jean Delay, *The Youth of André Gide*, abridged and trans. by June Guicharnaud (Chicago: University of Chicago Press, 1963), 487.

32. Beckett described Gide as always 'faithful to classical litotes' (MIC60, 47) and ascribed the older writer's individualism (the 'Classical artist is most intensely individual' (MIC60, 15)) as well as his typical 'restraint' to this quality (MIC60, 15). Gide's *L'École des femmes* (1929), for instance, was the product of a laudable but 'painful restraint of language and method' adopted by the author 'getting back to Racine' (MIC60, 15).

33. André Gide, *Morceaux choisis* (Paris: Éditions de la Nouvelle Revue Française, 1921), 453, my translation.

34. The three works Beckett identifies in this regard are *Paludes, Le Prométhée mal enchaîné*, and *Les caves du Vatican* (MIC60, 31).

35. *Paludes* was written after Gide's first journey to Africa, in the interim before his second voyage there and the confirmation of his sexual tendencies. And it was perhaps inevitable that Gide's rejection of his faith was followed by his loss of confidence in Symbolism. As Catherine Savage has shown, if Mallarmé's teachings served as a complementary or substitute mysticism for the ascetic Protestantism of Gide's upbringing, the emphases Symbolism shared with that Protestantism and made it an initially agreeable fit – purity, self-sacrifice, duty, an attention to the inner life – also meant that it, too, would dissipate as Gide's Christianity eroded. See Catherine H. Savage, 'Gide's Criticism of Symbolism', *Modern Language Review* 61, no. 4 (Oct. 1966), 601–9, 601. For Beckett, Gide's subsequent enthusiasm for engaging with life led to some slippage in his classical ideal; he 'let himself go in *Les Nourritures terrestres* ([with] some unfortunate results)' (MIC60, 15).

36. André Gide, Letter to H. Drain, 18/7/1932, in Yvonne Davet, *Autour des Nourritures terrestres: histoire d'un livre* (Paris: Gallimard, 1948), 90, my translation.

37. André Gide, 'Feuillets', *Oeuvres Complètes*, Édition augmentée de texts inédits, établie par Martin-Chauffier, 15 volumes (Paris: Nouvelle Revue Française, 1932–39), *XIII*, 439–40; trans. and qtd. in Walker, *Gide*, 25.

38. Germaine Brée, *André Gide l'insaisissable Protée* (Paris: Les Belles Lettres, 1953), 161, my translation.

39. Gide admitted as much to his friend Henri Ghéon. Musing about *L'Immoraliste*, he admitted that despite his 'belles théories', his early récits still involved an unhappy, deterministic 'empirisme'. André Gide, Henri Ghéon, *Correspondance: 1897–1903*, 2 vols. (Paris: Gallimard, 1976), vol. 1, 27/9/1901, 363.

40. J. M. Coetzee, 'The Comedy of Point of View in Beckett's Murphy', *Doubling the Point: Essays and Interviews*, ed. David Atwell (Cambridge, MA: Harvard University Press, 1992), 31–42, 36.

41. Edouard Dujardin's deployment of interior monologue in *Les Lauriers sont coupés* (1888) went largely unnoticed until Joyce acknowledged Dujardin in 1922 as a source for the technique in *Ulysses*.

42. At the end of his lectures Gide admitted that '[in Dostoevsky's work] I have sought, consciously or unconsciously, what had most intimate connection with my own ideas. Others no doubt will be able to discern different things'. André Gide, *Dostoïevsky*, trans. Dorothy Bussy (London: Secker and Warburg, 1949), 162. Germaine Brée confirms that 'what Gide had to say about Dostoevsky in his lectures offers little that was not already in [his] mind' (Brée, *Gide*, 191). As we shall see, Beckett also acknowledged that Gide was talking about himself in the latter's lectures on Dostoevsky.

43. The notion of 'abnegation' or 'renunciation' also derives from Gide's Christianity (it is related to the 'Evangelistic paradox' mentioned earlier) and his reading of Dostoevsky as a believer. In *Feuillets d'Automne*, Gide recalls discussing such 'Christian virtues' with Paul Valéry while lying in bed with a fever (a topic which the younger writer did not approach with the same reverence): 'and, as I was rising to their defence, the word *abnegation* having escaped me, there was Paul jumping up, leaping from his seat, rushing toward the hall door in an assumed frenzy: "Ice! Bring some ice, quick! … The invalid is raving! He ABNEGATES!"' (Gide, *Feuillets*, 111).

44. Most apparently, *Les Faux-Monnayeurs* and *Les Caves du Vatican* are much more ironically self-reflexive than Dostoevsky's novels (for example, in the way that they reflect on the act of narration).

45. 'To disturb is my function', he famously claimed (*LC*, 50).

46. Alain Robbe-Grillet, *Le miroir qui revient* (Paris: Minuit, 1984), 212; my translation.

47. Friedrich Schiller, *On the Aesthetic Education of Man: In a Series of Letters*, trans. Elizabeth Wilkinson and L. A. Willoughby; ed. Walter Hindered and Daniel O. Dahlstrom (Oxford: Clarendon Press, 1967), 17.

48. Most recently, Brigitte Le Juez has given an account of the lectures with summaries and some transcriptions in *Beckett before Beckett*, trans. Ros Schwartz (London: Souvenir Press, 2008).

1 'THE INTEGRITY OF INCOHERENCE': THEORY AND *DREAM OF FAIR TO MIDDLING WOMEN*

1. Proust remained a complex, even ambivalent figure for Beckett. See, for example, Shane Weller's analysis of Beckett's two Prousts of 1930 in *A Taste for the Negative: Beckett and Nihilism* (London: Legenda, Modern Humanities Research Association and Maney Publishing, 2005), 35–49. See also Beckett's later account of Proust in his 1934 review 'Proust in Pieces' in which he defends Proust's work as one in which 'conflict' is 'only rarely to be resolved' (*Dis*, 63–65).

2. Beckett continued to be interested in these writers in the following years. He read Dostoevsky's *The Possessed* – in a French translation – in May of 1931 as he was writing *Dream*, and made several attempts to write a monograph on Gide (a subject addressed in the next chapter).

3. 'Naturalist' as used here is Beckett's own terminology for the writers being discussed. Please see footnote 7 for further clarification.

4. See Shane Weller's account of Beckett's *Three Dialogues* in *A Taste*, 61–67. Rupert Wood's essay 'An Endgame of Aesthetics: Beckett as Essayist' is also helpful in this regard (see his essay in *The Cambridge Companion to Beckett*, ed. John Pilling (Cambridge: Cambridge University Press 2004), 1–16), as is John Pilling's chapter 'Writings on Literature and Art' in his *Samuel Beckett* (London: Routledge and Kegan Paul, 1976), 13–24.

5. Le Juez has recognised Beckett's reliance on Gide's text for his lectures on the novel: '[In his lectures on the modern novel] Beckett dwells at length on Gide's essay on Dostoevsky ... and Rachel Burrows's notes show that he scrupulously follows the order of the essay chapters'. Brigitte Le Juez, *Beckett before Beckett*, trans. Ros Schwartz (London: Souvenir Press, 2008), 35. Gide's book was derived from his own lectures (published with additional essays), given in the early months of 1922 before Jacques Copeau's School of Dramatic Art at the *Vieux-Colombier*.

6. Burrows's note 'read Gide on Dostoevsky for Gide himself' indicates Beckett's self-acknowledged source for his commentary on the Russian writer (MIC60, 8).

7. As David Walker reminded me, it would be misleading to call Balzac a Naturalist. The Naturalist school emerged toward the end of the nineteenth-century and is best represented by Zola; Balzac was closer to what might be termed a 'romantic realist'. In the following, however, I use Beckett's distinction between the 'Pre-Naturalists' and the 'Naturalists' to try to follow his own theory as closely as possible.

8. Jacques Rivière, *Nouvelle Revue Française*, Feb 1922, 176–7; qtd. in *D*, 100.

9. Consider, for example, Ackerley and Gontarski's claims that '[p]arallels may be adduced from classical doctrines of the tripartite soul; divisions of the soul into sensitive, rational, and spiritual components; Dante's *Divine Comedy*; or Spinoza's three levels of knowledge, the third being the identification of the self with the intellectual love of God. Also manifest is Leibniz's distinction between virtual and actual, the unconscious realm of confused perception,

the conscious realm of relatively clear perception, and the self-conscious realm of apperception. Schopenhauer's manifestation of the Will accentuates the three forms of space, time, and causality. The tripartite division is incommensurate with Cartesian dualism and thereby critiques the rationalist tradition' (*GC*, 388–9). Whether or not such parallels suggest influence, the scheme for *Murphy*'s mind would not be 'SB's own' if I am correct regarding Gide's impact here (*GC*, 389).

10. Gide's comment was published for the first time in Delay's biography of Gide (which appeared in the late 1950s), so it would not have been available to Beckett until then. But it is worth noting Beckett's comparable challenge to Stendhal in *Les Deux Besoins* (1938): 'Il y a des jours, surtout en Europe, où la route reflète mieux que le miroir' (*Dis*, 55).

11. Leslie Daiken, 'Student notes', held by the Beckett International Foundation at the University of Reading. Unaccessioned holding; Daiken's emphasis.

12. Though Beckett made a significant distinction between Corneille and Racine, the force of his contrast here is between the modern novel and French classical drama.

13. According to Beckett, 'Gide [was] interested in liminal consciousness ([which was] sneered at by [Max] Nordau)' (MIC60, 42). In his *Dream* Notebook, Beckett noted an 'inchoate liminal erotico-mystic presentation (of St. John of the Cross & St. Teresa)' – a paraphrase of a passage from his reading of Nordau's *Degeneration* (1895) joined by Beckett with elements drawn from W. R. Inge's *Christian Mysticism*. See also *Dream*'s 'erotico-mystic' (*DFMW*, 30), and 'innumerable other inchoate liminal presentations' (*DFMW*, 32–33) (*DN, 91*).

14. James Joyce, *A Portrait of the Artist as a Young Man* (London: Penguin Books, 1992), 3.

15. Like his forbears in the *Bildungsroman*, Belacqua leaves the constrained atmosphere of home (here Beckett's Ireland, figured in the censorious, uncultivated authority figures of the wharfinger and policeman), makes his way to the city, experiences urban life, has amorous affairs, concocts aesthetic theories, and writes verse. Belacqua's love affairs also gesture toward the pattern appropriated by nineteenth-century novels like *Middlemarch* from the chivalric romance ('this frail world that is all temptation and knighthood' (*DFMW*, 3)), presenting Belacqua with the path of the flesh and the path of the spirit embodied by two women: the Smeraldina-Rima and the ethereal Alba. Unlike Eliot's Lydgate, who easily chooses between the gift of the gods (Dorothea) and the rose of the world (Rosamond), Belacqua's tastes seem to swing toward the ethereal, though (to use Belacqua's own terms, which are derived from Mario Praz's *The Romantic Agony* (1930; trans. 1933 by Angus Davidson, 2nd ed., (London: Oxford University Press, 1970), not Eliot's novel) neither the Rosa Munda nor the Rosa Mundi is preferable to 'Nothing' (*DN*, 46).

16. Thomas L. Jeffers, *Apprenticeships: The Bildungsroman from Goethe to Santayana* (New York: Palgrave Macmillan, 2005), 18.

17. Beckett had not read *Wilhelm Meister* by 1930/1, but he did in 1934 at around the same time he showed a renewed interest in writing his monograph on Gide (John Pilling, personal communication).

18. By 'humility' Beckett refers to the novelist-narrator's admission of his lack of control over his creatures or narrative. For example, in *Dream* Belacqua's complexity poses problems for the 'novelist's' conjugation of the verb 'to be', a difficulty he acknowledges in another nod to Gide: 'We find we have written *he is* when of course we meant *he was*. For a postpicassian man ... it is frankly out of the question ... to conjugate *to be* without a shudder.... Now he is once more a mere outside, façade, penetrated, if we may pilfer to reapply the creditable phrase of Monsieur Gide, by his façade' (*DFMW*, 46). As Pilling notes, the phrase 'penetrated by his façade' is 'pilfered' from Gide's *Journal des Faux-Monnayeurs* (1926), where it is applied to Gide's character Lucien Bercail (perhaps anticipating *Dream*'s Lucien). See André Gide, *Logbook of the Coiners,* trans. Justin O'Brien (London: Cassell, 1952), 25. Beckett also reapplied Gide's phrase to his Walter Draffin in 'What a Misfortune' in *More Pricks Than Kicks* (*DN*, 90).

19. Though originally described by Gide, this technique is perhaps best known through its revival in the sixties and seventies by the new novelists (especially Robbe-Grillet, Simon, Sarraute and Butor); however, it has not been recognised that Beckett was one of the first writers to have taken cognisance of Gide's innovations. In using the term here I refer to Gide's definition, which first occurs in an 1893 entry in his *Journal,* specifically referring to *La Tentative amoureuse*: 'In a work of art', Gide wrote, 'I rather like to find thus transposed, at the level of the characters, the subject of the work itself. Nothing sheds more light on the work or displays the proportions of the whole work more accurately' (*J*, 30–1). As Lucien Dällenbach has written, the mise en abyme can be described as *'any aspect enclosed within a work that shows a similarity with the work that contains it'*. Lucien Dällenbach, *The Mirror in the Text,* trans. Jeremy Whiteley with Emma Hughes (Chicago: University of Chicago Press, 1989), 8.

20. 'What have I to do with the *état-civil*? *L'état c'est moi*!', Edouard contends. '[M]y work doesn't purport to rival anything' (*C*, 167).

21. Belacqua's virtual artwork remains untitled and he does not keep a journal within the novel.

22. Like Gide's 'novelist', Mr Beckett is guilty of all kinds of transgressions of 'incoherence', such as the 'Overstatement' he acknowledges was done in imitation of Dickens (*DFMW*, 159).

23. André Gide, *The Notebooks of André Walter,* trans. Wade Baskin (London: Peter Owen, 1986), 122.

24. Edouard claims that 'The only existence that anything (including myself) has for me, is poetical. I restore this word to its full signification' (*C*, 68).

25. Albert Sonnenfeld, 'Readers and Reading in *La Porte Étroite*', *Romantic Review* 67 (1976), 172–80, 149.

2 'AN IRONICAL RADIANCE': *MURPHY*
AND THE MODERN NOVEL

1. John Pilling, *A Samuel Beckett Chronology* (New York: Palgrave Macmillan, 2006), 39.
2. Beckett was clearly still thinking about Gide at the time of *Murphy*: he quoted a modified version of Gide's dictum that 'Il est bon de suivre sa pente, pourvu que ce soit en montant' as 'poursuivre ta pente pourvu qu'elle soit en montant' in a letter to McGreevy on 8 September 1934 (*LSB 1*, 222). For Gide's saying, see *C*, 310.
3. Samuel Beckett, *Murphy* (London: John Calder, 2003), 65.
4. Andrew Gibson, *Beckett and Badiou: The Pathos of Intermittency* (Oxford: Oxford University Press, 2007), 143. See Hugh Kenner, *Samuel Beckett: A Critical Study* (New York: Grove Press, 1962), 75.
5. John Fletcher, *The Novels of Samuel Beckett*, 2nd edition (London: Chatto and Windus, 1970), 41. For J. M. Coetzee's reading of *Murphy* as a meta-fiction see his 'The Comedy of Point of View in Beckett's *Murphy*' in *Doubling the Point: Essays and Interviews*, ed. David Atwell (Cambridge, MA: Harvard University Press, 1992), 31–42.
6. Hugh Kenner, *Ulysses* (London: George Allen and Unwin, 1980), 64.
7. Speaking of Beckett's early fictions, the Unnamable points out that 'it was clumsily done, you could see the ventriloquist'. Samuel Beckett, *Molloy, Malone Dies, The Unnamable* (London: John Calder, 1994), 85.
8. C. J. Ackerley, *Demented Particulars: The Annotated* Murphy (Tallahassee, FL: Journal of Beckett Studies Books, 1998), 19.
9. Beckett's readers have argued for Racine's treatment of plot as an important influence on *Murphy* for some time and Ackerley, for one, tentatively places Beckett's second novel in Racine's tradition before all others (*DP*, 23). Beckett's ironic use of Racine in *Murphy* is a subject for another time, but it should be recognized that it is very possible that the reason Racine shows up in *Murphy* at all is because Beckett considered that Gide had already appropriated him in the interests of modernizing the novel – and it was *this* model that Beckett sought to emulate.
10. Gide labeled *Les Caves du Vatican* a *sotie* to differentiate it from his idea of the novel. The *sotie* is a term 'borrowed from a burlesque a satirical form of medieval drama which [Gide] also applied retrospectively to *Paludes* and *Le Prométhée Mal Enchaîné*' (Walker, *Gide*, 137). Beckett's lectures indicate he knew *Les Caves du Vatican* well and devoted a significant amount of instruction time to it and its related topics, such as Gide's adaptation of Dostoevsky's 'mental conflict' (the 'coexistence of apparently mutually exclusive states in the same organ'), and Lafcadio's 'act that cannot be reduced to motive' (MIC60, 14). Beckett's attention to this latter theme also indicates his awareness that Gide's confrontation with what Germaine Brée has described as 'the interaction between chance, will and necessity' in his fiction was not confined to his experiments in *Les Faux-Monnayeurs*, but

found other expressions (Brée, 'On Time Sequences and Consequences in the Gidian World', 43). Note also Beckett's mention of 'Gide's *Lafcadio*' in his 1934 review of Leishmann's translation of Rilke's *Poems* (*Dis*, 66), and his playful mention of Gide and '*crime immotivé*' to Nuala Costello in a letter of 27 February 1934 (*LSB 1*, 186). Beckett was still thinking about Gide's novel in the year after he finished *Murphy*; he puns on the name of writer and teacher Patrick Lafcadio Hearn in a letter of 18 January 1937 (SB to Mary Manning Howe, *LSB 1*, 423).

11. André Gide, *Les Caves du Vatican*, translated as *Lafcadio's Adventures*, trans. Dorothy Bussy (New York: Vintage Intl., 2003), 216.

12. The comparison between revising a work of literature and correcting an action in life is initiated in Lafcadio's discussion with Julius in book II, but is picked up again in Lafcadio's conversation with Protos (who has 'revised' Lafcadio's crime) in book IV. Lafcadio argues that life is superior to art because it does not allow touch-ups. 'In life one corrects *oneself,*' he tells Julius, 'but one can't correct what one *does*. It is the power of revising that makes writing such a colourless affair.... Yes! That's what seems to me so fine about life. It's like fresco-painting–erasures aren't allowed' (*L*, 86).

13. *Caves* also suggests the novelist's limitations but as Babcock has pointed out, these gestures are perhaps also a part of the novelist's game – they may even reveal a higher level of control and subtlety on the part of the novelist. For example, though the novelist seems to regret that Lafcadio can apparently fall in love against his wishes, when this actually happens at the end of the novel he interrupts the scene and starts writing a new volume. 'The Novelist's rather broad gestures at the autonomy of his characters serve only to demonstrate that it is he who pulls the strings, that there can be no such thing as novelistic autonomy.' Arthur E. Babcock, *Portraits of Artists: Reflexivity in Gidean Fiction, 1902–1946* (York, SC: French Literature Publications, 1982), 79.

14. See Kenner's argument that *Murphy* is an attempt to emulate 'the workman-like linkages of Flaubertian fiction' in its use of 'coincidence' to resolve the narrative. Hugh Kenner, *Samuel Beckett: A Critical Study* (New York: Grove Press, 1962), 75. Citing Celia's identification of Murphy by his birthmark, Kenner suggests that 'In Flaubertian fiction, of which *Ulysses* and *Finnegans Wake* are supreme examples, a myriad of unimportant matters are not scattered like sand over the text but nestle into it perfectly' (Kenner, *Samuel Beckett*, 75). In contrast, John Fletcher argues that 'the finicky precision with which the simultaneities of the action are pointed out, as well as the virtuosity with which the different events of the intrigue are harmonized and the characters made to converge, would seem to constitute a deliberate *défi de maître*' (Fletcher, 41). The source of this technique has hitherto remained unclear. *Murphy*'s apparently inevitable progression toward its dénouement has often been attributed to Racine's influence (Ludovic Janvier, for example, describes the novel as '*Andromaque jouée par les* Marx Brothers' (qtd. in *DP*, 38)), but this answer fails to satisfy. The complex arrangement of

Beckett's plot serves to reveal the machinations of an *individual* – Murphy's sardonic 'novelist'– who is quite unlike the chthonic powers that govern Racine's universe.

15. Even as he details Murphy's regretful birth, the 'novelist' promises us this satisfyingly cruel end as an eventual payoff: 'His rattle will make amends' (*M*, 44). The phrase 'Racinian lightning' appears in Beckett's *Whoroscope* notebook (entry #3) in his early sketches for the fiction that would become *Murphy*. Samuel Beckett, *Whoroscope Notebook*, Beckett International Foundation, Reading University Library, MS 3000.

16. Wolfgang W. Holdheim, *Theory and Practice of the Novel: A Study of André Gide* (Geneva: Librairie Droz, 1968), 213–4. Alain Goulet, *Les Caves du Vatican d'André Gide: Etude méthodologique* (Paris: Larousse, 1972), 27.

17. Arthur E. Babcock, *Portraits of Artists: Reflexivity in Gidean Fiction, 1902–1946* (York, SC: French Literature Publications, 1982), 76.

18. Jonathan Culler, *Structuralist Poetics* (London: Routledge and Kegan Paul, 1975), 238. Broome also points out that this was an important aspect of the novel's historical position. Published on the brink of the First World War, its critique of a host of belief systems, and certainty in general, figures a deepening 'crisis of values' in Europe (Broome, 11–12).

19. Wylie considers his theory a sceptical one. '"I greatly fear", said Wylie, "that the syndrome known as life is too diffuse to admit of palliation. For every symptom that is eased, another is made worse. The horse leech's daughter is a closed system. Her quantum of wantum cannot vary"' (*M*, 36). But as Murphy reflects following the loss of his biscuits, Wylie's theory, like Neary's, is consolatory: 'Wylie in Murphy's place might have consoled himself with the thought that the Park was a closed system in which there could be no loss of appetite; Neary with the unction of an *Ipse dixit*' (*M*, 60).

20. The answer, for Murphy as with Fleurissoire, is of course 'his irrevocable Destiny'. This last point also highlights the fact that both works include types of the novel in their critique of systems, for both Murphy and Fleurissoire are quixotic figures whose follies parody the quest novel. Consider also Counihan's version: *Murphy* is a romance with the eponymous hero as her 'knight errant' (*M*, 33). Of course the type of novel most consistently attacked by both authors is the realist one, and this critique arguably governs *Murphy*'s style.

21. I take this term and my account of Gide in the following from Walker's argument for the significance of Gide's interest in evolutionary theory to his narrative approach (see Walker, *Gide*, 106–19).

22. Beckett read *Origin of Species* in 1932 and felt that he had 'never read such badly written cat lap' (qtd. in *DF*, 161).

23. It is possible that Beckett was aware of these evolutionary ideas directly through Bergson; in his lectures he described Gide's debts to the philosopher in some detail. (Beckett was already quite familiar with Bergson by 1930. He adapted Bergson's *Le Rire* for *Le Concentrisme*, and had read at least two of the philosopher's books.) For Gide, Beckett argued, 'thought goes

further than science'; he then pointed out that Gide derived his concepts of inconsistency in *Les Caves du Vatican* (specifically the *crime immotivé*) from Bergson's idea of *imprévisibilité* (MIC60, 14). Note also Beckett's argument for the presence of *imprévisibilité* in other forerunners of the modern novel Gide mentioned in *Dostoïevsky*; for example, Beckett (literally) highlighted *l'imprevu* three times in his annotations of Stendhal's *Le Rouge et le Noir* in his *Dream* notebook (*DN*, 128–9).

24. '[D]o not despair', Neary tells Counihan and Wylie in the course of their frustrated search, 'Remember there is no triangle, however obtuse, but the circumference of some circle passes through its wretched vertices' (*M*, 120).

25. It is worth noting that Neary's position at the end is an obvious example of the way both *Les Caves du Vatican* and *Murphy* present a 'skewed parody of narrative resolution' in the way they ironically deflate their characters' expectations and desires (Walker, *Gide*, 130). Through a set of 'random' convergences, Neary is finally granted Counihan (by this point she is only a pest for him) through the death of Murphy (who had replaced Counihan as the object of his fixation) just as Neary is informed that his wife, the other main obstacle to his former passion for Counihan, is also dead ('for some time', Cooper points out) (*M*, 153).

26. *Murphy*'s protagonist in this sense represents a parodic rewriting of *Dostoïevsky*'s antiheroic type in more general ways. In centring on themes of idleness and madness, Beckett assents to Gide's argument (referring to the protagonist of *Notes from Underground* – according to Gide the 'summit' of Dostoevsky's achievement) that 'action presupposes a certain intellectual inferiority' (*D*, 109).

3 'THE CREATIVE CONSCIOUSNESS': THE *WATT* NOTEBOOKS

1. See Gide's comment that 'imagination (in my case) rarely precedes the idea; it is the latter, and not at all the former, that excites me; but the latter without the former produces nothing in itself; it is a fever without virtue. *The idea of a work is its composition*' (Gide qtd. in Delay, 487).

2. Beckett noted to Gottfried Büttner in 1978 that '*Watt* was begun in Paris 1942, then continued evenings mostly in Rousillon and finished 1945 in Dublin & Paris.' Gottfried Büttner, *Samuel Beckett's Novel* Watt, trans. Joseph P. Dolan (Philadelphia: University of Pennsylvania Press, 1984), Letter, 12 April 1978; qtd. in Büttner, 5–6. The novel was actually begun in 1941 (the date on *Watt*'s Notebook 1) and though Beckett was sending off the novel to publishers in 1945, he continued revising it for several more years. The prevalent reading of *Watt* as a philosophical parody can be traced back to Jacqueline Hoefer's influential article on *Watt* and Wittgenstein in *Perspective* (1959). See Jacqueline Hoefer, 'Watt', *Perspective* 11, no. 3 (autumn 1959), 166–82; rpt. in *Samuel Beckett: A Collection of Critical Essays*, ed. Martin Esslin (Englewood Cliffs, NJ: Prentice Hall, 1965), 62–76. Since Hoefer's article, the novel has been described as a 'comic attack on [Cartesian] rationality' (*DF*, 303) and

even a caricature 'of all philosophical concepts that govern man's undertakings'. Raymond Federman, *Journey to Chaos: Samuel Beckett's Early Fiction* (Berkeley: University of California Press, 1965), 119.

3. John Pilling, 'Beckett's *Letters*', *Journal of Beckett Studies*, 18 (Sept. 2009), 178–91; 180.

4. Thomas Rudmose-Brown was also fond of antithesis and his erstwhile student uses this technique in his essays on Joyce and Proust, as well as his lectures on Gide. It was a strategy Beckett would eventually redeploy – when the *painter* had become the dominant subject of his criticism – in *Three Dialogues*.

5. In 'Dante and the Lobster' (in *More Pricks than Kicks* (1931–33; pub. 1934)), Carducci's emulation of Pindar is described as the clucking of an old hen (*MPTK*, 16).

6. Samuel Beckett, 'Notes on Literature' (Giosuè Carducci), Beckett Manuscript Collection, Trinity College Dublin Library, TCD MS 10965, 30–32.

7. Beckett criticizes the 'academic' privileging of poetic 'scenery' over an authentic exploration of the self in 'Recent Irish Poetry' (1934) (*Dis*, 71). Note also his attack on Prof. Albert Feuillerat's *Comment Proust a composé son Roman* in 1934 (*Dis*, 63–5). Like Carducci's imitation of Pindar, Feuillerat's rigidity in approaching an inspired artist results in a form of what Beckett earlier called 'book-keeping' rather than an aesthetically rewarding response (*Dis*, 19).

8. Samuel Beckett, *The Complete Dramatic Works*. (London: Faber and Faber, 1990), 70.

9. The following are all from a single page of his fiction: 'At the same time we are bound to admit, placing ourselves for the moment in the thick of the popular belief that there are two sides to every question … '; 'Consequently, we are rather anxious to dilate briefly … '; 'Shall we consider then in the first instance … ' (*DFMW*, 113).

10. Samuel Beckett, '*Watt* Notebooks', Harry Ransom Center, University of Texas at Austin, Box 6 (folders 5–7); Box 7 (folders 1–4), NB3, 1–2.

11. Knowlson and others have documented the ways that Beckett's approach to novel-writing in *Dream* and *Murphy* was reliant on source-gathering and 'grafting' methods (the joining of external source material with the developing fiction) he learned from Joyce. See *DN*, xii–xxi.

12. Beckett later described *Dream* as the product of a young man with 'nothing to say and an itch to make' (qtd. in *GC*, 287), and the 'chest into which [he] threw [his] wild thoughts' (qtd. in *DFMW*, xiii). No manuscript exists for Beckett's first novel, and it is possible the typescript is all there ever was. It is also worth noting that the *Dream* typescript does not show major differences from the final version (Pilling, personal communication).

13. 'My poems are worthless', Beckett told A. J. Leventhal on 28 July 1934 (qtd. in Pilling, 'Beckett's *Letters*', 181). This letter is not in the *Letters*.

14. Beckett's Joyce of 1929 is an 'innovator' who builds a 'machine' by conjoining conflicting 'elements'; this device proceeds toward a 'recurrent'

'explosion' (*Dis*, 31). Like Beckett's account of *Work in Progress*, Gide's *Les Faux-Monnayeurs* is also a carefully constructed apparatus joining inner 'antagonisms' (which Beckett dismantled in his account of Gide's '*New structure*' for the novel only to reconstruct it as the imploding engine at the heart of *Dream*'s Joycean gizmos). Beckett also conceptualises the artist as a demolitionist in his 1934 review of Sean O'Casey's *Windfalls*. The poet and playwright 'discerns the principle of disintegration in even the most complacent solidities, and activates it to their explosion'. In O'Casey's play *The End of the Beginning* 'the entire set comes to pieces' (*Dis*, 82–3).

15. Samuel Beckett, *Collected Poems in English and French* (New York: Grove Press, 1977), 7.

16. In late September of 1937 Beckett wrote to Thomas McGreevy that his getting 'the job in Cape town' and his accepting it were 'two conditions unlikely to be satisfied' (SB to TM, 21/9/1937, *LSB 1*, 550).

17. It seems that Beckett filled up his first two Johnson notebooks in late May/early June. On 22 May he told Mary Manning Howe that he had been working all the time since his return home on his Johnson play in the National Library (*BC*, 67).

18. On 5 June, Beckett wrote to McGreevy that 'The only thing resembling work has been in the library on Johnson' (*LSB 1*, 504).

19. Mark Nixon, *Samuel Beckett's 'German Diaries': 1936–7* (London: Continuum, 2010), 107.

20. Beckett eventually filled three large notebooks with material for the Johnson play. Joyce also lingers in the *Watt* manuscript. (One of the names of Beckett's protagonist in Notebook 1 is 'James John Macevoy'.) Joyce's death in January of 1941 and his birthday (celebrated posthumously by Beckett) on 2 February would have reminded Beckett of his vow to 'get over' his mentor when he sat down to begin *Watt*'s Notebook 1 on 11 February – a little over a week after he listened to a recording of Joyce's voice with Paul and Lucy Léon.

21. John Pilling, *Beckett before Godot* (Cambridge: Cambridge University Press, 1997), 87.

22. C. J. Ackerley, *Obscure Locks, Simple Keys: The Annotated* Watt (Tallahassee, FL: Journal of Beckett Studies Books, 2005). SB qtd. in *OLSK*, 12.

23. See *David Hayman*'s 'Getting Where? Beckett's Opening Gambit for *Watt*', *Contemporary Literature* 43, no. 1 (2002), 28–49.

24. In this connection, the fragmentation of the previous pages, though unintentional, suggests the opening of *Dream*'s second chapter with its ellipses and the breaks sown between paragraphs. It is conceivable that, as in *Dream*, Beckett here considers dramatising his *own* difficulties in beginning as his *narrator*'s inability to control or comprehend his characters. ('The fact of the matter is we do not quite know where we are in this story' (*DFMW*, 9).)

25. The 'we' who carries out this task is in fact a researcher who intends to write a realistic fiction about Quin's home. Beckett's impulse toward documentary realism rises at the end of Notebook 1, dominates the opening of Notebook

2, and resurges at page 42 of Notebook 2 in a tedious descriptive section cataloguing various doors, steps, bells, doorknobs, and so on in the Quin household.

26. One night Quin finds he cannot locate the lavatory. In the 'strange' darkness of his home, he encounters a shadowy hunchbacked intruder who tells Quin that he used to work for Quin's father, and speaks of the traumatic experience of falling off a ladder. This figure survives in the *Watt* text as Mr Hackett.

27. Quin's experience walking in his garden anticipates Arthur's encounter with the aged gardener as recorded in *Watt*'s addenda (*W*, 252–4).

28. There are obvious differences between these pieces of writing, most importantly in the area of form. *Three Dialogues* is a sophisticated comic work (and one which Beckett intended for publication). By means of a dialogistic exchange, and the use of a caricatural mask (B.), Beckett complicates any straightforward identification with *either* position in a way that is different from the diaristic, first-person narration of the 'creative consciousness' passage.

29. As Pilling points out, there is some debate concerning the date of 'the vision at last' but summer of 1945 is the most likely date (*BC*, 94).

30. *Watt* anticipates concerns that remained on Beckett's mind as he composed *Three Novels* in more than one sense: 'Molloy' had already come to him in the early forties – his being 'The Name!' Beckett had stumbled across for his protagonist early in *Watt*'s Notebook 1 (NB1, 11).

31. It is also worth noting that 'Jesus' here anticipates Watt, the protagonist (perhaps with the exception of Hamm) who is most overtly compared to Christ in Beckett's work. Ackerley acknowledges this in his claim that 'Mr Knott is a God-figure, and the novel is fundamentally an allegory; in Christian terms (the mythology with which Beckett claimed to be most familiar), of mankind's quest for salvation, and the inevitable frustration of that quest' (*OLSK*, 87).

32. 'Mr Beckett' notes the way his novel is 'degenerating into a kind of Commedia Dell'Arte, a form of literary statement to which we object particularly' (*DFMW*, 117).

33. At the time he was exploring the 'change' in Notebook 1 Beckett's old man was named Molloy. Meditating on his name as the last words that will desert him at the time of his death, Beckett's protagonist listens to the words fade in the silence and begins 'Feeling within him an unwanted change as when with stillness an unuttered <still> murmur ceases' (NB1, 19–20).

34. Samuel Beckett, *Watt* Typescript, Harry Ransom Center, University of Texas at Austin, Box 7 (folders 5–6), WTS, 211; NB3, 29.

35. Elements from 'we's' description of these paintings survive. The music room in Mr Knott's home (*W*, 68) was initially part of Art Conn O'Connery's picture of Mr Alexander Quin sitting at his piano. Dum Spiro's question about the rat and the consecrated wafer (*W*, 26–7) was originally part of a story relating how Matthew David McGilligan, Master of the Leopardstown Halflengths, got to Rome.

36. This sequence originally developed from a lengthy and complicated discussion about cross-breeding Irish Setters and Palestine Retrievers to produce the ideal famished dog. The Lynch family supervises this 'spectacle'.

4 'TELLING THE TALE': NARRATORS AND
NARRATION (1943–1946)

1. See Matthew Winston, '*Watt*'s First Footnote', *Journal of Modern Literature*, no. 6, 1971, 69–82.
2. Jonathan Swift, *A Tale of a Tub* (Oxford: Oxford University Press, 1999), 10.
3. For example, Smith introduces the quoted 'Haemophilia' note with 'Beckett says', and suggests that the Addenda is a coy pretence at a 'lack of authorial control' (Smith, 41–2). This perspective is more understandable coming from Ackerley because he traces many of the lacunae in the *Watt* text to earlier drafts (where it often seems that Beckett intended to replace the empty spaces with quotations or other information). But Ackerley's account of these and other textual elements does not quite justify his statements that the 'thirty-seven Addenda to *Watt* represent, *according to Beckett*, precious and illuminating material', or that Addenda item 10's suggestion to 'Note that Arsene's declaration gradually came back to Watt' is somehow the same as 'Beckett's reminder to himself, as recorded at the end of NB5 (182)' (*OLSK*, 205; my emphasis, 209).
4. To my knowledge, Beer is the only commentator who suggests that Sam is a narrated figure. See her article 'Watt, Knott and Beckett's Bilingualism', *Journal of Beckett Studies*, no. 10 (Autumn 1983), 37–76.
5. Sam says: 'For there we have to do with events that resisted all Watt's efforts to saddle them with meaning, and a formula, so that he could neither think of them, nor speak of them, but only suffer them, when they recurred, though it seems probable that they recurred no more, at the period of Watt's revelation, to me, but were as though they had never been' (*W*, 75–6).
6. For example, the gap that reads 'He could not see the stands, the grand, the members', the people's, so ? when empty with their white and red' (*W*, 27) originally read 'so (Indian artist)ish when empty' in the late drafts (NB4, 228). As Ackerley points out, maybe Beckett simply could not recall the Indian artist by the time he reread and revised this passage (*OLSK*, 51).
7. Is it possible that Watt communicated with Mr Hackett about the latter's private thoughts on the day of Watt's journey to Knott's (his memories of the 'sunlit fields' on the day of his 'fall' (*W*, 14)), or that the newsagent Evans told Watt about what he did later that evening (play a game of chess with himself out of Mr Staunton's handbook (*W*, 24))?
8. Ackerley suggests that this late 'we' can be differentiated from the earlier 'we' (in Notebook 2, for example), presumably on the basis that the late 'we' is no longer a pervasive presence in the text – the focus having shifted to Watt – or an embodied character (*OLSK*, 123).

9. Consider also that these two notes appear to be connected, for if any elements of the novel are 'intended' as 'symbols' by the composer of the Addenda and *Watt*, the main characters' names (a seeker named 'Watt' who confronts an ontological 'Knott'/naught) must be among them.

10. One of the most convincing arguments for the existence of a 'plural self' 'over' Sam is of course that the Watt-like tendency to exhaust propositions and serialise is general, and extends to the behaviour of all the major characters, as well as their *own* acts of narration. The Louit/Bando story as told by Arthur, and Arsene's 'short statement' are some examples. Consider also Knott's dressing/shaving/sleeping procedures, or Sam's speculations regarding the 'bull'. And note the way that several characters play at being the novel's narrator: for example, Arsene takes over the narration from Sam, describing Watt's entry, sojourn, and an exit in the third person for twenty-five pages in a mode scarcely dissimilar from *his* narrator.

11. Samuel Beckett, *The Complete Short Prose 1929–1989*, ed. S. E. Gontarski (New York: Grove Press, 1995), 278.

12. Beckett's protagonist may have been virtually fully formed at the time of composition, but the story itself was to be plagued by publication difficulties. Beckett began 'Suite' in English on 17 February 1946, continued in French on 13 March, and was finished with a first French/English version by 27 May. At some point, though probably after he had finished translating the first half into French, he titled the piece, inscribing the words 'Suite/1946' on the cover. He then translated and revised approximately half of the manuscript length version (the half completed in English) for publication as 'Suite' on 1 July in volume 10 of *Les Temps modernes*, expecting, so the story goes, to print the remainder of the work as Fin in a subsequent edition. Beckett had to wait for nine years for the story to be printed as a whole in *Nouvelles et textes pour rien*. The story did not appear in English until Beckett collaborated with Richard Seaver on a translation for the Parisian magazine *Merlin* (No. 2, Summer–Autumn, 1954) though, as he complained to Pamela Mitchell in late August of 1955, this version was full of errors. Clearly dissatisfied not only with the printer but also with the existing English version, Beckett significantly reworked the 1954 text and published another version in the November–December edition of *Evergreen Review* in 1960.

13. Samuel Beckett, 'Holograph of 'Suite' manuscript (1946)', Calvin Israel Samuel Beckett Collection, John J. Burns Library, Boston College, MS 91–1, Box 1 (folder 9), 1.

14. Samuel Beckett, *First Love and Other Novellas* (London: Penguin Books, 2000), 9.

15. See, for example, James Acheson's argument that French allowed Beckett to escape Joyce's influence and the 'flamboyant English of *Murphy* and *Watt*' James Acheson, *Samuel Beckett's Artistic Theory and Practice: Criticism, Drama and Early Fiction* (London: Macmillan, 1997), 80–1. Leslie Hill puts it rather differently when he posits that French released Beckett to 'construct

the world differently' in the postwar fiction, generating 'a productive distance or difference between his writing and the stresses at work in *Watt*' Leslie Hill, *Beckett's Fiction: In Different Words* (Cambridge: Cambridge University Press, 1990), 38. '[I]t is no surprise that when Beckett turns to French', Hill argues, 'he also turns unreservedly to the use of the first person. The French language functions here as a cryptic idiom which allows Beckett to articulate a new position in language and a new relation to fiction. There is clear evidence of this new turn in Beckett's work in the first texts written in his adopted language, his four *Novellas* ... ' (Hill, 38–9). Coetzee is typically more reserved, acknowledging the change in Beckett's style without arguing for a causal connection: 'The style of even Beckett's first published French work, the *Novellas*, is more jagged and paratactic then the style of *Watt*. While still as recognisably his own as his English prose, his French prose has freed itself from the stylisation, or automatism of style, of *Watt*.' J. M. Coetzee, 'Samuel Beckett and the Temptations of Style', *Doubling the Point: Essays and Interviews*, ed. David Atwell (Cambridge, MA: Harvard University Press, 1992), 43–9, 49.

16. Samuel Beckett, 'Suite', *Les Temps Modernes*, 10 (July 1946), 107–19, 111.

17. Typescript of 'The End'. Richard Seaver Collection of Samuel Beckett Materials. Harry Ransom Center, University of Texas at Austin. Box 1 (folder 1), 6.

18. Beckett mentions *La Nausée* for the first time in a letter of 26 May 1938 where he expresses an uncharacteristic enthusiasm for the book as 'extraordinarily good' (*DF*, 295). He was still thinking of the novel in August 1954 when he recommended it to Pamela Mitchell (incidentally at the same time as he was reading over the Merlin printing of 'The End') (*BC*, 124–5).

19. Jean-Paul Sartre, *Nausea*, trans. Robert Baldick (London: Penguin Books, 2000), 9–10.

20. Martin Esslin, 'Towards the Zero of Language', *Beckett's Later Fiction and Drama*, ed. J. Acheson and K. Arthur (New York: St. Martin's Press, 1987) 35–49, 44.

21. Samuel Beckett, *Mercier and Camier* (London: John Calder, 1999), 9.

22. Denis Diderot, *Jacques the Fatalist and His Master*, trans. David Coward (Oxford: Oxford University Press, 1999), 73.

23. Louis-Ferdinand Céline, *Death on Credit*, trans. Ralph Manheim (London: John Calder, 1989), 16.

5 IMAGES OF THE AUTHOR

1. Some readers have also argued that Moran authors *Molloy* I. For example, Edith Kern suggests that '[Moran's] reflections in anticipation of the Molloy mission reveal Moran as the artist wrestling with the task of creation in the manner of the hero setting out on a superhuman quest'. Edith Kern, 'Moran-Molloy: The Hero as Author', *Twentieth-Century Interpretations of Molloy, Malone Dies and The Unnamable*, ed. J. D. O'Hara (Inglewood Cliffs, NJ: Prentice-Hall, 1970), 35–45, 36. She also avers that 'Molloy originated ...

as Moran's artistic vision' (Kern, 37). David Hesla argues that 'just as Moran is a writer in search of a character to put in a story, so Molloy is a character in search of an author who has a story capable of accommodating him.' David Hesla, *The Shape of Chaos: An Interpretation of the Art of Samuel Beckett* (Minneapolis: University of Minnesota Press, 1971), 102.

2. I thank Shane Weller for pointing out Adorno's note to me; it is also Weller's translation that I use in the following sentence from Adorno's notes on *The Unnamable* as published in '"Gegen den Trug der Frage nach dem Sinn": Eine Dokumentation zu Adornos Beckett-Lecktuere', in *Frankfurter Adorno Blaetter* III, (Munich: edition text+kritik, 1994), 18–77: 'Die clownhaften Reflexionen aufs Werk selbst erinnern an Gides Paludes, ueberhaupt vieles – es ist ausser Kafka die wichtigste Brueke' ('The clownish reflections on the work itself recall Gide's *Paludes* to a considerable degree – besides Kafka, that work is the most important connection'.) Beckett lectured on *Paludes* in 1930, and as John Pilling has noted, in *Dream* Beckett referred to Dublin's 'paludal heavens' (*DFMW*, 111). Pilling also notes the possible importance of *Paludes* in *Dream*'s nonending: see his note in *A Companion to* Dream of Fair to Middling Women (Tallahassee, FL: Journal of Beckett Studies Books, 2004), 206.

3. Youdi's messenger Gaber recalls the messenger-angel Gabriel; Youdi lives at '8 Acacia Square' (a number Beckett early on associated with the infinity symbol – see his review of Denis Devlin's verse (*Dis*, 91–4)); Youdi speaks in the 'simple prophetic present' in his commands to his underlings, and so on.

4. As Delay points out, 'Gide wrote his first notebooks on a Louis XVI writing desk, with a mirror attached, which Anna Shackleton had left him in her will' (Delay, 173).

5. Justin O'Brien, 'Gide's Fictional Technique', *French Literary Horizon* (New York: Rutgers University Press, 1967), 91–102, 82.

6. H. Porter Abbott, *Diary Fiction: Writing as Action* (Ithaca: Cornell University Press, 1984), 49.

7. André Gide, *Paludes*, translated as *Marshlands. Marshlands and Prometheus Misbound*, trans. George D. Painter (London: Secker and Warburg, 1953), 15.

8. Certainly by the winter of 1948 (when he was writing *Malone Dies*), Beckett had this new treatment of form in mind. In January, Beckett described *Molloy* to McGreevy as 'the second last of the series begun with *Murphy*, if it can be said to be a series' (SB to TM, 14/1/48, qtd. in Deirdre Bair, *Samuel Beckett: A Biography* (New York: Harcourt Brace Jovanovich, 1978), 372). He went on to describe *Malone Dies* as '[t]he last' instalment of this sequence, after which he hoped he would 'hear no more of him' – meaning the avatar he had conceived as the diarist/narrator of all of his previous fictions (SB to TM, 14/1/48, qtd. in Bair, 372).

6 'OH IT'S ONLY A DIARY': *MOLLOY*

1. Michael Holquist, *Dostoevsky and the Novel* (Evanston, IL: Northwestern University Press, 1986), 50.

2. John N. Morris, *Versions of the Self: Studies in English Autobiography from John Bunyan to John Stuart Mill* (New York: Bove Books, 1996), 12.

3. See Mark Nixon's account of Beckett's reading of diaries and his attempt to begin a work entitled *Journal of a Melancholic* in the late thirties (Nixon, 110–31). Nixon also provides a brief reading of *Malone Dies* as a diary novel in his 'Conclusion' (Nixon, 187–92). H. Porter Abbott argues that in *Malone Dies* Beckett 'took the available genre of the diary novel and reduced it to its skeletal parts. The violence he did to the form is an extreme version of that inflicted on the diary novel by Sartre and Bellow. But in breaking down the genre, he was self-consciously undoing the book itself through its most primitive representative' (Abbott, *Diary*, 185). Lorna Martens is more reserved. For the Beckett of *Molloy* and *Malone Dies*, she argues, the 'idea of the diary itself is incidental'; Beckett uses the form to 'question more or less pointedly the traditional claims and purposes of writing'. Lorna Martens, *The Diary Novel* (Cambridge: Cambridge University Press, 1985), 192.

4. As Louis Untermeyer puts it in his 'Introduction' to *A Treasury of the World's Great Diaries*, ed. Philip Dunaway and Mel Evans (New York: Doubleday, 1957), 'When we read a diary [we] are looking into [the writer's] inmost mind, his hidden heart: here everything is forthright and without subterfuge.... [E]verything is spontaneous, unpremeditated, and completely convincing' (v).

5. C. G. Jung, 'The Tavistock Lectures', in *The Collected Works of C. G. Jung*, trans. R. F. C. Hull, 20 vols. (Princeton: Princeton University Press, 1976), Vol. 18, 173.

6. C. G. Jung, 'The Transcendent Function,' in *The Collected Works of C. G. Jung*, trans. R. F. C. Hull, 20 vols. (Princeton: Princeton University Press, 1976), Vol. 8, 90.

7. J. D. O'Hara, 'Jung and the Molloy Narrative', *The Beckett Studies Reader*, ed. S. E. Gontarski (Tallahassee: University Press of Florida, 1993), 129–45, 139. O'Hara's reading acknowledges an interesting fact: if Beckett's novel involves itself with such 'analogues', it does do so through a deeply 'comic', even 'absurd' distortion of them (O'Hara, 132). In the following I take O'Hara's insight further to argue that this dynamic underpins *Molloy*'s treatment of seriousness and meaning throughout.

8. As his final work 'comment dire' testifies, this was a notion of enduring importance to Beckett: in this poem, a voice reaches out for a world that can never be captured in words, all the while acknowledging the very attempt as 'folly'. Samuel Beckett, 'what is the word', *As the Story Was Told* (London: John Calder, 1990), 131–4.

9. As noted, Beckett pointed out that 'if the subject of my novels could be expressed in philosophical terms, there would have been no reason for my writing them' (qtd. in d'Aubarède, 217).

10. C. G. Jung, *The Archetypes and the Collective Unconscious*, 2nd edition (London: Routledge, 1990), 82.

11. Thomas Pynchon, *Slow Learner: Early Stories* (New York: Back Bay Books, 1984), 5.
12. Giacomo Leopardi, *The Canti*, trans. J. G. Nichols (Manchester: Carcanet Press, 2003), 118.
13. Beckett's house in Cooldrinagh had a stand of larches and in 'Sanies I' they recall his birth: he was 'born with a pop with the green of the larches' – an event the trees preside over again in 'A Piece of Monologue'. Like Molloy, Belacqua cannot tell an oak from an elm but he can recognize the larch. The tree appears also in Arsene's speech in *Watt* (where the changing of the leaves figures 'the whole bloody business' of death and regeneration) and in 'Draff' and 'Serena II'.
14. 'And every time I say, I said this, or, I said that, or speak of a voice saying, far away inside me, Molloy ... I am merely complying with the convention that demands you either lie or hold your peace. For what really happened was quite different' (*T*, 87–8).
15. Alfred Tennyson, *In Memoriam*, ed. Susan Shatto and Marion Shaw (Oxford: Clarendon Press, 1982), Section 128, ll.22–4, 140.
16. Anaïs Nin, *On Writing* (Yonkers: Oscar Baradinski, 1947), 22.
17. Beckett also noted this topic in summing up his key lecture points: point three is 'Influences of Nietzsche and Dostoyevsky [on Gide's novels]' (MIC60, 44).
18. Beckett realized that this book should be read in the light of Gide's argument about abnegation. Concluding his discussion of *La Symphonie pastorale*, he outlined the importance of a rejection of Nietzsche's philosophy to Gide's fiction (MIC60, 13). He also noted the importance of the speaker's self-evasion in the diary, pointing out the Pastor's self-induced 'ignorance' (MIC60, 13).
19. André Gide, *La Symphonie pastorale* and *Isabelle*, trans. Dorothy Bussy (London: Penguin, 1963), 30.
20. One thinks of the rules the Pastor insists must be preserved regarding his private room 'which the children call [his] "sanctum" and into which they are forbidden to enter' (*PS*, 42). Note the similar policies Moran imposes concerning his bedchamber. Once again, Moran avers that these rules exist to protect his son, though they are actually intended to protect Moran from the embarrassment of being caught masturbating: 'Father with yawning fly and starting eyes toiling to scatter on the ground his joyless seed, that was no sight for a small boy. Harshly I recalled him to the proprieties' (*T*, 103).
21. Beckett's firsthand knowledge of these writers is less important than his formative encounter with Sartre's response, but he certainly knew Mauriac. Beckett first refers to this author – whom he 'decidedly did not like' – in an undated letter to McGreevy in the summer of 1929, where he describes *Le Desert de l'Amour* (1925) as 'a patient tenuous snivel that one longs to see projected noisily into a handkerchief' (*LSB 1*, 11). In a letter to Arland Ussher on 25 March 1936, he playfully denigrates Seán O'Sullivan by describing him as an individual who 'reads Mauriac with relish' (*LSB 1*, 328). Mauriac's novel

Le Noeud de Vipères has been described by David Lodge as 'a classic example of the genre [of the Catholic diary novel]' with its critique of materialism and 'the tireless pursuit of the erring soul by God' (David Lodge, 'Introduction' to *The Knot of Vipers*, 7).

22. George Bernanos, *The Diary of a Country Priest*, trans. Pamela Morris (London: Bodley Head, 1975), 33.

23. François Mauriac, *The Knot of Vipers*, trans. Gerald Hopkins (New York: Penguin, 1985), 116.

24. François Mauriac, *Journal* (Paris: Bernard Grasset, 1934), Vol. 1, 188.

25. See Frank Kermode, *The Sense of an Ending: Studies in the Theory of Fiction*. (New York: Oxford University Press, 2000), 133–52.

26. Jean-Paul Sartre, *Literary Essays*, trans. Annette Nicholson (New York: Philosophical Library, 1957), 23.

27. Samuel Beckett, 'The Capital of the Ruins', in *The Complete Short Prose 1929–1989*, ed. S. E. Gontarski (New York: Grove Press, 1995), 278.

28. A statement Moran-narrator typically then doubts and retracts.

29. Phil Baker, *Beckett and the Mythology of Psychoanalysis* (Basingstoke: Macmillan, 1997), 37–47.

30. In this sense, we should see Moran through the lens of Beckett's early novelistic theory: Moran literally *is* that 'French character', who, like the authors who have so far preserved him and his ilk, seeks 'sharp outlines', rejects 'inwardness' and represents a lust for 'the complete absence of indistinctness, and the lack of shading' (*D*, 108). (As Moran puts it, 'Vagueness I abhor' (*T*, 99).) In *Molloy*, this quintessentially rule-bound character is compelled to live through and to *write* a narrative that must come to terms with the 'black gulfs' of the 'incoherent' counterreality that have been ignored in the novel as a genre, yet *comprise* the Molloy terrain (and the inner reality of Moran himself).

7 'THE ART OF INCARCERATION': *MALONE DIES*

1. The opposite extreme – too much information – must also be avoided, for this, too, will be unlike a 'real life'. 'I told myself … that I must make better speed. True lives do not tolerate this excess of circumstance' (*T*, 197).

2. Malone's comment that 'I don't like those gull's eyes. They remind me of an old shipwreck, I forget which' also takes on the discomforting resonance of Beckett's encounter with past selves in his own writings linking death/suicide by water and a vision of gulls (*T*, 193). Just as the shipwreck here suggests Malone's (unconscious) dread of the gaze of his own 'father' (Samuel Beckett), this sense of 'sinking' recalls the drowing scene in 'The End', which closes with the narrator listening to the cries of the gulls as he recalls an image of *his* father as he 'sinks' in his overturned boat. And this narrator's memory of drowning is at least partly the fictionalisation of one of Beckett's own memories of a suicidal moment as recorded in 'Enueg I': 'Blotches of doomed yellow in the pit of the Liffey;/the fingers of the ladders hooked over the parapet,/

soliciting;/a slush of vigilant gulls in the grey spew of the sewer'. Samuel Beckett, *Collected Poems in English and French* (New York: Grove Press, 1977), 10–12.

3. See James Acheson, *Samuel Beckett's Artistic Theory and Practice: Criticism, Drama and Early Fiction* (London: Macmillan, 1997), and Lawrence Miller, *Samuel Beckett: The Expressive Dilemma* (London: Palgrave Macmillan, 1992).

4. Honoré de Balzac, *Louis Lambert*, trans. Clara Bell and James Waring (Milton Keynes, UK: Lightning Source, n.d.), 60.

5. Samuel Taylor Coleridge, *Biographia Literaria: or, Biographical Sketches of My Literary Life and Opinions* (New York: Leavitt, Lord, 1834), Thesis IX, 159.

6. Jonathan Wordsworth, 'The Romantic Imagination', *A Companion to Romanticism*, ed. Duncan Wu (Oxford: Blackwell, 1999), 486–94, 486.

7. George Gordon, Lord Byron, *The Complete Poetical Works*, ed. Jerome J. McGann (Oxford: Clarendon Press, 1980), *Childe Harold's Pilgrimage*, III, 46–9.

8. See James Acheson's *Samuel Beckett's Artistic Theory and Practice: Criticism, Drama and Early Fiction* (London: Macmillan, 1997), 120–5.

9. See Chapter Three in Mario Praz, *The Romantic Agony*, 2nd edition, trans. Angus Davidson (London: Oxford University Press, 1970).

10. *The Letters of Samuel Beckett: 1941–1956*, vol. 2, ed. George Craig, Martha Dow Fehsenfeld, Dan Gunn, and Lois More Overbeck (Cambridge: Cambridge University Press, 2011), SB to GD, Friday, possibly the end of December 1950, 211. It is unclear to what end Beckett was translating Blanchot's essay as no publication came of this labour.

11. Beckett's admiration for Sade endured and he was still ready to discuss him enthusiastically in the late sixties after watching Peter Brooks's Royal Shakespeare production of *Marat/Sade* with pleasure (*DF*, 514).

12. Maurice Blanchot, 'Sade', *Justine, Philosophy in the Bedroom and Other Writings*, trans. Richard Seaver and Austryn Wainhouse (New York: Grove Press, 1965), 40.

13. Marquis de Sade, *Juliette*, trans. Austryn Wainhouse (New York: Grove Press, 1968), 525.

14. Sade, Marquis de, *The 120 Days of Sodom and Other Writings,* compiled and trans. Austryn Wainhouse and Richard Seaver (New York: Grove Press, 1966), 234.

CONCLUSION: BECKETT AND THE MODERN NOVEL

1. Martha Nussbaum, 'Narrative Emotions: Beckett's Genealogy of Love', *Ethics* 98, no. 2 (1988), 225–54, 229.

2. Philip Fisher, *The Vehement Passions* (Princeton: Princeton University Press, 2002), 251.

3. Samuel Beckett, *Nohow On: Company, Ill Seen Ill Said, Worstward Ho* (New York: Grove Press, 1996), 24.

4. Jenefer Robinson, *Deeper than Reason: Emotion and Its Role in Literature, Music, and Art* (New York: Oxford University Press, 2005), 159.

5. For Beckett's comment see J. D. O'Hara, *Samuel Beckett's Hidden Drives: Structural Uses of Depth Psychology* (Gainesville: University of Florida Press, 1997), 301.

6. See Georges Bataille, '*Molloy*', *Critique*, 15 May 1951, 387–96; rpt. in *Samuel Beckett: The Critical Heritage*, 55–63.

Bibliography

WORKS BY SAMUEL BECKETT

Beckett, Samuel, *As the Story Was Told*, London: John Calder, 1990.

Beckett's Dream Notebook, ed. John Pilling, Reading: Beckett International Foundation, 1999.

Collected Poems in English and French, New York: Grove Press, 1977.

The Complete Dramatic Works, London: Faber and Faber, 1990.

The Complete Short Prose 1929–1989, ed. S. E. Gontarski, New York: Grove Press, 1995.

Disjecta, London: John Calder, 2001.

Dream of Fair to Middling Women, London: John Calder, 1993.

Eleutheria, trans. Barbara Wright, London: Faber and Faber, 1996.

First Love and Other Novellas, London: Penguin Books, 2000.

'German Literature': MS 10971/1, Beckett Manuscript Collection, Trinity College Library, Dublin.

Holograph of 'Suite' manuscript (1946), MS 91–1, Calvin Israel Samuel Beckett Collection, John J. Burns Library, Boston College, Box 1, folder 9.

How It Is, London: John Calder, 1964.

The Letters of Samuel Beckett: 1929–1940, vol. 1, Martha Dow Fehsenfeld and Lois More Overbeck, eds., Cambridge: Cambridge University Press, 2009.

The Letters of Samuel Beckett: 1941–1956, vol. 2, George Craig, Martha Dow Fehsenfeld, Dan Gunn, and Lois More Overbeck, eds., Cambridge: Cambridge University Press, 2011.

Letters to Thomas McGreevy: MS 10402, Beckett Manuscript Collection, Trinity College Library, Dublin.

Mercier and Camier, London: John Calder, 1999.

Murphy, London: John Calder, 2003.

Nohow On: Company, Ill Seen Ill Said, Worstward Ho, New York: Grove Press, 1996.

'Notes on Literature (Giosuè Carducci)', TCD MS 10965, Beckett Manuscript Collection, Trinity College Dublin Library.

'Notes on Philosophy', MS 10967, Beckett Manuscript Collection, Trinity College Library, Dublin.

'Notes on Samuel Beckett's lectures' taken by Leslie Daiken, Beckett International Foundation, Reading University Library, unaccessioned holding.

'Notes on Samuel Beckett's lectures' taken by Rachel Burrows: MIC60, Beckett Manuscript Collection, Trinity College Dublin Library.

Proust and Three Dialogues with Georges Duthuit, London: John Calder, 1999.

Stories and Texts for Nothing, New York: Grove Press, 1967.

'Suite' in *Les Temps Modernes*, vol. 10, July, 1946, 107–19.

Trilogy: *Molloy, Malone Dies, The Unnamable*, London: John Calder, 1994.

Typescript of 'The End', Richard Seaver Collection of Samuel Beckett Materials, Harry Ransom Center, University of Texas at Austin, Box 1, folder 1.

Watt, London: John Calder, 1998.

Watt Notebooks, Harry Ransom Center, University of Texas at Austin, Box 6, folders 5–7; Box 7, folders 1–4.

Watt Typescript, Harry Ransom Center, University of Texas at Austin, Box 7, folders 5–6.

Whoroscope Notebook: MS 3000, Beckett International Foundation, Reading University Library.

WORKS BY OTHER AUTHORS

Abbot, H. Porter. *Diary Fiction: Writing as Action*, Ithaca: Cornell University Press, 1984.

'Letters to the Self: The Cloistered Writer in Nonretrospective Fiction', *PMLA*, vol. 95, no. 1 (January 1980), 23–41.

'Narrative', *Palgrave Advances in Samuel Beckett Studies*, ed. Lois Oppenheim, New York: Palgrave Macmillan, 2004, 7–29.

Acheson, James, *Samuel Beckett's Artistic Theory and Practice: Criticism, Drama and Early Fiction*, London: Macmillan, 1997.

Ackerley, C. J., *Demented Particulars: The Annotated* Murphy, Tallahassee, FL: Journal of Beckett Studies Books, 1998.

Obscure Locks, Simple Keys: The Annotated Watt, Tallahassee, FL: Journal of Beckett Studies Books, 2005.

Ackerley, C. J. and S. E. Gontarski, *The Grove Companion to Samuel Beckett*, New York: Grove Press, 2004.

Adorno, Theodor, '"Gegen den Trug der Frage nach dem Sinn": Eine Dokumentation zu Adornos Beckett-Lecktuere', *Frankfurter Adorno Blaetter III*, Munich: edition text+kritik 1994, 18–77.

Amiran, Eyal, *Wandering and Home: Beckett's Metaphysical Narrative*, University Park: Penn State University Press, 1997.

Apter, Emily S., *André Gide and the Codes of Homotextuality, Stanford French and Italian Studies* 48, Saratoga, CA: Anma Libri, 1987.

Babcock, Arthur E., *Portraits of Artists: Reflexivity in Gidean Fiction, 1902–1946*, York, SC: French Literature Publications, 1982.

Bair, Deirdre, *Samuel Beckett: A Biography*, New York: Harcourt Brace Jovanovich, 1978.

Balzac, Honoré de, *Louis Lambert*, trans. Clara Bell and James Waring, Milton Keynes, UK: Lightning Source, n.d.

Baker, Phil, *Beckett and the Mythology of Psychoanalysis*, Basingstoke and New York: Macmillan Press, 1997.

Bataille, Georges, 'Molloy', *Critique* (15 May 1951), 387–96; reprinted in *Samuel Beckett: the Critical Heritage*, 55–63.

Beer, Ann, 'Watt, Knott and Beckett's Bilingualism', *Journal of Beckett Studies*, no. 10, (Autumn 1983), 37–76.

Begam, Richard, *Samuel Beckett and the End of Modernity*, Palo Alto, CA: Stanford University Press, 1996.

Bernanos, Georges, *The Diary of a Country Priest*, trans. Pamela Morris, London: Bodley Head, 1975.

Bixby, Patrick, *Samuel Beckett and the Postcolonial Novel*, Cambridge: Cambridge University Press, 2009.

Blanchot, Maurice, 'Sade', *Justine, Philosophy in the Bedroom and Other Writings*, trans. Richard Seaver and Austryn Wainhouse, New York: Grove Press, 1965.

Boulter, Jonathan, *Interpreting Narrative in the Novels of Samuel Beckett*, Gainesville: University Press of Florida, 2001.

Brée, Germaine, *André Gide l'insaisissable Protée*, Paris: Les Belles Lettres, 1953.

Gide, New Brunswick, NJ: Rutgers University Press, 1963.

'On Time Sequences and Consequences in the Gidian World', in *André Gide*, ed. David Walker, New York: Addison Wesley Longman, 1996, 43–51.

Brée, Germaine and Margaret Guiton, eds., *The French Novel from Gide to Camus*, New York: Harbinger Books, 1962.

Breton, André, *Nadja*, trans. Richard Howard, New York: Grove Press, 1960.

Oeuvres complètes, édition établie par Marguerite Bonnet, Paris: Éditions Gallimard, 1988, vol. 2.

'What Is Surrealism?', *Paths to the Present: Aspects of European Thought from Romanticism to Existentialism*, ed. E. Weber, New York: Dodd, Mead, 1963.

Broome, Peter, *Gide: Les Caves du Vatican*, Critical Guides to French Texts, Valencia: Grant & Cutler, 1995.

Burrows, Rachel, 'Interview with Rachel Burrows', Interview by S. E. Gontarski, Dougald McMillan, and Martha Fehsenfeld, *Journal of Beckett Studies*, vol. 11/12, 1–15.

Bush, Ronald, *TS Eliot: A Study in Character and Style*, Oxford: Oxford University Press, 1984.

Butler, Lance St. John, *Samuel Beckett and the Meaning of Being: A Study in Ontological Parable*, New York: Palgrave Macmillan, 1984.

Büttner, Gottfried, *Samuel Beckett's Novel* Watt, trans. Joseph P. Dolan, Philadelphia: University of Pennsylvania Press, 1984.

Byron, George Gordon, *The Complete Poetical Works*, ed. Jerome J. McGann, Oxford: Clarendon Press, 1980.

Carey, Phyllis and Ed Jewinski, *Joyce 'n Beckett*, New York: Fordham University Press, 1992.

Caselli, Daniela, *Beckett's Dantes: Intertexuality in the Fiction and Criticism*, Manchester: Manchester University Press, 2006.

Céline, Louis-Ferdinand, *Death on Credit*, trans. Ralph Manheim, London: John Calder, 1989.

Crocker, Lester G., *An Age of Crisis: Man and World in Eighteenth-Century French Thought*, Baltimore: Johns Hopkins University Press, 1959.

Coetzee, J. M., *Doubling the Point: Essays and Interviews*, ed. David Atwell, Cambridge, MA: Harvard University Press, 1992.

'The Comedy of Point of View in Beckett's Murphy', ed. David Atwell, 31–42.

'The Manuscript Revisions of Beckett's *Watt*', ed. David Atwell, 39–42.

Preface to *Samuel Beckett: The Grove Centenary Edition*, New York: Grove Press, 2006.

'Samuel Beckett and the Temptations of Style', ed. David Atwell, 43–9.

Coleridge, Samuel Taylor, *Biographia Literaria: or, Biographical Sketches of My Literary Life and Opinions*, New York: Leavitt, Lord, 1834.

Culler, Jonathan, *Structuralist Poetics*, London: Routledge and Kegan Paul, 1975.

Dällenbach, Lucien , *The Mirror in the Text*, trans. Jeremy Whiteley with Emma Hughes, Chicago: University of Chicago Press, 1989.

Davet, Yvonne, *Autour des Nourritures terrestres : histoire d'un livre*, Paris: Gallimard, 1948.

Diderot, Denis, *Jacques the Fatalist and His Master*, trans. David Coward, Oxford: Oxford University Press, 1999.

D'Aubarède, Gabriel, 'Interview with Beckett', in *Samuel Beckett: The Critical Heritage*, Lawrence Graver and Raymond Federman, eds., London: Routledge and Kegan Paul, 1979, 215–17.

Delay, Jean, *The Youth of André Gide*, abridged and trans. June Guicharnaud, Chicago: University of Chicago Press, 1963.

Driver, Tom, 'Interview with Beckett', in *Samuel Beckett: The Critical Heritage*, Lawrence Graver and Raymond Federman, eds., London: Routledge and Kegan Paul, 1979, 217–23.

Dunaway, Philip and Mel Evans, *A Treasury of the World's Great Diaries*, New York: Doubleday, 1957.

Dunn, Peter N., *The Spanish Picaresque Novel*, Boston: Twayne, 1979.

Esslin, M., 'Towards the Zero of Language', J. Acheson and K. Arthur, eds., *Beckett's Later Fiction and Drama*, New York: St Martin's Press, 1987, 35–49.

Federman, Raymond, *Journey to Chaos: Samuel Beckett's Early Fiction*, Berkeley: University of California Press, 1965.

Fielding, Henry, *Joseph Andrews and Shamela*, Oxford: Oxford University Press, 1999.

Tom Jones, Oxford: Oxford University Press, 1998.

Fisher, Philip, *The Vehement Passions*, Princeton: Princeton University Press, 2002.

Fletcher, John, *The Novels of Samuel Beckett*, 2nd edition, London: Chatto and Windus, 1970.

Gibson, Andrew, *Beckett and Badiou: The Pathos of Intermittency*, Oxford: Oxford University Press, 2007.

Gide, André, *André Gide, Henri Ghéon. Correspondance:1897–1903*, 2 vols., Paris: Gallimard, 1976.

Autumn Leaves, trans. Elsie Pell, New York: Philosophical Library, 1950.

The Counterfeiters, trans. Dorothy Bussy, London: Penguin Books, 1966.

Dostoevsky, trans. Dorothy Bussy, London: Secker and Warburg, 1949.

If It Die, trans. Dorothy Bussy, London: Random House, 2002.

Journals 1889–1949, trans. Justin O'Brien, Harmondsworth: Penguin Books, 1967.

Lafcadio's Adventures, trans. Dorothy Bussy, New York: Vintage International, 2003.

Littérature Engagée, Paris: Gallimard, 1950.

Logbook of the Coiners, trans. Justin O'Brien, London: Cassell, 1952.

Marshlands and Prometheus Misbound, trans. George D. Painter, London: Secker and Warburg, 1953.

Morceaux choisis, Paris: Éditions de la Nouvelle Revue Française, 1921.

The Notebooks of André Walter, trans. Wade Baskin, London: Peter Owen, 1986.

Oeuvres Complètes, édition augmentée de texts inédits, établie par Martin-Chauffier, 15 volumes, Paris: Nouvelle Revue Française, 1932–1939.

Pretexts. Reflections on Literature and Morality, selected, edited and introduced by Justin O'Brien, London: Secker and Warburg, 1959.

La Symphonie pastorale and Isabelle, trans. Dorothy Bussy, London: Penguin, 1963.

Gluck, Barbara Reich, *Beckett and Joyce: Friendship and Fiction*, Lewisburg, PA: Bucknell University Press, 1959.

Goethe, Johann Wolfgang von, *Aus meinem Leben: Dichtung und Wahrheit*, Munich: Carl Hanser, 1985.

The Autobiography of Johann Wolfgang von Goethe, trans. John Oxenford, London: Sidgwick and Jackson, 1971.

The Sorrows of Young Werther, trans. Michael Hulse, London: Penguin Books, 1989.

Gontarski, S. E., ed., *The Beckett Studies Reader*, Tallahassee: University Press of Florida, 1993.

Goulet, Alain, Les Caves du Vatican *d'André Gide: Etude méthodologique*, Paris: Larousse, 1972.

Graver, Lawrence and Raymond Federman, eds., *Samuel Beckett: The Critical Heritage*, London: Routledge and Kegan Paul, 1979.

Guillén, Claudio, *Literature as System: Essays toward the Theory of Literary History*, Princeton: Princeton University Press, 1971.

Harmon, Maurice, ed., *No Author Better Served: The Correspondence of Samuel Beckett and Alan Schneider*, Cambridge, MA: Harvard University Press, 1998.

Hartley, Anthony, 'Samuel Beckett', *Spectator* (23 October 1953), 148–9.

Hayman, David, 'Going Where? Beckett's Opening Gambit for *Watt*', *Contemporary Literature*, vol. 43, no. 1 (Spring 2002), 28–49.

Ulysses: *The Mechanics of Meaning*, Englewood Cliffs, NJ: Prentice-Hall, 1970.

Hesla, David, *The Shape of Chaos: An Interpretation of the Art of Samuel Beckett*, Minneapolis: University of Minnesota Press, 1971.

Hill, Leslie, *Beckett's Fiction: In Different Words*, Cambridge: Cambridge University Press, 1990.

Hoefer, Jacqueline, 'Watt', *Perspective*, vol. 11, no. 3 (Autumn 1959), 166–82. Rpt. in *Samuel Beckett: A Collection of Critical Essays*, ed. Martin Esslin, Englewood Cliffs, NJ: Prentice-Hall, 1965, 62–76.

Holdheim, Wolfgang W., *Theory and Practice of the Novel: A Study of André Gide*, Geneva: Librairie Droz, 1968.

Holquist, Michael, *Dostoevsky and the Novel*, Evanston, IL: Northwestern University Press, 1986.

Jeffers, Thomas L., *Apprenticeships: The Bildungsroman from Goethe to Santayana*, New York: Palgrave Macmillan, 2005.

Joyce, James, *A Portrait of the Artist as a Young Man*, London: Penguin Books, 1992.

Juliet, Charles, *Conversations with Samuel Beckett and Bram Van Velde*, trans. Janey Tucker, with an introduction and notes by Adriaan van der Weel and Ruud Hisgen, Leiden: Academic Press 1995.

Jung, Carl Gustav, *The Archetypes and the Collective Unconscious*, 2nd edition, London: Routledge, 1990.

'The Tavistock Lectures', *The Collected Works of C. G. Jung*, trans. R.F.C. Hull, 20 vols., Princeton: Princeton University Press, 1976, vol. 18.

'The Transcendent Function,' *The Collected Works of C. G. Jung*, trans. R.F.C. Hull, 20 vols., Princeton: Princeton University Press, 1976, vol. 8.

Keats, John, *Complete Poems and Selected Letters of John Keats*, New York: Modern Library, 2001.

Kenner, Hugh, *Samuel Beckett: A Critical Study*, New York: Grove Press, 1962.

Ulysses, London: George Allen and Unwin, 1980.

Kermode, Frank, *The Sense of an Ending: Studies in the Theory of Fiction*, New York: Oxford University Press, 2000.

Kern, Edith, 'Moran-Molloy: The Hero as Author', *Twentieth-Century Interpretations of Molloy, Malone Dies and The Unnamable*, ed. J. D. O'Hara, Inglewood Cliffs, NJ: Prentice-Hall, 1970, 35–45.

Knowlson, James, *Damned to Fame: The Life of Samuel Beckett*, London: Bloomsbury, 1996.

Knowlson, James and John Haynes, eds., *Images of Beckett*, Cambridge: Cambridge University Press, 2003.

Lawall, Sarah, *Critics of Consciousness: The Existential Structures of Literature*, Cambridge: Harvard University Press, 1968.

Le Juez, Brigitte, *Beckett before Beckett*, trans. Ros Schwartz, London: Souvenir Press, 2008.

Lejeune, Philippe, 'On André Gide and Autobiography', *André Gide*, ed. David Walker, New York: Addison Wesley Longman, 1996, 79–98.

Leopardi, Giacomo, *The Canti*, trans. J. G. Nichols, Manchester: Carcanet Press, 2003.

Lukács, Georg, *The Theory of the Novel*, trans. Anna Bostock, London: Merlin Press, 1971.

Mauriac, François, *Journal*, Paris: Bernard Grasset, 1934.

The Knot of Vipers, trans. Gerald Hopkins, New York: Penguin, 1985.

Martens, Lorna, *The Diary Novel*, Cambridge: Cambridge University Press, 1985.

Martin, Claude, *André Gide par lui-même*, Paris: Seul, 1963.

McDonald, Christie, 'The Proustian Revolution', *The Cambridge Companion to the French Novel: From 1800 to the Present*, ed. Timothy Unwin, Cambridge: Cambridge University Press, 1997, 111–25.

McMillan, Dougald and Martha Fehsenfeld, *Beckett in the Theatre*, London: Calder and Boyars, 1988.

Miller, Lawrence, *Samuel Beckett: The Expressive Dilemma*, London: Palgrave Macmillan, 1992.

Morris, John N., *Versions of the Self: Studies in English Autobiography from John Bunyan to John Stuart Mill*, New York: Bove Books, 1996.

Murphy, P. J., 'Beckett and the Philosophers', *The Cambridge Companion to Beckett*, ed. John Pilling, Cambridge: Cambridge University Press, 2004, 222–40.

Nicholls, Peter, *Modernisms: A Literary Guide*, London: Macmillan, 1995.

Nin, Anaïs, *On Writing*, Yonkers: Oscar Baradinski, 1947.

Nixon, Mark, *Samuel Beckett's 'German Diaries': 1936–7*, London: Continuum, 2010.

Nussbaum, Martha, 'Narrative Emotions: Beckett's Genealogy of Love', *Ethics*, vol. 98, no. 2 (1988), 225–54.

O'Brien, Justin, 'Gide's Fictional Technique', *The French Literary Horizon*, Piscataway, NJ: Rutgers University Press, 1967, 91–102.

O'Hara, J. D., *Samuel Beckett's Hidden Drives: Structural Uses of Depth Psychology*, Gainesville: University Press of Florida, 1997.

'Jung and the Molloy Narrative', *The Beckett Studies Reader*, ed. S. E. Gontarski, Gainesville: University Press of Florida, 1993, 129–45.

ed., *Twentieth-Century Interpretations of Molloy, Malone Dies and The Unnamable*, Inglewood Cliffs, NJ: Prentice-Hall, 1970.

Oppenheim, Lois, ed., *Palgrave Advances in Samuel Beckett Studies*, New York: Palgrave Macmillan, 2004.

Ovid, *Metamorphoses, Books I–VIII*, trans. Frank Justus Miller, revised G. P. Goold, Loeb Classical Library 42, London, and Cambridge, MA: Harvard University Press, 1999.

Parker, Alexander, *Literature and the Delinquent: The Picaresque Novel in Spain in Europe, 1599–1753*, Edinburgh: Edinburgh University Press, 1967.

Pasco, Allan H., *Novel Configurations. A Study of French Fiction*, Birmingham, AL: Summa, 1987.

Pattie, David, 'Beckett and Bibliography', *Palgrave Advances in Samuel Beckett Studies*, ed. Lois Oppenheim, New York: Palgrave Macmillan, 2004, 226–46.

Phiddian, Robert, *Swift's Parody*, Cambridge: Cambridge University Press, 1995.

Pilling, John, ed., *The Cambridge Companion to Beckett*, Cambridge: Cambridge University Press, 2004.

  A Companion to Dream of Fair to Middling Women, Tallahassee, FL: Journal of Beckett Studies Books, 2004.

  Samuel Beckett, London: Routledge and Kegan Paul, 1976.

  A Samuel Beckett Chronology, New York: Palgrave Macmillan, 2006.

  Beckett before Godot, Cambridge, New York: Cambridge University Press, 1997.

  'Beckett's *Letters*', *Journal of Beckett Studies* 18 (September 2009), 178–91.

Praz, Mario, *The Romantic Agony*, trans. Angus Davidson, 2nd ed., London: Oxford University Press, 1970.

Pultar, Gönül, *Technique and Tradition in Beckett's Trilogy of Novels*, Lanham, MD: United Press of America, 1996.

Pynchon, Thomas, *Slow Learner: Early Stories*, New York: Back Bay Books, 1984.

Rabinovitz, Rubin, *Innovation in Samuel Beckett's Fiction*, Urbana: University of Illinois Press, 1992.

Reid, James H., *Proust, Beckett and Narration*, Cambridge: Cambridge University Press, 2003.

Robbe-Grillet, Alain, *Le Miroir qui revient*, Paris: Minuit, 1984.

Robinson, Jenefer, *Deeper than Reason: Emotion and Its Role in Literature, Music, and Art*, New York: Oxford University Press, 2005.

Sade, Marquis de, *Juliette*, trans. Austryn Wainhouse, New York: Grove Press, 1968.

  The 120 Days of Sodom and Other Writings, compiled and trans. Austryn Wainhouse and Richard Seaver, New York: Grove Press, 1966.

Sartre, Jean-Paul, *Nausea*, trans. Robert Baldick, London: Penguin Books, 2000.

  Literary Essays, trans. Annette Nicholson, New York: Philosophical Library, 1957.

Savage, Catherine H., 'Gide's Criticism of Symbolism', *Modern Language Review*, vol. 61, no. 4 (October 1966), 601–9.

Sellin, Eric, 'Aspects of Surrealism: Surrealist Aesthetics and the Theatrical Event', *Books Abroad*, vol. 43, no. 2 (Spring 1969), 167–72.

Schiller, Friedrich, *On the Aesthetic Education of Man: In a Series of Letters*, trans. Elizabeth Wilkinson; ed. L. A. Willoughby, Walter Hindered, and Daniel O. Dahlstrom, Oxford: Clarendon Press, 1967.

Schopenhauer, Arthur, *The World as Will and Representation*, trans. E. F. J. Payne, 2 vols., New York: Dover, 1969.

Sharpe, Lesley, ed., *The Cambridge Companion to Goethe*, Cambridge: Cambridge University Press, 2002.

Shenker, Israel, 'An Interview with Beckett', *Samuel Beckett: The Critical Heritage*, ed. Lawrence Graver and Raymond Federman, London: Routledge and Kegan Paul, 1979, 146–9.

Sheridan, Alan, *André Gide: A Life in the Present*, London: Penguin, 1998.

Smith, Frederik N., *Beckett's Eighteenth Century*, Basingstoke: Palgrave, 2002.

Smollett, Tobias, *Roderick Random*, London: Penguin Books, 1995.

Sonnenfeld, Albert, 'Readers and Reading in *La Porte Étroite*', *Romantic Review*, vol. 67 (1976), 172–80.

Swales, Martin, 'Goethe's Prose Fiction', *The Cambridge Companion to Goethe*, ed. Lesley Sharpe, Cambridge: Cambridge University Press, 2002, 133–87.

Swift, Jonathan, *A Tale of a Tub*, Oxford: Oxford University Press, 1999.

Tennyson, Alfred, *In Memoriam*, ed. Susan Shatto and Marion Shaw, Oxford: Clarendon Press, 1982.

The Holy Bible Containing the Old and New Testaments, Authorised King James Version, London: Collins' Clear-Type Press, 1957.

Thomas, Duncan and Stephen Coppel, *Avigdor Arikha: Drawings and Prints 1965–2005*, London: British Museum Press, 2006.

Tindall, William York, *Samuel Beckett*, New York: Columbia University Press, 1964.

Trezise, Thomas, *Into the Breach: Samuel Beckett and the Ends of Literature*, Princeton: Princeton University Press, 1990.

Uhlmann, Anthony, *Beckett and Poststructuralism*, Cambridge: Cambridge University Press, 1999.

Unwin, Timothy, ed., *The Cambridge Companion to the French Novel: From 1800 to the Present*, Cambridge: Cambridge University Press, 1997.

Walker, David, 'Challenging the Novel in *Les Faux-Monnayeurs*', *André Gide*, ed. David Walker, New York: Addison Wesley Longman, 1996, 202–20.

'Formal Experiment and Innovation', *The Cambridge Companion to the French Novel: From 1800 to the Present*, ed. Timothy Unwin, Cambridge: Cambridge University Press, 1997, 126–44.

André Gide, London: Macmillan, 1990.

ed., *André Gide*, New York: Addison Wesley Longman, 1996.

Weller, Shane, *Beckett, Literature and the Ethics of Alterity*, New York: Palgrave Macmillan, 2006.

A Taste for the Negative: Beckett and Nihilism, London: Legenda, Modern
  Humanities Research Association and Maney Publishing, 2005.
Winston, Matthew, 'Watt's First Footnote', *Journal of Modern Literature* vol. 6
  (1971), 69–82.
Wood, Rupert, 'An Endgame of Aesthetics: Beckett as Essayist', *The Cambridge
  Companion to Beckett*, ed. John Pilling, Cambridge: Cambridge University
  Press, 2004, 1–16.
Wordsworth, Jonathan, 'The Romantic Imagination', *A Companion to
  Romanticism*, ed. Duncan Wu, Oxford: Blackwell, 1999, 486–94.

Index